HELP YOUR CHILD GROW WITH THE
Core Knowledge Series

What Your Kindergartner Needs to Know (1996)
What Your First Grader Needs to Know (*Revised Edition, 1997**)
What Your Second Grader Needs to Know (1991)
What Your Third Grader Needs to Know (1992)
What Your Fourth Grader Needs to Know (1992)
What Your Fifth Grader Needs to Know (1993)
What Your Sixth Grader Needs to Know (1993)

FOR MORE INFORMATION, WRITE OR CALL:
Core Knowledge Foundation
2012-B Morton Drive
Charlottesville, VA 22903

804-977-7550

*PARENTS AND TEACHERS: Please note that this **Revised Edition** of *What Your First Grader Needs to Know* is the follow-up volume to *What Your Kindergartner Needs to Know*. Older editions of the First Grade book contain some material now in the Kindergarten book. (See in this book the General Introduction to the Core Knowledge Series for a discussion of the research leading to the development and revision of the curricular guidelines on which these books are based.)

The Core Knowledge™ Series

Resource Books for Kindergarten Through Grade Six

DOUBLEDAY
New York London Toronto Sydney Auckland

THE·CORE·KNOWLEDGE
SERIES

What Your First Grader Needs to Know

FUNDAMENTALS OF A GOOD FIRST-GRADE EDUCATION
(Revised Edition)

Edited by

E. D. HIRSCH, JR.

PUBLISHED BY DOUBLEDAY
a division of Bantam Doubleday Dell Publishing Group, Inc.
1540 Broadway, New York, New York 10036

DOUBLEDAY and the portrayal of an anchor with a dolphin
are trademarks of Doubleday, a division of
Bantam Doubleday Dell Publishing Group, Inc.

BOOK DESIGN BY BONNI LEON-BERMAN

Library of Congress Cataloging-in-Publication Data
What your first grader needs to know: fundamentals of a good first-grade education /
    edited by E. D. Hirsch, Jr. — Rev. ed.
        p.   cm. — (The core knowledge series; bk. 1)
    1. First grade (Education)—United States—Curricula.   2. Curriculum planning—
United States.   I. Hirsch, E. D. (Eric Donald), 1928–   . II. Series.
LB1571 1st.W53   1997
372. 19—dc20   96-24454
                                                                    CIP

10   9   8   7   6   5   4   3   2

Editor-in Chief of the Core Knowledge Series: E. D. Hirsch, Jr.

Text Editor: John Holdren

Art Editor and Project Manager: Tricia Emlet

Writers: Curriculum Concepts, Inc. (Mathematics); Diane Darst (Visual Arts); John Holdren (Language and Literature, History and Geography, Music , Mathematics, Science); Susan Tyler Hitchcock (Science); Mary Beth Klee (History and Geography); Janet Smith (Music); Linda Williams (Reading, Writing, and Your First Grader)

Artists and Photographers: Catherine Bricker, Leslie Evans, Jonathan Fuqua, Julie Grant, Steve Henry, Hannah Holdren, Sara Holdren, Phillip Jones, Bob Kirchman, Gail McIntosh, Nic Siler

Art and Photo Research, Art and Text Permissions: Martha Clay Sullivan, Jeanne Nicholson Siler

Research Assistant: Deborah Hyland

Acknowledgments

This series has depended on the help, advice, and encouragement of some two thousand people. Some of those singled out here already know the depth of our gratitude; others may be surprised to find themselves thanked publicly for help they gave quietly and freely for the sake of the enterprise alone. To helpers named and unnamed we are deeply grateful.

Advisors on Multiculturalism: Minerva Allen, Barbara Carey, Frank de Varona, Mick Fedullo, Dorothy Fields, Elizabeth Fox-Genovese, Marcia Galli, Dan Garner, Henry Louis Gates, Cheryl Kulas, Joseph C. Miller, Gerry Raining Bird, Connie Rocha, Dorothy Small, Sharon Stewart-Peregoy, Sterling Stuckey, Marlene Walking Bear, Lucille Watahomigie, Ramona Wilson

Advisors on Elementary Education: Joseph Adelson, Isobel Beck, Paul Bell, Carl Bereiter, David Bjorklund, Constance Jones, Elizabeth LaFuze, J. P. Lutz, Sandra Scarr, Nancy Stein, Phyllis Wilkin

Advisors on Technical Subject Matter: Marilyn Jager Adams, Karima-Diane Alavi, Richard Anderson, Judith Birsh, Cheryl Cannard, Paul Gagnon, David Geary, Andrew Gleason, Blair Jones, Connie Juel, Eric Karell, Morton Keller, Joseph Kett, Mary Beth Klee, Michael Lynch, Sheelagh McGurn, Joseph C. Miller, Jean Osborn, Margaret Redd, Nancy Royal, Mark Rush,

Janet Smith, Ralph Smith, Nancy Strother, Nancy Summers, Marlene Thompson, James Trefil, Patricia Wattenmaker, Nancy Wayne, Linda Williams, Lois Williams

Conferees, March 1990: Nola Bacci, Joan Baratz-Snowden, Thomasyne Beverley, Thomas Blackton, Angela Burkhalter, Monty Caldwell, Thomas M. Carroll, Laura Chapman, Carol Anne Collins, Lou Corsaro, Henry Cotton, Anne Coughlin, Arletta Dimberg, Debra P. Douglas, Patricia Edwards, Janet Elenbogen, Mick Fedullo, Michele Fomalont, Mamon Gibson, Jean Haines, Barbara Hayes, Stephen Herzog, Helen Kelley, Brenda King, John King, Elizabeth LaFuze, Diana Lam, Nancy Lambert, Doris Langaster, Richard LaPointe, Lloyd Leverton, Madeline Long, Allen Luster, Joseph McGeehan, Janet McLin, Gloria McPhee, Marcia Mallard, Judith Matz, William J. Maloney, John Morabito, Robert Morrill, Roberta Morse, Karen Nathan, Dawn Nichols, Valeta Paige, Mary Perrin, Joseph Piazza, Jeanne Price, Marilyn Rauth, Judith Raybern, Mary Reese, Richard Rice, Wallace Saval, John Saxon, Jan Schwab, Ted Sharp, Diana Smith, Richard Smith, Trevanian Smith, Carol Stevens, Nancy Summers, Michael Terry, Robert Todd, Elois Veltman, Sharon Walker, Mary Ann Ward, Charles Whiten, Penny Williams, Clarke Worthington, Jane York

Schools: Special thanks to Three Oaks Elementary for piloting *Core Knowledge Sequence* in 1990. And thanks to the schools that have offered their advice and suggestions for improving the *Core Knowledge Sequence,* including (in alphabetical order): Academy Charter School(CO); Coleman Elementary (TX); Coral Reef Elementary (FL); Coronado Village Elementary (TX); Crooksville Elementary (OH); Crossroads Academy (NH); Gesher Jewish Day School (VA); Hawthorne Elementary (TX); Highland Heights Elementary (IN); Joella Good Elementary (FL); Mohegan School-CS 67 (NY); The Morse School (MA); Nichols Hills Elementary (OK); Ridge View Elementary (WA); R. N. Harris Elementary (NC); Southside Elementary (FL); Three Oaks Elementary (FL); Washington Core Knowledge School (CO). And to the many other schools teaching Core Knowledge—too many to name here, and some of whom we have yet to discover—our heartfelt thanks for "sharing the knowledge"!

Benefactors: The Brown Foundation, The Challenge Foundation, Mrs. E. D. Hirsch, Sr., The Walton Family Foundation

Our grateful acknowledgment to these persons does not imply that we have taken their (sometimes conflicting) advice in every case, or that each of them endorses all aspects of this project. Responsibility for final decisions must rest with the editors alone. Suggestions for improvements are very welcome, and we wish to thank in advance those who send advice for revising and improving this series.

This book is dedicated to the memory of
Paul Bell
late superintendent of Dade County Public Schools.

"Because he kept the Divine Vision in time of trouble."
(William Blake, *Jerusalem*, II:30)

A Note to Teachers

We hope you will find this book useful, especially those of you who are teaching in the growing network of Core Knowledge schools. Throughout the book, we have addressed the suggested activities and explanations to "Parents," since you as teachers know your students and will have ideas about how to use the content of this book in relation to the lessons and activities you plan. If you are interested in the ideas of teachers in Core Knowledge schools, please write or call the Core Knowledge Foundation (801 East High St., Charlottesville, VA 22902; 804-977-7550) for information on ordering collections of lessons created and shared by teachers in Core Knowledge schools. Many of these teacher-created lessons are available through the Core Knowledge Home Page on the Internet at the following address:

http://www.coreknowledge.org

Author's earnings from sales of the Core Knowledge Series go to the non-profit Core Knowledge Foundation. E.D. Hirsch, Jr. receives no remuneration for editing the series nor any other remuneration from the Core Knowledge Foundation.

Contents

I. Language and Literature

II. History and Geography

Introduction 109

III. Visual Arts
Introduction 179

IV. Music
Introduction 201

V. Mathematics
Introduction   233

VI. Science
Introduction   269

CONTENTS

Introduction
to the Revised Edition

This is a revision of the first edition of *What Your First Grader Needs to Know*, first published in 1991. Almost nothing in that earlier book, which elicited wide praise and warm expressions of gratitude from teachers and parents, has become outdated. Why, then, revise the earlier book at all?

Because good things can be made better. In the intervening years since 1991, we at the Core Knowledge Foundation have had the benefit of a great deal of practical experience that can improve the contributions of these Core Knowledge books to early education. We have worked with and learned from an ever-growing network of Core Knowledge schools. At this writing, we can build on the experiences of well over two hundred schools in more than thirty states that are following the Core Knowledge curriculum guidelines. We have also received many suggestions from parents who are using the books. And besides conducting our own research, we have continued to seek advice from subject-matter experts and multicultural advisors.

All these activities have enabled us to field-test and refine the original *Core Knowledge Sequence*, the curriculum guidelines on which the Core Knowledge books are based. Perhaps most significant of all for the revision of this book, we have now published a Core Knowledge book for kindergarten, *What Your Kindergartner Needs to Know*, which includes some of the topics included in the original first-grade book of 1991. That transfer of topics has enabled us to enhance what is presented to first graders—following the principle that guides our whole initiative, that each grade in the *Core Knowledge Sequence* should build carefully upon the previous grade.

What kind of knowledge and skills can your child be expected to learn in first grade at school? How can you help your child at home? These are questions that we try to answer in this book. It presents the sort of knowledge and skills—in language and literature, history and geography, visual arts, music, mathematics, and science—that should be at the core of a challenging first-grade education.

Because children and localities differ greatly across this big, diverse country, so do first-grade classrooms. But all communities, including classrooms, require some common ground for communication and learning. In this book, we present the specific shared knowledge that hundreds of parents and teachers across the nation have agreed upon for American first graders. This core is not a comprehensive prescription for everything that every first grader needs to know. Such a complete prescription would be rigid and undesirable. But the book does offer a solid common ground that will enable young students to become active, successful learners in their classroom communities and later in the larger communities we live in—town, state, nation, and world.

In this revised edition, we have retold some stories in more detail, as well as provided guidance about how children learn to read. We have added more activities to the Mathematics section, and placed a more engaging emphasis on the story in history. These improvements reflect contributions from many hands and minds. Our gratitude to all these advisors and contributors is great indeed.

A special and emphatic acknowledgment is owed to the director of the entire revision project, John Holdren of the Core Knowledge Foundation. He oversaw the research and consensus-building that led to the changes made in the underlying *Core Knowledge Sequence*. He sought and found excellent contributors to this revised edition. He devised ways to overcome what I and others had felt to be a shortcoming in the stories of the earlier edition—their too great brevity and lack of narrative tension. He edited the contributions of our various writers, and himself wrote considerable portions of the book. For all of the improvements, I owe a large debt of thanks to John. As is customary with an editor-in-chief, however, I accept responsibility for any defects that may still be found in this book, and I invite readers to send criticisms and suggestions to the Core Knowledge Foundation.

We hope you and your child will enjoy this book, and that it will help lay the foundations upon which to build a lifetime of learning.

E. D. Hirsch, Jr.

General Introduction
to the Core Knowledge Series

I. WHAT IS YOUR CHILD LEARNING IN SCHOOL?

A parent of identical twins sent me a letter in which she expressed concern that her children, who are in the same grade in the same school, are being taught completely different things. How can this be? Because they are in different classrooms; because the teachers in these classrooms have only the vaguest guidelines to follow; in short, because the school, like many in the United States, lacks a definite, specific curriculum.

Many parents would be surprised if they were to examine the curriculum of their child's elementary school. Ask to see your school's curriculum. Does it spell out, in clear and concrete terms, a core of specific content and skills all children at a particular grade level are expected to learn by the end of the school year?

Many curricula speak in general terms of vaguely defined skills, processes, and attitudes, often in an abstract, pseudotechnical language that calls, for example, for children to "analyze patterns and data," or "investigate the structure and dynamics of living systems," or "work cooperatively in a group." Such vagueness evades the central question: what is your child learning in school? It places unreasonable demands upon teachers, and often results in years of schooling marred by repetitions and gaps. Yet another unit on dinosaurs or "pioneer days." *Charlotte's Web* for the third time. "You've never heard of the Bill of Rights?" "You've never been taught how to add two fractions with unlike denominators?"

When identical twins in two classrooms of the same school have few academic experiences in common, that is cause for concern. When teachers in that school do not know what children in other classrooms are learning on the same grade level, much less in earlier and later grades, they cannot reliably predict that children will come prepared with a shared core of knowledge and skills. For an elementary school to be successful, teachers need a common vision of what they want their students to know and be able to do. They need to have *clear, specific learning goals*, as well as the sense of mutual accountability that comes from shared commitment to helping all children achieve those goals. Lacking both specific goals and mutual accountability, too many schools exist in a state of curricular incoherence, one result of which is that they fall far short of developing the full potential of our children.

To address this problem, I started the nonprofit Core Knowledge Foundation in 1986. This book and its companion volumes in the Core Knowledge Series are designed to give parents, teachers—and through them, children—a guide to clearly defined learning goals in the form of a carefully sequenced body of knowledge, based upon the specific content guidelines developed by the Core Knowledge Foundation (see below, "The Consensus Behind the *Core Knowledge Sequence*").

Core Knowledge is an attempt to define, in a coherent and sequential way, a body of widely used knowledge taken for granted by competent writers and speakers in the United States. Because this knowledge is taken for granted rather than being explained when it is used, it forms a necessary foundation for the higher-order reading, writing, and thinking skills that children need for academic and vocational success. The universal attainment of such knowledge should be a central aim of curricula in our elementary schools, just as it is currently the aim in all world-class educational systems.

For reasons explained in the next section, making sure that all young children in the United States possess a core of shared knowledge is a necessary step in developing a first-rate educational system.

II. WHY CORE KNOWLEDGE IS NEEDED

Learning builds on learning: children (and adults) gain new knowledge only by building on what they already know. It is essential to begin building solid foundations of knowledge in the early grades when children are most receptive because, for the vast majority of children, academic deficiencies from the first six grades can *permanently* impair the success of later learning. Poor performance of American students in middle and high school can be traced to shortcomings inherited from elementary schools that have not imparted to children the knowledge and skills they need for further learning.

All of the highest-achieving and most egalitarian elementary school systems in the world (such as those in Sweden, France, and Japan) teach a specific core of knowledge in each of the first six grades, thus enabling all children to enter each new grade with a secure foundation for further learning. It is time American schools did so as well, for the following reasons:

(1) Commonly shared knowledge makes schooling more effective.

We know that the one-on-one tutorial is the most effective form of schooling, in part because a parent or teacher can provide tailor-made instruction for the individual child. But in a nontutorial situation—in, for example, a typical classroom with twenty-five or more students—the instructor cannot effectively impart new knowledge to all the students unless each one shares the background knowledge that the lesson is being built upon.

Consider this scenario: In third grade, Ms. Franklin is about to begin a unit on early explorers—Columbus, Magellan, and others. In her class, she has some students who were in Mr. Washington's second-grade class last year, and some students who were in Ms. Johnson's second-grade class. She also has a few students who moved in from other towns. As Ms. Franklin begins the unit on explorers, she asks the children to look at a globe and use their fingers to trace a route across the Atlantic Ocean from Europe to North America. The students who had Mr. Washington look blankly at her: they didn't learn that last year. The students who had Ms. Johnson, however, eagerly point to the proper places on the globe, while two of the students who came from other towns pipe up and say, "Columbus and Magellan again? We did that last year."

When all the students in a class *do* share the relevant background knowledge, a classroom can begin to approach the effectiveness of a tutorial. Even when some children in a class do not have elements of the knowledge they were supposed to acquire in previous grades, the existence of a specifically defined core makes it possible for the teacher or parent to identify and fill the gaps, thus giving all students a chance to fulfill their potentials in later grades.

(2) Commonly shared knowledge makes schooling more fair and democratic.

When all the children who enter a grade can be assumed to share some of the same building blocks of knowledge, and when the teacher knows exactly what those building blocks are, then all the students are empowered to learn. In our current system, children from disadvantaged backgrounds too often suffer from unmerited low expectations that translate into watered-down curricula. But if we specify the core of knowledge that all children should share, then we can guarantee equal access to that knowledge and compensate for the academic advantages some students are offered at home. In a Core Knowledge school *all* children enjoy the benefits of important, challenging knowledge that will provide the foundation for successful later learning.

(3) Commonly shared knowledge helps create cooperation and solidarity in our schools and nation.

Diversity is a hallmark and strength of our nation. American classrooms are usually made up of students from a variety of cultural backgrounds, and those different cultures should be honored by all students. At the same time, education should create a *school-based* culture that is common and welcoming to all because it includes knowledge of many cultures and gives all students, no matter what their background, a common foundation for understanding our cultural diversity.

In the next section, I will describe the steps taken by the Core Knowledge Foundation to develop a model of the commonly shared knowledge our children need (which forms the basis for this series of books).

III. The Consensus Behind the Core Knowledge Sequence

The content in this and other volumes in the Core Knowledge Series is based on a document called the *Core Knowledge Sequence*, a grade-by-grade sequence of specific content guidelines in history, geography, mathematics, science, language arts, and fine arts. The *Sequence* is not meant to outline the whole of the school curriculum; rather, it offers specific guidelines to knowledge that can reasonably be expected to make up about *half* of any school's curriculum, thus leaving ample room for local requirements and emphases. Teaching a common core of knowledge, such as that articulated in the *Core Knowledge Sequence*, is compatible with a variety of instructional methods and additional subject matters.

The *Core Knowledge Sequence* is the result of a long process of research and consensus-building undertaken by the Core Knowledge Foundation. Here is how we achieved the consensus behind the *Core Knowledge Sequence*.

First, we analyzed the many reports issued by state departments of education and by professional organizations—such as the National Council of Teachers of Mathematics and the American Association for the Advancement of Science—that recommend general outcomes for elementary and secondary education. We also tabulated the knowledge and skills through grade six specified in the successful educational systems of several other countries, including France, Japan, Sweden, and West Germany.

In addition, we formed an advisory board on multiculturalism that proposed a specific knowledge of diverse cultural traditions that American children should all share as part of their school-based common culture. We sent the resulting materials to three independent groups of teachers, scholars, and scientists around the country, asking them to create a master list of the knowledge children should have by the end of grade six. About 150 teachers (including college professors, scientists, and administrators) were involved in this initial step.

These items were amalgamated into a master plan, and further groups of teachers and specialists were asked to agree on a grade-by-grade sequence of the items. That sequence was then sent to some one hundred educators and specialists who participated in a national conference that was called to hammer out a working agreement on an appropriate core of knowledge for the first six grades.

This important meeting took place in March 1990. The conferees were elementary school teachers, curriculum specialists, scientists, science writers, officers of national organizations, representatives of ethnic groups, district superintendents, and school principals from across the country. A total of twenty-four working groups decided on revisions in the *Core Knowledge Sequence*. The resulting provisional *Sequence* was further fine-tuned during a year of implementation at a pioneering school, Three Oaks Elementary in Lee County, Florida.

In only a few years many more schools—urban and rural, rich and poor, public and private—joined in the effort to teach Core Knowledge. Based largely on suggestions from these schools, the *Core Knowledge Sequence* was revised in 1995: separate guidelines were added for kindergarten, and a few topics in other grades were added, omitted, or moved from one grade to another in order to create an even more coherent sequence for learning. Revised editions of the books in the Core Knowledge Series reflect the revisions in the *Sequence*. Based on the principle of learning from experience, the Core Knowledge Foundation continues to work with schools and advisors to fine-tune the *Sequence,* and it is also conducting research that will lead to the publication of guidelines for grades seven and eight, as well as for preschool. (The *Core Knowledge Sequence* may be ordered from the Core Knowledge Foundation; see the end of this Introduction for the address.)

IV. THE NATURE OF THIS SERIES

The books in this series are designed to give a convenient and engaging introduction to the knowledge specified in the *Core Knowledge Sequence.* These are resource books, addressed primarily to parents, but which we hope will be useful tools for both parents and teachers. These books are not intended to replace the local curriculum or school textbooks, but rather to serve as aids to help children gain some of the important knowledge they will need to make progress in school and to be effective in society.

Although we have made these books as accessible and useful as we can, parents and teachers should understand that they are not the only means by which the *Core Knowledge Sequence* can be imparted. The books represent a single version of the possibilities inherent in the *Sequence,* and a first step in the Core Knowledge reform effort. We hope that publishers will be stimulated to offer educational videos, computer software, games, alternative books, and other imaginative vehicles based on the *Core Knowledge Sequence.*

These books are not textbooks or workbooks, though when appropriate they do suggest a variety of activities you can do with your child. In these books, we address your child directly, and occasionally ask questions for him or her to think about. The earliest books in the series are intended to be read aloud to children. Even as children become able to read the books on their own, we encourage parents to help their children read more actively by reading along with them and talking about what they are reading.

You and your child can read the sections of this book in any order, depending on your child's interests or depending on the topics your child is studying in school, which this book may sometimes complement or reinforce. You can skip from section to section and reread as much as your child likes.

We encourage you to think of this book as a guidebook that opens the way to many paths you and your child can explore. These paths may lead to the library, to many other good books, and, if possible, to plays, museums, concerts, and other opportunities for knowledge and enrichment. In short, this guidebook recommends places to visit and describes what is important in those places, but only you and your child can make the actual visit, travel the streets, and climb the steps.

V. WHAT YOU CAN DO TO HELP IMPROVE AMERICAN EDUCATION

The first step for parents and teachers who are committed to reform is to be skeptical about oversimplified slogans like "critical thinking" and "learning to learn." Such slogans are everywhere, and unfortunately for our schools, their partial insights have been elevated to the level of universal truths. For example: "What students learn is not important; rather, we must teach students to learn *how* to learn." "The child, not the academic subject, is the true focus of education." "Do not impose knowledge on children before they are developmentally ready to receive it." "Do not bog children down in mere facts, but rather, teach critical-thinking skills."

Who has not heard these sentiments, so admirable and humane, and—up to a point—so true? But these positive sentiments in favor of "thinking skills" and "higher understanding" have been turned into negative sentiments against the teaching of important knowledge. Those who have entered the teaching profession over the past forty years have been taught to scorn important knowledge as "mere facts," and to see the imparting of this knowledge as somehow injurious to children. Thus it has come about that many educators, armed with partially true slogans, have seemingly taken leave of common sense.

Many parents and teachers have come to the conclusion that elementary education must strike a better balance between the development of the whole child and the more limited but fundamental duty of the school to ensure that all children master a core of knowledge and skills essential to their competence as learners in later grades. But these parents and teachers cannot act on their convictions without access to an agreed-upon, concrete sequence of knowledge. Our main motivation in developing the *Core Knowledge Sequence* and this book series has been to give parents and teachers something concrete to work with.

It has been encouraging to see how many teachers, since the first volume in this series was published, have responded to the Core Knowledge reform effort. If you would like more information about the growing network of Core Knowledge schools, please call or write the Director of School Programs at the Core Knowledge Foundation.

Parents and teachers are urged to join in a grassroots effort to strengthen our elementary schools. The place to start is in your own school and district. Insist that your school clearly state the core of *specific* knowledge and skills that each child in a grade must learn. Whether your school's core corresponds exactly to the Core Knowledge model is less important than the existence of *some* core—which, we hope, will be as solid, coherent, and challenging as the *Core Knowledge Sequence* has proved to be. Inform members of your community about the need for such a specific curriculum, and help make sure that the people who are elected or appointed to your local school board are independent-minded people who will insist that our children have the benefit of a solid, specific, world-class curriculum in each grade.

You are invited to become a member of the Core Knowledge Network by writing or calling the Core Knowledge Foundation, 801 East High St., Charlottesville, VA 22902; 804-977-7550.

Share the knowledge!

E. D. Hirsch, Jr.
Charlottesville, Virginia

I.

Language and Literature

Reading, Writing, and Your First Grader

PARENTS: *Before we present a selection of poems and stories for your child, we want to address you directly. This section, Reading, Writing, and Your First Grader, is intended to help you understand how children are—or should be—taught to read and write in a good first-grade classroom, and to suggest a few ways that you can help at home. The first section below, Teaching Children to Read: The Need for a Balanced Approach, summarizes a discussion presented in* What Your Kindergartner Needs to Know. *If you have already read this, then you may wish to skip ahead to page 5 and begin with the section Goals for Reading and Writing: From Kindergarten to First Grade.*

Teaching Children to Read: The Need for a Balanced Approach

Everyone agrees that children should learn to read. But not everyone agrees how to achieve that goal. Many studies have demonstrated,* however, that while fashions come and go in education, pulling schools toward one extreme or another, there is a reasonable middle ground that is best for children.

This middle ground *balances* two approaches that some educators mistakenly see as mutually exclusive. The first approach emphasizes the systematic teaching of the "nuts and bolts" of written language: phonics and decoding skills (turning written letters into spoken sounds), spelling, handwriting, punctuation, grammar, vocabulary, sentence structure, paragraph form, and other rules and conventions. The second approach emphasizes the need for children to be nourished on a rich diet of poetry, fiction, and nonfiction. It focuses attention on the meanings and messages conveyed by written words, and insists that children be given frequent opportunities to use language in creative and expressive ways.

Schools need to embrace *both* of these approaches. In particular, at the time of this writing, many elementary schools need to pay much more attention to the "nuts and bolts": they need to take steps to balance a worthwhile emphasis on literature and creative expression with an equally necessary emphasis on the basic how-to skills of reading and writing.

---

*See, for example, Marilyn Jager Adams, *Beginning to Read: Thinking and Learning about Print* (Cambridge: MIT Press, 1990). A convenient summary of this authoritative analysis of research on early reading is available from the Center for the Study of Reading, University of Illinois, 51 Gerty Drive, Champaign, IL 61820. (Call 217-244-4083 for current pricing.)

Learning to Read and Write

To learn to read is to learn to understand and use our language, specifically our *written* language. Learning to read is not like learning to speak. While speech seems to come naturally, reading is a very different story. It is not enough just to see or hear others reading. Learning to read takes effort and instruction, because reading is not a natural process. Our written language is not a natural thing—it is an artificial code. There is no natural reason why when you see this mark—A—you should hear in your mind a sound that rhymes with "day." But you do, because you have learned the code. A few

children seem to figure out this code for themselves, but most children need organized, systematic, direct instruction in how to *decode* the words on the page, that is, to turn the written symbols, the letters, into the speech sounds they represent.

The key to helping children unlock the code of our written language is to help them understand the relationships between individual letters, and combinations of letters, and the sounds they make. True, sometimes these relationships seem odd: consider, for example, the different sounds of the letters "ough" in "though" and "enough." Despite these occasional oddities, there is a logic to the written English alphabet: its basic symbols, the letters, represent the basic speech sounds, or phonemes, of our spoken language. The relationships between letters and sounds exhibit many regular patterns, as in, for example, "cat," "hat," "sat," "mat," "fat," "rat."

So, part of learning to read means learning the predictable letter-sound patterns in written words. Learning these letter-sound patterns enables a child who confronts a page of print to *decode* the written words into the sounds of spoken language they represent. The other side of the coin here is learning the basic skills of writing, which enable a child who faces a blank page to *encode* the sounds of spoken language by putting on paper the corresponding written letters to form words, and by following other conventions of writing (such as capitalization and punctuation) that allow us to get across our meanings, even when the person to whom we are communicating is not present before us.

All this talk about decoding and encoding may sound very mechanical and a little intimidating. It should be kept in mind that instruction in decoding and encoding is all in the service of meaning and understanding. If children are to communicate their ideas, thoughts, and desires in writing, as well as to understand what others are saying in print—whether it's a traffic sign, a movie poster, a letter from a relative, or a story by Dr. Seuss or Beverly Cleary—then they need to have the tools to encode and decode written English.

Goals for Reading and Writing: From Kindergarten to First Grade

In *What Your Kindergartner Needs to Know*, we stated that a reasonable goal for instruction in kindergarten is to have all children beginning to read and write on their own by the end of the kindergarten year. By this we meant that kindergartners should:

- become comfortably familiar with the letters of the alphabet so that they can readily recognize and name the letters.
- develop a deliberate and conscious awareness of some of the sounds of oral language, and begin to make explicit connections between spoken sounds and printed letters.
- print both uppercase and lowercase letters with some proficiency, and write using some phonetic spelling (that is, spelling based on what they have learned so far about how words sound, for example, "bot" for "boat").
- be comfortable reading simple words they can sound out, as well as a few common "sight words," words that occur very often in writing but do not conform to the usual letter-sound patterns, such as "the," "an," "of," etc.

A reasonable goal for first grade is for children to become *independent readers and writers*—which, of course, doesn't mean that they ought to be able to read any book in the library or write a polished, perfectly spelled essay. By the end of the year, however, it is reasonable to expect that, with only limited assistance, first graders will read books appropriate to beginning readers and express themselves comfortably and legibly in writing.

What Does a Good First-Grade Program Do?

A good first-grade program can help children become independent readers and writers by taking a balanced approach that emphasizes both meaning and decoding. In a good first-grade class, children will be provided many opportunities to communicate and express themselves in speech and writing. As the year advances, they will be presented with appropriate "beginner books" and other print materials to read, with some assistance as needed, but with the goal of reading independently. They will continue to listen to interesting poetry, fiction, and nonfiction, and will be asked to talk about them and respond to them in thoughtful ways. Such literature gives children insight into a world of meaning expressed in words that they may not be able to read entirely on their own, but that they understand when the words are read aloud and discussed with an adult.

But for children to learn to read, it's not enough just to have good books read aloud to them. Listening to books does help children acquire a sense of what makes up a story, and motivates them to want to read. But it will not teach them how to read the words on the page. For that, children need repeated practice in working with letters and sounds in order to develop a good initial understanding of how language works. This does not mean mindless drill; rather, it means providing repeated and varied opportunities for children to work and play with letters and sounds.

There are many ways for a school to put together a good first-grade program in reading and writing, and many good materials for schools to use. Whatever the local approach or materials, any good first-grade program will do much of the following:

- A good first-grade program helps children develop their oral language, including speaking and listening. Children continue to hear good literature, both fiction and nonfiction, read aloud, often with the written text displayed so they can "follow along." They are asked to talk about books that have been read to them, to ask and answer questions, and sometimes to retell or summarize the story.
- A good first-grade program continues the practice begun in kindergarten of explicitly and systematically developing children's phonemic awareness, that is, the understanding that the sounds of a word can be thought of as a string of smaller, individual sounds. Children participate in a variety of listening and speaking activities designed to help them recognize and compare sounds that make up words. For example, they may be asked to listen to a word, such as "take," then to "say it again but start with *mmm*" ("make"); "say it again but start with *rrr*" ("rake"). Or they may be asked which word has the short *a* sound as in "apple": "mat" or "mate"? Which word has the long *o* sound as in "hope": "mop" or "mope"?

  In first grade, in addition to developing phonemic awareness through listening and speaking activities, children should consistently practice associating specific sounds with particular written letters and combinations of letters. They should be given regular opportunities to "sound out," read, and write words that correspond to the letter-sound patterns they have been taught. *Parents take note:* Some schools discourage children from sounding out words and urge them instead to "guess" the words based on "clues" from pictures or what's going on in the story. This is a serious mistake. Children need to learn a systematic, reliable way to figure out words they don't know, and this can come only from giving them explicit instruction in the code of our written language. It is important that this instruction be systematically organized to make *explicit* the letter-sound patterns and present them in a way that builds logically and sequentially, not in a haphazard or occasional fashion. Phonics instruction is most effective when it is regular, if not daily, with one skill building on another and with plenty of practice and review.

- As children master individual letter-sound patterns and become able to sound out words, a good program provides phonetically controlled reading materials. These are simple stories written in a controlled vocabulary that corresponds to the letter-sound patterns that a child has been taught in preparation for reading the story. For example, after being taught how a silent "e" at the end of a word can make a vowel long, a child might read a story about how "Jake made a cake." While such stories are of course not great literature, they are very helpful in teaching children to read, especially in providing the early and tremendously satisfying experience of being able "to read it all by myself." In preparation for reading these stories, children also need to add to their stock of sight words, such as "of," "was," "do," "the."

- Once children have demonstrated some success with phonetically controlled reading materials, they should be introduced to and asked to read, with occasional assistance, stories that are not phonetically controlled but are written for beginning readers, such as Arnold Lobel's *Frog and Toad* books or Peggy Parish's *Amelia Bedelia* books. (See below, pages 13–14, for more titles of books for beginning readers.)

- A good first-grade program provides regular handwriting practice through which children refine letter size and legibility, and learn to make appropriate use of the space on a page to present written information. (See charts, pages 8 and 9.)

- A good program introduces a few conventions and rules of capitalization, punctuation, and spelling. (You can reinforce some basic rules by reading aloud the information in the box on page 10, and by gently reminding your child of these rules when she writes.)

- A good first-grade program provides a classroom environment in which children are surrounded by written language that is meaningful to them, such as posters with the children's names and birthdays, name labels on desks or storage cubbies, and word labels on objects in the classroom ("door," "blackboard," "map," etc.). A good program recognizes that reading and writing reinforce each other, and it provides children with many opportunities to practice writing. Learning to read may be coordinated with learning to spell and write through regular dictation exercises in which

Handwriting chart: uppercase (capital) letters

the teacher calls out words that the children have practiced reading and asks the children to spell them (that is, correctly write the words, or sometimes short sentences, on paper). Other writing is more for purposes of communication or creativity, such as writing letters, descriptions, short stories, poems, captions to pictures, and the like. First graders will often want to say more than they can write correctly, so in some cases the children should be encouraged to use phonetic spelling, that is, "to spell it the way they think it sounds" (so that a child may write, for example, "bot" for "boat"). This *occasional* practice of phonetic spelling is beneficial for first graders because it engages them in actively thinking about the sounds of words and how they are represented, and can make them more interested in writing and more willing to put their thoughts on paper. Of course, children need regular practice with conventional, correct spellings as well.

That, in brief, describes some of what a good first-grade program will do to help chil-

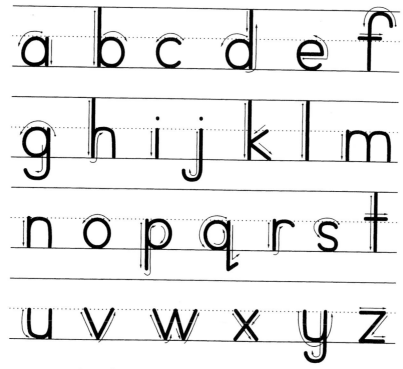

Handwriting chart: lowercase (small) letters

dren achieve the goal of becoming independent readers and writers. Some children will surpass this goal; others may come close but not quite achieve it. But *every* child should receive appropriate instruction, materials, and support, and should be guided and encouraged to do his or her best to meet the goal. If a child is having difficulty, a school should not rationalize his difficulty by saying that the child is "not developmentally ready." You do not wait for readiness to happen. Rather, the child who is less ready should be given even *more* support, encouragement, and practice in the areas posing difficulty.

What about the children who surpass the goals for first grade? Children who surpass the goals should of course not be held back. There will always be, as proud parents are delighted to report, a few first graders, and even kindergartners, who are "reading everything they can get their hands on," even books like *Charlotte's Web* and *Little House on the Prairie*. These few children who are reading dramatically beyond grade level should be encouraged, and their appetite for books should be fed with appropriately challenging material. At the same time, they can still benefit from explicit, systematic instruction in letter-sound correspondences, because such instruction gives them conscious knowledge of the conventions of written English, which is one of the tools they will need as they confront more challenging tasks in reading and writing.

A FEW RULES FOR WRITING

First graders should practice using the following rules, though they should not be expected to use them with 100 percent accuracy in all their writings. As part of their practice and review, children should sometimes be asked in school to apply what they have learned by proofreading and correcting selected samples of their written work.

- *Capital letters:* Use a capital letter at the beginning of a sentence and at the beginning of names, such as: Abraham Lincoln was born in Kentucky. When you refer to yourself, capitalize "I."
- *End punctuation:* When you write a sentence, use a punctuation mark to show where the sentence stops.

  Use a little dot called a period to end most sentences.

  If you're asking a question, use a question mark.

  To show excitement, use an exclamation point, as in "I hit a home run!"

- *Contractions:* We sometimes combine two words into one short word called a *contraction.* To show that letters have been left out in a contraction, use the punctuation mark called an *apostrophe.* For example:

  I am = I'm   do not = don't   it is = it's

- *Making words plural:* "Plural" means "more than one." "Singular" means "just one." You can put an "s" at the end of many words and change them from singular to plural. For example:

Singular	*Plural*
leg	legs
horse	horses
book	books

What Parents Can Do to Help

As parents, you can help your first grader become a more independent reader and writer. Here are a few suggestions:

- Without question, the single most important and helpful thing you can do is to set aside fifteen or twenty minutes regularly, daily if possible, to *read aloud to your child.* See pages 16–17 in this book for suggested activities.
- In addition to reading aloud good literature *to* your first grader, you can help him make the transition to independent reading through *shared reading* sessions in which he reads *with* you. See Suggested Resources, listed below, for some phonetically controlled readers and popular beginner books. While these books are only several pages long and may look very simple to you, they will be challenging for many first graders, so we suggest you start by shared reading in which you take turns reading. How much your child reads will depend on the difficulty of the book and the progress he has made. You may want to begin by reading most of the book and asking him to read a familiar refrain or only a final rhyming word at the end of a line. Later, he might read aloud the even-numbered pages to you, and you read aloud the odd-numbered pages to him. The idea is to make your child's portion manageable, not overwhelming. Of course, if your child is reading confidently and accurately, offer praise and encouragement and let him keep going! As your child reads, have him point with his finger to each word. This will help focus his attention, keep his place, and reinforce the idea that each spoken word corresponds to a written word. (You should run your finger under the words when you read, too.)
- As you read with your child, make special note of any difficulties. If she misreads a word, come back to it after she finishes the sentence. If it is a word she should be able to decode based on the letter-sound patterns she has been taught before reading the book, then use a pencil tip to point under each letter as she sounds out the word. If she hesitates, do it with her. If she misreads a sight word ("the," "an," "of," etc.), point to it, say the correct word, and ask her to repeat it.
- Designate a special notebook or writing tablet as your child's writing notebook, and encourage him to write in it once or twice a week (in school, your child should be writing more frequently). In this notebook he can write down, for example, a funny joke, a few sentences about a favorite book or TV show or sports activity, something interesting he has learned in school, captions for pictures that he draws or cuts out of old magazines, or a made-up story or poem. If he likes, he can draw pictures to go along with his writing. Many children need to feel that they have something to say in order to make the effort to write it down, so talk with your child about what he might write: the more he thinks aloud, the more willing he will be to put words on paper. If while writing he seems unsure about the spelling of a word and asks for your

help, first ask him to "sound out" the word and try to write it the way it sounds, but if this proves too frustrating, then provide the correct spelling. When he has finished writing, ask him to read aloud what he has written. Praise and encourage! Show an interest in the *content* of what he has written by asking questions and engaging him in conversation about the topic. Once you've affirmed your interest in *what* he has written, then you can ask him to take a closer look at *how* he has said it, and help him correct errors of spelling and punctuation. At first do not try to correct every error. Instead, focus on the most familiar words and the most basic rules, such as ending a statement with a period. In helping him make corrections, the point is not to dwell on what's wrong but to show him that "this is how that word is spelled" or "this is how we begin a sentence, with a capital letter, remember?"

- Take advantage of unplanned moments to engage in spontaneous language games. Tell jokes. Ask riddles. Try tongue twisters. While driving in the car, you can play rhyming games and memory games, recite favorite poems, and point to different signs and talk about what they mean. While shopping for groceries, ask your child to cross items off the shopping list, or to try reading the names on a few labels.
- You can send an important message about the value you place on reading and writing by talking with your child about the schoolwork he brings home. Set aside time to look at his papers with him. Be supportive; praise the effort and do not dwell on the errors. (In school, the teacher should be observing your child's progress and working to correct any consistent pattern of errors.)

Suggested Resources

The resources recommended here are meant *to complement, not substitute for,* the reading programs and associated materials that schools use to teach reading and writing. Our suggestions are directed to parents, though some teachers may find these additional resources helpful as well, especially if their school has adopted a philosophy or set of materials that neglects the systematic early teaching of decoding skills and the conventions of written language.

The following list is intended to help you get started in locating a few of the many good resources available. There are *many* phonics materials available from many sources. In recommending a few here, we do not mean to exclude others. Here we suggest materials that are time-tested and/or readily available, generally at a reasonable cost, and usable by those without special training in the teaching of reading and writing.

Besides the books suggested below, other useful supplies are generally available from teacher supply stores and some toy stores:

- magnetic letters and letter-sound flash cards
- letter-picture cards (cards with simple pictures and a corresponding letter, for example, the letter "a" with a picture of an apple) and word-picture cards

- workbooks to practice handwriting
- word games, puzzles, and activity books
- computer software for teaching letter-sound patterns, words, and early reading and writing skills, such as *Beginning Reading* (Sierra On-Line), *Kid Phonics* (Davidson), *Reader Rabbit* (Level 2) and *Reader Rabbit's Interactive Reading Journey* (The Learning Company), and *Storybook Weaver Deluxe* (MECC)

General Resources

Bob Books; More Bob Books; Even More Bob Books by Bobby Lynn Maslen (Bob Books Publications/Scholastic, 1976). These three sets of little books might especially appeal to parents whose children are showing signs of interest in reading on their own. The phonetically controlled books—occasionally whimsical, quirky, and fun—offer cute stories and line drawings that verge on silly but which most children will probably like for that very reason. The books begin with short words and simple consonant sounds, and go on through the three sets to introduce new sounds in a nicely sequenced fashion. The first set may be easy for first graders if they have been taught phonics in kindergarten.

Dover Publications, 31 East 2nd Street, Mineola, NY 11501. Dover produces many attractive and inexpensive activity books, including many word games and alphabet books. Write and request a Children's Book Catalog.

Educators Publishing Service (EPS), 31 Smith Place, Cambridge, MA 02138-1000. This mail-order company has many good teacher-created resources, including such favorites as the *Primary Phonics* series of workbooks and storybooks (described below). Call 800-225-5750 for a catalogue.

Ladybug and *Spider*. Colorful, attractive artwork illustrates each issue of these monthly magazines for children, which feature many stories, activities, and puzzles, with no advertising. *Ladybug* is for children about three to six years old, with good read-aloud stories, simple poems, and some simple texts for beginning readers. *Spider* is for children about six to eight years old, with longer and more challenging stories. Many libraries carry the magazines. For subscription information, write to Cricket Magazine Group, 315 Fifth Street, Peru, IL 61354; or call 800-827-0227.

Primary Phonics Workbooks and Storybooks by Barbara Makar (Educators Publishing Service). These five sets of workbooks and coordinated readers have simple line drawings for many short stories using words with short vowels, long vowels, *r*-controlled vowels, and other vowel combinations in a carefully controlled sequence. Taken as a whole, they form a fairly comprehensive phonics program, more than most parents are likely to undertake at home (unless, of course, they are home schooling). For kindergartners, the *Primary Phonics Consonant Lessons Workbook* and the first set of storybooks, which focus on short vowels, might be used at home to complement reading instruction in school. First graders who have mastered the consonants and short vowel sounds might want to proceed to *Primary Phonics Workbook 2* and the second set of storybooks, which introduce long vowel sounds. *Primary Phonics* is only one of many sets of phonics materials available from Educators Publishing Service (address above). Call 800-225-5750 for a catalog.

Beginning Reader Books (not phonetically controlled)

Ready . . . Set . . . Read: The Beginning Reader's Treasury and *Ready . . . Set . . . Read—and Laugh! A Funny Treasury for Beginning Readers*, compiled by Joanna Cole and Stephanie Calmenson (Doubleday, 1990 and 1995). Two nicely illustrated collections containing stories, poems, riddles, and word games by well-known writers like Arnold Lobel and Eve Merriam. These are good books to turn to for the child who is growing more confident as a reader and ready for challenges beyond phonetically controlled texts.

Note: The following authors have written many stories for beginning readers. We suggest a few to get you started; look in the "Beginning or Easy Readers" section of your library, or ask your child's teacher or librarian to suggest more titles by these and other authors.

Dr. Seuss:
  The Cat in the Hat Comes Back
  Green Eggs and Ham
  Marvin K. Mooney Will You Please Go Now!

P. D. Eastman:
  Are You My Mother?
  Go, Dog, Go
  Sam and the Firefly

Lillian Hoban:
  Arthur's Honey Bear
  Arthur's Loose Tooth
  Arthur's Prize Reader

Syd Hoff:
  Danny and the Dinosaur
  Oliver
  Sammy the Seal

Arnold Lobel:
  Frog and Toad Are Friends
  Frog and Toad Together
  Owl at Home

Edward Marshall:
  Fox at School
  Fox in Love
  Three by the Sea

James Marshall:
  Fox on Stage
  Fox on the Job
  Three Up a Tree

Else Holmelund Minarik:
  Little Bear
  Little Bear's Friend
  Little Bear's Visit

Peggy Parish:
  Amelia Bedelia
  Amelia Bedelia Helps Out
  Come Back, Amelia Bedelia

Literature

INTRODUCTION

There is one simple practice that can make a world of difference for your first grader. *Read aloud to your child often*, daily if possible. Reading aloud opens the doors to a world of meaning that most children are curious to explore but in first grade are still beginning to enter on their own. In reading aloud, you can offer your child a rich and varied selection of literature, including poetry, fiction, and nonfiction.

For your first grader, we offer a selection of poetry, including some traditional rhymes, Mother Goose favorites, and familiar tongue twisters. We also include some poems by favorite modern and contemporary writers. All of these selections should be considered a starting point. We encourage you to read many more poems with your child, to delight in the play of language, and occasionally to help your child memorize a personal favorite.

The stories presented here are written in language more complex than most first graders will be able to read on their own, though they can readily be understood and enjoyed when the words are read aloud with expression, and talked about with an adult. These stories are meant to complement, not replace, the stories with controlled vocabularies and syntax that children should be given as part of their instruction in learning to read. (See Reading, Writing, and Your First Grader, page 7.)

In this book, we present many familiar and traditional tales that have stood the test of time. Some of the selections from other lands may not be familiar to American readers, but by including them here we hope to make them so.* Among the stories, you will find favorite folktales from many lands and cultures. We have paired two stories—"Issun Boshi: One-Inch Boy" and "Tom Thumb"—to help children see that people in different lands tell similar stories. We also include some modern classics of children's literature, such as *The Tale of Peter Rabbit* and a selection from *The House at Pooh Corner*.

Some of the stories in this first-grade volume build upon the selection of fairy tales by the Brothers Grimm and others presented in *What Your Kindergartner Needs to Know*. For children, such fairy tales can delight and instruct, and provide ways of dealing with darker human emotions like jealousy, greed, and fear. As G. K. Chesterton observed, fairy tales "are not responsible for producing in children fear, or any of the shapes of fear. . . . The baby has known the dragon intimately ever since he had an imagination. What the fairy tale provides for him is a St. George to kill the dragon." And as the celebrated writer of children's tales, Wanda Gag, wrote in 1937, "A fairy

---

*For a description of the process that led to the selection of poems and stories included in this book, see "The Consensus Behind the *Core Knowledge Sequence*," page xix.

story is not just a fluffy puff of nothing . . . nor is it merely a tenuous bit of make believe. . . . Its roots are real and solid, reaching far back into man's past . . . and into the lives and customs of many people and countries." Whatever the geographical origin of the traditional tales we tell here—Africa, Japan, Europe, America, etc.—the stories have universal messages and lasting appeal across cultures and generations.

Consider this selection of stories a starting point for further exploration. Beyond stories and poems, you can share appropriate works of nonfiction with your child. Many first graders enjoy, for example, illustrated books that explain what things are and how they work, books about animals and how they live, and biographies of famous people.

Your local library has a treasury of good books, and you might want to consult the lists of recommended works in such guides as:

Books That Build Character by William Kilpatrick et al. (Simon and Schuster/Touchstone, 1994)

Books to Build On: A Grade-by-Grade Resource Guide for Parents and Teachers, edited by John Holdren and E. D. Hirsch, Jr. (Dell, 1996)

The New Read-Aloud Handbook by Jim Trelease (Penguin Books, 1995)

The New York Times Parent's Guide to the Best Books for Children by Eden Ross Lipson (Times Books, revised and updated 1991)

Read-Aloud Activities

Try to set aside a regular time for reading aloud, a time free from other obligations or distractions (including the television, which must be off). When you read aloud, don't feel embarrassed about hamming it up a bit. Be expressive; try giving different characters different voices.

If your child is not used to hearing stories read aloud, you may want to begin by reading some poems or some of the shorter selections in this book. If your child starts to squirm as you read longer stories, take a break from reading and get your child involved: have him look at a picture, or ask him some questions, or ask him to tell you what he thinks about what has happened so far, or have him draw a picture to go with the part of the story you've read.

When you read aloud, most of the time your child will be involved in the simple pleasure of listening. At other times, you can involve your child in some additional activities to encourage comprehension and interest. Remember, these activities are not tests. Use them with a gentle touch: relax, have fun together.

- Let your child look through the book before you read it. Let him skim the pages and look at pictures.
- Direct your child's attention to the book's title page. Point to the author's name and read it as written, for example, "Written by Peggy Parrish." If the book is illustrated,

also read the illustrator's name, for example, "Illustrated by Jerry Pinkney." Discuss what the words "author" and "illustrator" mean. As you read more and more books, talk with your child about her favorite authors or illustrators. Look in the library for more works by your child's favorite authors and illustrators.

- Sometimes let your child pick the books for reading aloud. If your child has picked a book or books from the library, she may soon learn the lesson that "you can't tell a book by its cover." If you begin a book that she has chosen and she expresses dislike or lack of interest, don't force her to finish hearing it. Just put the book aside with the understanding that "maybe we'll like this better later."

- As you read, sometimes run your finger below the words as you say them. This will help confirm your child's sense of the left-to-right direction of print. In rereading a selection, you can direct your child's attention to individual words as you say them aloud. You can also ask your child to try to read occasional words and phrases, especially ones that he is likely to have some success with.

- After reading a story, discuss the *sequence* of events. "Can you tell me what happened first?" "What did he do next?" You can draw three or four simple pictures representing scenes in the story, then ask your child to arrange the pictures in the proper sequence as she retells the story.

- After reading a poem or a story or a segment of a longer book, help your child *recall details* by asking questions. Keep in mind the five W's: Who? What? When? Where? Why? For example, after reading "The Boy at the Dike," ask, "Where did Peter live?" "Whom did Peter go to visit?" "Why did he go there?" "What happened on the way home?" "Why couldn't he leave the dike?" "When did somebody find him?" (Maintain a playful, conversational tone; this is not a test!)

- In talking about stories, occasionally use words that are common in the discussion of literature, such as "character," "hero," and "heroine." For example, you might ask, "Who is your favorite character in *The House at Pooh Corner*?" Not all stories have heroes or heroines, but you can bring up the terms when appropriate, for example by asking, "Isn't it surprising that the hero of 'Issun Boshi' is no bigger than your thumb (at least for most of the story)?" Or, "That was a brave thing for Gretel to do. She's a real heroine, isn't she?"

- Engage your child in a discussion of the story by asking questions that go beyond recall of details and take her into interpretation. For example, after reading "It Could Always Be Worse," ask, "Why do you think the story has that title? What do you think it means?"

- Help your child memorize a favorite poem.

- Act out a story or scenes from a story. Your child doesn't need to memorize a set script; she can use her own language to express a character's thoughts. A few simple props can help: paper bags for masks, old shirts for costumes, a broomstick for a horse—all can be transformed by your child's active imagination.

Poetry

Traditional Rhymes

Little Sally Walker

Little Sally Walker
Sitting in the saucer
Rise, Sally, rise
Wipe your weepy eyes.
Put your hands on your hips
And make your backbone slip.
Oh, shake it to the east
Oh, shake it to the west
Oh, shake to the one
    that you love the best.

If Wishes Were Horses

If wishes were horses, beggars would ride.
If turnips were watches, I would wear one
   by my side,
And if "ifs" and "ands" were pots and pans,
There'd be no work for tinkers!

The Queen of Hearts

The Queen of Hearts
She made some tarts,
    All on a summer's day.
The Knave of Hearts
He stole the tarts,
    And took them clean away.

The King of Hearts
Called for the tarts,
    And beat the Knave full sore.
The Knave of Hearts
Brought back the tarts,
    And vowed he'd steal no more.

Three Wise Men of Gotham

Three wise men of Gotham
Went to sea in a bowl;
If the bowl had been stronger
My song had been longer.

Solomon Grundy

Solomon Grundy,
Born on a Monday,
Christened on Tuesday,
Married on Wednesday,
Took ill on Thursday,
Worse on Friday,
Died on Saturday,
Buried on Sunday:
This is the end
Of Solomon Grundy.

Thirty Days Hath September

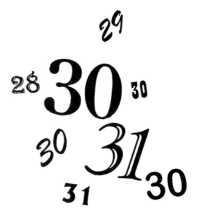

Thirty days hath September,
April, June, and November.
All the rest have thirty-one,
But February has twenty-eight alone,
Except in leap year, that's the time
When February's days are twenty-nine.

Tongue Twisters

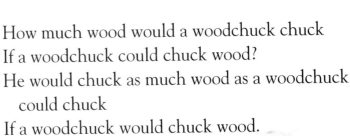

Peter Piper picked a peck of pickled peppers;
A peck of pickled peppers Peter Piper picked.
If Peter Piper picked a peck of pickled peppers,
Where's the peck of pickled peppers Peter Piper picked?

Moses supposes his toeses are roses,
But Moses supposes erroneously;
For nobody's toeses are posies of roses,
As Moses supposes his toeses to be.

How much wood would a woodchuck chuck
If a woodchuck could chuck wood?
He would chuck as much wood as a woodchuck
    could chuck
If a woodchuck would chuck wood.

Swan swam over the sea;
Swim, swan, swim.
Swan swam back again;
Well swum, swan.

She sells seashells by the seashore.

Riddle Rhymes
(For answers, turn this page upside down.)

Riddle me, riddle me, what is that
Over the head, and under the hat?

(*hair*)

Higher than a house, higher than a tree,
Oh, whatever can it be?

(*a star*)

A hill full, a hole full,
Yet you cannot catch a bowl full.

(*mist or smoke*)

Thirty white horses upon a red hill,
Now they tramp, now they champ,
  now they stand still.

(*teeth*)

More Poems for First Grade

The Pasture
by Robert Frost

I'm going out to clean the pasture spring;
I'll only stop to rake the leaves away
(And wait to watch the water clear, I may):
I shan't be gone long.—You come too.

I'm going out to fetch the little calf
That's standing by the mother. It's so young
It totters when she licks it with her tongue.
I shan't be gone long.—You come too.

Hope
by Langston Hughes

Sometimes when I'm lonely,
Don't know why,
Keep thinkin' I won't be lonely
By and by.

A Good Play
by Robert Louis Stevenson

We built a ship upon the stairs
All made of the back-bedroom chairs,
And filled it full of sofa pillows
To go a-sailing on the billows.

We took a saw and several nails,
And water in the nursery pails;
And Tom said, "Let us also take
An apple and a slice of cake";
Which was enough for Tom and me
To go a-sailing on, till tea.

We sailed along for days and days,
And had the very best of plays;
But Tom fell out and hurt his knee,
So there was no one left but me.

The Swing
by Robert Louis Stevenson

How do you like to go up in a swing,
  Up in the air so blue?
Oh, I do think it the pleasantest thing
  Ever a child can do!

Up in the air and over the wall,
  Till I can see so wide,
Rivers and trees and cattle and all
  Over the countryside—

Till I look down on the garden green,
  Down on the roof so brown—
Up in the air I go flying again,
  Up in the air and down!

The Frog
by Hilaire Belloc

Be kind and tender to the Frog,
  And do not call him names,
As "Slimy skin," or "Polly-wog,"
  Or likewise "Ugly James,"
Or "Gape-a-grin," or "Toad-gone-wrong,"
  Or "Billy Bandy-knees":
The Frog is justly sensitive
  To epithets like these.
No animal will more repay
  A treatment kind and fair;
At least so lonely people say
Who keep a frog (and, by the way,
  They are extremely rare).

The Purple Cow
by Gelett Burgess

I never saw a Purple Cow,
I never hope to see one;
But I can tell you, anyhow,
I'd rather see than be one.

I Know All the Sounds That the Animals Make
by Jack Prelutsky

I know all the sounds that the animals make,
and make them all day from the moment I wake,
I roar like a mouse and I purr like a moose,
I hoot like a duck and I moo like a goose.

I squeak like a cat and I quack like a frog,
I oink like a bear and I honk like a hog,
I croak like a cow and I bark like a bee,
no wonder the animals marvel at me.

The Owl and the Pussy-cat
by Edward Lear

The Owl and the Pussy-cat went to sea
    In a beautiful pea-green boat,
They took some honey, and plenty
of money,
    Wrapped up in a five-pound note.
The Owl looked up to the stars above,
    And sang to a small guitar,
"O lovely Pussy! O Pussy, my love,
    What a beautiful Pussy you are,

You are,
    You are!
What a beautiful Pussy you are!"

Pussy said to the Owl, "You elegant fowl!
    How charmingly sweet you sing!
O let us be married! too long we have tarried:
    But what shall we do for a ring?"
They sailed away, for a year and a day,
    To the land where the Bong-tree grows
And there in a wood a Piggy-wig stood
    With a ring at the end of his nose,
        His nose,
        His nose,
With a ring at the end of his nose.

"Dear Pig, are you willing to sell for one shilling
    Your ring?" Said the Piggy, "I will."
So they took it away, and were married next day
    By the Turkey who lives on the hill.
They dined on mince, and slices of quince,
    Which they ate with a runcible spoon;
And hand in hand, on the edge of the sand,
    They danced by the light of the moon,
        The moon,
        The moon,
They danced by the light of the moon.

My Shadow
by Robert Louis Stevenson

I have a little shadow that goes in and out with me,
And what can be the use of him is more than I can see.
He is very, very like me from the heels up to the head;
And I see him jump before me, when I jump into my bed.

The funniest thing about him is the way he likes to grow—
Not at all like proper children, which is always very slow;
For he sometimes shoots up taller like an india-rubber ball,
And he sometimes gets so little that there's none of him at all.

He hasn't got a notion of how children ought to play,
And can only make a fool of me in every sort of way.
He stays so close beside me, he's a coward you can see;
I'd think shame to stick to nursie as that shadow
       sticks to me!

One morning, very early, before the sun was up,
I rose and found the shining dew on every
    buttercup;
But my lazy little shadow, like an arrant
    sleepy-head,
Had stayed at home behind me and was fast asleep
    in bed.

Rope Rhyme
by Eloise Greenfield

Get set, ready now, jump right in
Bounce and kick and giggle and spin
Listen to the rope when it hits the ground
Listen to that clappedy-slappedy sound
Jump right up when it tells you to
Come back down, whatever you do
Count to a hundred, count by ten
Start to count all over again
That's what jumping is all about
Get set, ready now,
    jump
        right
           out!

Table Manners
by Gelett Burgess

The Goops they lick their fingers,
    And the Goops they lick their knives;
They spill their broth on the tablecloth—
    Oh, they lead disgusting lives!
The Goops they talk while eating,
    And loud and fast they chew;
And that is why I'm glad that I
    Am not a Goop—are you?

Sing a Song of People
by Lois Lenski

Sing a song of people
   Walking fast or slow;
People in the city,
   Up and down they go.

People on the sidewalk,
People on the bus;
People passing, passing,
In back and front of us.
People on the subway
Underneath the ground;
People riding taxis
Round and round and round.

People with their hats on,
Going in the doors;
People with umbrellas
When it rains and pours.
People in tall buildings
And in stores below;
Riding elevators
Up and down they go.

People walking singly,
People in a crowd;
People saying nothing,
People talking loud.
People laughing, smiling,
Grumpy people too;
People who just hurry
And never look at you!

Sing a song of people
   Who like to come and go;
Sing of city people
   You see but never know!

Washington
by Nancy Byrd Turner

He played by the river when he was young,
He raced with rabbits along the hills,
He fished for minnows, and climbed and swung,
And hooted back at the whippoorwills.
Strong and slender and tall he grew—
And then, one morning, the bugles blew.

Over the hills the summons came,
Over the river's shining rim.
He said that the bugles called his name,
He knew that his country needed him,
And he answered, "Coming!" and marched away
For many a night and many a day.

Perhaps when the marches were hot and long
He'd think of the river flowing by
Or, camping under the winter sky,
Would hear the whippoorwill's far-off song.
Boy or soldier, in peace or strife,
He loved America all his life!

Wynken, Blynken, and Nod
by Eugene Field

Wynken, Blynken, and Nod one night
   Sailed off in a wooden shoe—
Sailed on a river of crystal light,
   Into a sea of dew.
"Where are you going, and what do you wish?"
   The old moon asked the three.
   "We have come to fish for the herring fish
   That live in this beautiful sea:
   Nets of silver and gold have we!"
      Said Wynken,
      Blynken,
      And Nod.

The old moon laughed and sang a song,
   As they rocked in the wooden shoe,
And the wind that sped them all night long
   Ruffled the waves of dew.
The little stars were the herring fish

That lived in that beautiful sea—
"Now cast your nets wherever you wish—
Never afeard are we";
So cried the stars to the fishermen three:
    Wynken,
    Blynken,
    And Nod.

All night long their nets they threw
    To the stars in the twinkling foam—
Then down from the skies came the wooden shoe
    Bringing the fishermen home;
'Twas all so pretty a sail it seemed
    As if it could not be,
And some folks thought 'twas a dream they'd dreamed
    Of sailing that beautiful sea—
    But I shall name you the fishermen three:
    Wynken,
    Blynken,
    And Nod.

Wynken and Blynken are two little eyes,
    And Nod is a little head,
And the wooden shoe that sailed the skies
    Is a wee one's trundle-bed.
So shut your eyes while mother sings
    Of wonderful sights that be,
And you shall see the beautiful things
    As you rock in the misty sea,
    Where the old shoe rocked the fishermen three:
    Wynken,
    Blynken,
    And Nod.

Thanksgiving Day
by Lydia Maria Child

Over the river and through the
    wood,
To grandfather's house we go;
The horse knows the way
To carry the sleigh
Through the white and drifted snow.

Over the river and through the
    wood—
Oh, how the wind does blow!
It stings the toes
And bites the nose,
As over the ground we go.

Over the river and through the
    wood,
To have a first-rate play.
Hear the bells ring,
"Ting-a-ling-ding!"
Hurrah for Thanksgiving Day!

Over the river and through the
    wood,
Trot fast, my dapple-gray!
Spring over the ground,
Like a hunting-hound!
For this is Thanksgiving Day.

Over the river and through the
    wood,
And straight through the barn-yard
    gate.
We seem to go
Extremely slow—
It is so hard to wait!

Over the river and through the
    wood—
Now grandmother's cap I spy!
Hurrah for the fun!
Is the pudding done?
Hurrah for the pumpkin-pie!

Aesop's Fables

A fable is a special kind of story that teaches a lesson. People have been telling some fables over and over for hundreds of years. It is said that many of these fables were told by a man named Aesop [EE-sop], who lived in Greece a very, very long time ago.

Aesop knew bad behavior when he saw it, and he wanted people to be better. But he knew that we don't like to be told when we're bad. That is why many of his fables have animals in them. The animals sometimes talk and act like people. In fact, the animals behave just as well and just as badly as people do. That's because, even when a fable is about animals, it is really about people. Through these stories about animals, Aesop teaches us how we should act as people.

At the end of the fable, Aesop often tells us a lesson we should learn. The lesson is called the *moral* of the story.

Here are six of Aesop's fables, most with animals in them. The moral of the story is stated at the end of each fable. As you read the fables, try saying what you think the lesson might be before you read the moral.

The Boy Who Cried Wolf

There was once a young shepherd boy who tended his sheep at the foot of a mountain near a dark forest. It was lonely for him watching the sheep all day. No one was near, except for three farmers he could sometimes see working in the fields in the valley below.

One day the boy thought of a plan by which he could get a little company and have some fun. He ran down toward the valley crying, "Wolf! Wolf!"

The men ran to meet him, and after they found out there was no wolf after all, one man remained to talk with the boy awhile.

The boy enjoyed the company so much that a few days later he tried the same trick again, and again the men ran to help him.

A few days later, a real wolf came from the forest and began to steal the sheep. The boy ran toward the valley, and more loudly than ever he cried, "Wolf! Wolf!"

But the men, who had been fooled twice before, thought that he was tricking them again. No one came to help the boy. And so the wolf had a very good meal.

MORAL: If you often lie, people won't believe you even when you are telling the truth.

The Fox and the Grapes

One hot summer day, a fox was strolling along when he noticed a bunch of juicy grapes, just turning ripe, hanging on a vine high above. "Mmm, that's just the thing to take care of my thirst," said the fox. He trotted back a few steps, then ran forward and *jumped*, but he missed the grapes. He turned around and tried again. "One, two, three, *go*," he said, and he leaped with all his might. But again he missed the grapes.

Again and again he tried, but at last he gave up. And he walked away with his nose in the air, saying, "I didn't want those old grapes anyway. I'm sure they are sour."

MORAL: When people cannot get what they want, they sometimes tell themselves that what they want is no good anyway.

"Sour grapes" has become a common saying. People say "It's just sour grapes" to refer to griping or unkind remarks someone makes about something he or she can't have. For example:

Jim turned to his teacher, Mr. Rodriguez, and asked, "Why did Mark say our class play isn't going to be any good?"

"Oh, that's just sour grapes," said Mr. Rodriguez. "Mark wanted to be the star, but he's playing a smaller part. But once he sees how much fun it is, he'll change his mind."

The Dog in the Manger

There was once a dog who liked to nap on hot days in the cool barn. He liked to sleep in the manger, the long wooden box where hay was put for the farm animals to eat.

One hot day after a long afternoon pulling the plow, the oxen returned to the barn, hungry for their dinner. But the dog was lying in the manger on the hay.

"Excuse me," said a tired ox, "would you please move so that I can eat my hay?"

The dog, angry at being awakened from his nap, growled and barked at the ox.

"Please," said the ox, "I've had a hard day and I'm very hungry."

But the dog, who of course did not eat hay, only barked and snapped at the ox, and refused to budge. At last the poor ox had to give up, and went away tired and hungry.

MORAL: *Don't be mean and stingy when you have no need of things yourself. Don't be a dog in the manger.*

The Maid and the Milk Pail

Peggy, the milk maid, was going to market. There she planned to sell the fresh sweet milk in the pail that she had learned to carry balanced on her head.

As she went along, she began thinking about what she would do with the money she would get for the milk. "I'll buy some chickens from Farmer Brown," she said, "and they will lay eggs each morning. When those eggs hatch, I'll have more chickens. Then I'll sell some of the chickens and some of the eggs, and that will get me enough money to buy the blue dress I've wanted, and some blue ribbon to match. Oh, I'll look so lovely that all the boys will want to dance with me at the fair, and all the girls will be jealous. But I don't care; I'll just toss my head at them, like this!"

She tossed back her head. The pail flew off, and the milk spilled all over the road. So Peggy had to return home and tell her mother what had happened. "Ah, my child," said her mother, "don't count your chickens before they're hatched."

MORAL: Don't count your chickens before they're hatched. Have you heard this saying before? It means: Do not count on getting everything you want, or having everything turn out exactly as you plan, because you may be disappointed.

The Wolf in Sheep's Clothing

Night after night a wolf prowled around a flock of sheep looking for one to eat, but the shepherd and his dogs always chased him away. But one day the wolf found the skin of a sheep that had been thrown aside. He pulled the skin carefully over him so that none of his fur showed under the white fleece. Then he strolled among the flock. A lamb, thinking that the wolf was its mother, followed him into the woods—and there the wolf made a meal of the lamb!

So for many days the wolf was able to get a sheep whenever he pleased. But one day the shepherd decided to cook lamb for his own dinner. He chose the biggest, fattest sheep he could find and killed him on the spot. Guess who it was—the wolf!

TWO MORALS: (1) Beware of a wolf in sheep's clothing: things are not always what they appear to be. (2) If you pretend to be what you are not, you might get caught.

People sometimes use the phrase "a wolf in sheep's clothing" to describe someone who appears to be harmless or friendly but who is really dangerous or untrustworthy. For example:

"I can't believe Ronnie took my idea for his art poster. He said he just wanted to know what I was working on, so I told him, but then he did it himself. What a wolf in sheep's clothing!"

The Goose That Laid the Golden Eggs

Once a farmer went to the nest of his goose and found there an egg, all yellow and shiny. When he picked it up, it was heavy as a rock. He was about to throw it away because he thought that someone was playing a trick on him. But on second thought, he took it home, and there he discovered to his delight that it was an egg of pure gold!

He sold the egg for a handsome sum of money. Every morning the goose laid another golden egg, and the farmer soon became rich by selling eggs.

As he grew rich, he grew greedy. "Why should I have to wait to get only one egg a day?" he thought. "I will cut open the goose and take all the eggs out of her at once."

And so he killed the goose and cut her open, only to find—nothing.

MORAL: He who wants more often loses all. When you want something, be patient. If you are greedy, you might lose what you already have.

Stories

All Stories Are Anansi's

(A tale from West Africa)

PARENTS: *Anansi [ah-NAHN-see], the spider, is a popular figure in the folklore of parts of West Africa (the stories later came with slaves to the Caribbean islands). Like Brer Rabbit in America (see below, page 43), Anansi is a "trickster" figure—clever, cunning, sometimes mischievous—who uses his wits to make up for what he lacks in size and strength. This story tells how Anansi became the "owner" of all stories.*

In the beginning, all tales and stories belonged to Nyame [NYAH-meh], the Sky God. But Kwaku Anansi, the spider, yearned to be the owner of all the stories known in the world, and he went to Nyame and offered to buy them.

The Sky God said: "I am willing to sell the stories, but the price is high. Many people have come to me offering to buy, but the price was too high for them. Rich and powerful families have not been able to pay. Do you think you can do it?"

Anansi replied to the Sky God: "I can do it. What is the price?"

"My price is three things," the Sky God said. "I must first have Mmoboro [mmmoh-BOH-roh], the hornets. I must then have Onini [oh-NEE-nee], the great python. I must then have Osebo [oh-SAY-boh], the leopard. For these things I will sell you the right to tell all stories."

Anansi said: "I will bring them."

He went home and made his plans. He first cut a gourd from a vine and made a small hole in it. He took a large calabash [like a bowl], and filled it with water. He went to the tree where the hornets lived. He poured some of the water over himself, so that he was dripping. He threw some water over the hornets, so that they too were dripping. Then he put the calabash on his head, as though to protect himself

from a storm, and called out to the hornets: "Are you foolish people? Why do you stay in the rain that is falling?"

The hornets answered: "Where shall we go?"

"Go here, in this dry gourd," Anansi told them.

The hornets thanked him and flew into the gourd through the small hole. When the last of them had entered, Anansi plugged the hole with a ball of grass, saying: "Oh, yes, but you are really foolish people!"

He took his gourd full of hornets to Nyame, the Sky God. The Sky God accepted them. He said: "There are two more things."

Anansi returned to the forest and cut a long bamboo pole and some strong vines. Then he walked toward the house of Onini, the python, talking to himself. He seemed to be talking about an argument with his wife. He said: "My wife is wrong. I say he is longer and stronger. My wife says he is shorter and weaker. I give him more respect. She gives him less respect. Is she right or am I right? I am right, he is longer. I am right, he is stronger."

When Onini, the python, heard Anansi talking to himself, he said: "Why are you arguing this way with yourself?"

The spider replied: "Ah, I have had a dispute with my wife. She says you are shorter and weaker than this bamboo pole. I say you are longer and stronger."

Onini said: "It's useless and silly to argue when you can find out the truth. Bring the pole and we will measure."

So Anansi laid the pole on the ground, and the python came and stretched himself out beside it.

"You seem a little short," Anansi said.

The python stretched further.

"A little more," Anansi said.

"I can stretch no more," Onini said.

"When you stretch at one end, you get shorter at the other end," Anansi said. "Let me tie you at the front so you don't slip."

He tied Onini's head to the pole. Then he went to the other end and tied the tail to the pole. He wrapped the vine all around Onini, until the python couldn't move.

"Onini," Anansi said, "it turns out that my wife was right and I was wrong. You are shorter than the pole and weaker. My opinion wasn't as good as my wife's. But you were even more foolish than I, and you are now my prisoner."

Anansi carried the python to Nyame, the Sky God, who said: "There is one thing more."

Osebo, the leopard, was next. Anansi went into the forest and dug a deep pit where the leopard liked to walk. He covered it with small branches and leaves and put dust on it, so that it was impossible to tell where the pit was. Anansi went away and hid. When Osebo came prowling in the black of night, he stepped into the trap Anansi had prepared and fell to the bottom. Anansi heard the sound of the leopard falling, and he said: "Ah, Osebo, you are half-foolish!"

When morning came, Anansi went to the pit and saw the leopard there.

"Osebo," he asked, "what are you doing in this hole?"

"I have fallen into a trap," Osebo said. "Help me out."

"I would gladly help you," Anansi said. "But I'm sure that if I bring you out, I will have no thanks for it. You will get hungry, and later on you will be wanting to eat me and my children."

"I promise it won't happen!" Osebo said.

"Very well. Since you promise it, I will take you out," Anansi said.

He bent a tall green tree toward the ground, so that its top was over the pit, and he tied it that way.

Then he tied a rope to the top of the tree and dropped the other end of it into the pit.

"Tie this to your tail," he said.

Osebo tied the rope to his tail.

"Is it well tied?" Anansi asked.

"Yes, it is well tied," the leopard said.

"In that case," Anansi said, "you are not merely half-foolish, you are all-foolish."

And he took his knife and cut the other rope, the one that held the tree bowed to the ground. The tree straightened up with a snap, pulling Osebo out of the hole. He hung in the air head downward, twisting and turning.

As he twisted and turned, he got so dizzy that Anansi had no trouble tying the leopard's feet with vines.

Anansi took the dizzy leopard, all tied up, to Nyame, the Sky God, saying: "Here is the third thing. Now I have paid the price."

Nyame said to him: "Kwaku Anansi, great warriors and chiefs have tried, but they have been unable to do it. You have done it. Therefore, I will give you the stories. From this day onward, all stories belong to you. Whenever a man tells a story, he must acknowledge that it is Anansi's tale."

And that is why, in parts of Africa, the people love to tell, and love to hear, the stories they call "spider stories." And now, you have heard one too.

> Check your library for more stories about Anansi, such as:
>
> *Anansi and the Moss-Covered Rock* and *Anansi Goes Fishing*, retold by Eric A. Kimmel (Holiday House, 1988 and 1992)
> *Anansi Finds a Fool* by Verna Aardema (Dial Books for Young Readers, 1992)

The Boy at the Dike

PARENTS: *If you have access to a world map or globe, help your child locate Holland (also called the Netherlands).*

Many years ago, there lived a boy who did a brave deed. His name was Peter, and he lived in Holland, a country by the sea.

In Holland, the sea presses in on the land so much that the people built big walls of earth and stone to hold back the waters. Every little child in Holland was taught that these big walls, called dikes, must be watched at every moment. No water must be allowed to come through the dikes. Even a hole no larger than your little finger was a very dangerous thing.

One afternoon in the early fall, when Peter was seven years old, his mother called to him. "Come, Peter," she said. "I want you to go across the dike and take these cakes to your friend the blind man. If you go quickly, you will be home again before dark."

Peter was happy to go, because his friend the blind man lived alone and was always glad to have a visitor. When he got to the blind man's home, Peter stayed awhile to tell him of his walk along the dike. He told about the bright sun and the flowers and the ships far out at sea. Then Peter remembered that his mother wanted him to return home before dark. So he said good-bye and set out for home.

As he walked along, he noticed how the water beat against the side of the dike. There had been much rain, and the water was higher than before. Peter remembered how his father always spoke of the "angry waters."

"I suppose Father thinks they are angry," thought Peter, "because we have been keeping them out for so long. Well, I am glad these dikes are so strong. If they gave way, what would become of us? All these fields would be covered with water. Then what would happen to the flowers, and the animals, and the people?"

Suddenly Peter noticed that the sun was setting. Darkness was settling on the land. "Mother will be watching for me," he said. "I must hurry." But just then he heard a noise. It was the sound of trickling water! He stopped, looked down, and saw a small hole in the dike, through which a tiny stream was flowing.

A leak in the dike! Peter understood the danger at once. If water ran through a little hole, it would soon make a larger one, then the waters could break through and the land would be flooded!

Peter saw what he must do. He climbed down the side of the dike and thrust his finger in the tiny hole. The water stopped!

"The angry waters will stay back now," said Peter. "I can keep them back with my finger. Holland will not be drowned while I am here."

But then he thought, "How long can I stay here?" Already it was dark and cold. Peter called out, "Help! Is anyone there? Help!" But no one heard him. No one came to help.

It grew darker and colder still. Peter's arm began to grow stiff and numb. "Will no one come?" he thought. Then he shouted again for help. And when no one came, he cried out, "Mother! Mother!"

Many times since sunset, his mother had looked out at the dike and expected to see her little boy. She was worried, but then she thought that perhaps Peter was spending the night with his blind friend, as he had done before. "Well," she thought, "when he gets home in the morning, I will have to scold him for staying away from home without permission."

Poor Peter! He would rather have been home than anywhere else in the world, but he could not move from the dike. He tried to whistle to keep himself company, but he couldn't because his teeth chattered with cold. He thought of his brother and sister in their warm beds, and of his father and mother. "I must not let them be drowned," he thought. "I must stay here until someone comes."

The moon and stars looked down on the shivering child. His head was bent and his eyes were closed, but he was not asleep. Now and then he rubbed the hand that was holding back the angry waters.

Morning came. A man walking along the dike heard a sound, something like a groan. He bent down and saw the child below. He called out, "What's the matter, boy? Are you hurt? Why are you sitting there?"

In a voice faint and weak, the boy said, "I am keeping the water from coming in. Please, tell them to come quickly!"

The man ran to get help. People came with shovels to fix the dike, and they carried Peter, the little hero, home to his parents.

> 'Tis many a year since then; but still,
>   When the sea roars like a flood,
> The children are taught what a child can do
>   Who is brave and true and good.
> For all the mothers and fathers
>   Take their children by the hand
> And tell them of brave little Peter
>   Whose courage saved the land.

Brer Rabbit Gets Brer Fox's Dinner

PARENTS: *The Brer Rabbit stories are African American folktales collected and retold in the late nineteenth century by the American writer Joel Chandler Harris. Harris wrote the tales in the speech of a character he called Uncle Remus, an old black man who speaks to a young boy on a Southern plantation. The tales reflect the speech of the teller, and so use words like "ain't." The stories are rich in humor and come alive when read aloud. The story we present here is a modern retelling by Julius Lester, whose volumes of Uncle Remus tales include* Tales of Uncle Remus *and* More Tales of Uncle Remus *(Dial, 1987 and 1988).*

If you ain't never heard about Brer Rabbit and Brer Fox, you might get the idea from these stories that they are enemies. Well, that ain't the way it is. On the other hand they weren't friends either. Brer Rabbit was Brer Rabbit, which meant he couldn't help it if he woke up some mornings and the first thing he thought about was creating devilment. And Brer Fox was Brer Fox. Wasn't his fault if he woke up thinking about the same thing. So they weren't enemies and they weren't friends. They were who they were. Another way of putting it is: They ain't who they wasn't. Now that that's all clear, let's get on with the story.

Not having anything better or worse to do one day, Brer Rabbit decided to see what Brer Fox was up to. As he got close to Brer Fox's house, he heard a lot of hammering. When he got there, he saw Brer Fox on the roof nailing shingles as fast as he could.

Well, Brer Rabbit treated work like he did his mamma, and he wouldn't hit his mamma a lick. So he looked around to see what else he could see, and there by the fence post was Brer Fox's dinner pail. Brer Rabbit knew there was more food in it than there was in his stomach. That didn't seem right. How was he going to get Brer Fox's dinner from where it wasn't doing no good to where it would do a whole lot of good?

"Brer Fox! How you doing today?" Brer Rabbit called up.

"Busy. Ain't got time to be flapping gums with you."

"What you doing up there?"

"Putting on a new roof before winter come."

"You need some help?"

"I do, but where am I going to get it at?"

"I'm a powerful man with a hammer, Brer Fox. I'll give you a hand."

Brer Rabbit climbed up to the roof and set to work. Pretty soon he was out-hammering Brer Fox. He was putting roofing on like winter was on the outskirts of town. He nailed and nailed and nailed until he was right up to Brer Fox's tail.

Brer Rabbit pushed the tail to one side, but, a tail being a tail, it just swished right back.

"Don't know how come folks got to have such long tails," Brer Rabbit mumbled to himself.

He brushed the tail aside again and resumed nailing. He nailed under Brer Fox. He nailed around Brer Fox. He nailed beside Brer Fox. He nailed and he nailed until all of a sudden Brer Fox dropped his hammer and let out a yell, "Ow! Brer Rabbit! You done nailed my tail!"

Brer Rabbit looked at him, eyes big. "I done what? You got to be joking, Brer Fox. Don't be accusing me of something I ain't done."

Brer Fox hollered and squalled and kicked and squealed. "Have mercy, Brer Rabbit! Unnail my tail! Unnail my tail!"

Brer Rabbit started down the ladder, shaking his head. "I must be losing my aim, my stroke, or something. Maybe my eyes is getting weak. I ain't never nailed nobody's tail before. Doing something like that upsets me. Doing something like that upsets me so much, it makes me hungry."

All the while Brer Fox is hollering and screaming and squalling.

Brer Rabbit climbed down the ladder, still muttering to himself about how getting upset made him hungry. He opened up Brer Fox's dinner pail and helped himself to the fried chicken, corn, and biscuits inside. When he finished, he wiped his mouth on his coattail, belched a time or two, and went on down the road, hoping he hadn't done no permanent damage to Brer Fox's long, pretty tail.

The Frog Prince
(A tale from the Brothers Grimm, retold by Wanda Gag)

In the olden days when wishing was still of some use, there lived a King. He had several beautiful daughters, but the youngest was so fair that even the sun, who sees so many wonders, could not help marveling every time he looked into her face.

Near the King's palace lay a large dark forest and there, under an old linden tree, was a well. When the day was very warm, the little Princess would go off into this forest and sit at the rim of the cool well. There she would play with her golden ball, tossing it up and catching it deftly in her little hands. This was her favorite game and she never tired of it.

Now it happened one day that, as the Princess tossed her golden ball into the air, it did not fall into her uplifted hands as usual. Instead, it fell to the ground, rolled to the rim of the well and into the water. *Plunk, splash!* The golden ball was gone.

The well was deep and the Princess knew it. She felt sure she would never see her beautiful ball again, so she cried and cried and could not stop.

"What is the matter, little Princess?" said a voice behind her. "You are crying so that even a hard stone would have pity on you."

The little girl looked around and there she saw a frog. He was in the well and was stretching his fat ugly head out of the water.

"Oh, it's you—you old water-splasher!" said the girl. "I'm crying over my golden ball. It has fallen into the well."

"Oh, as to that," said the frog, "I can bring your ball back to you. But what will you give me if I do?"

"Whatever you wish, dear old frog," said the Princess. "I'll give you my dresses, my beads and all my jewelry—even the golden crown on my head."

The frog answered: "Your dresses, your beads and all your jewelry, even the golden crown on your head—I don't want them. But if you can find it in your heart to like me and take me for your playfellow, if you will let me sit beside you at the table, eat from your little golden plate and drink from your little golden cup, and if you are willing to let me sleep in your own little bed besides: if you promise me all this, little Princess, then I will gladly go down to the bottom of the well and bring back your golden ball."

"Oh yes," said the Princess, "I'll promise anything you say if you'll only bring back my golden ball to me." But to herself she thought: "What is the silly frog chattering about? He can only live in the water and croak with the other frogs; he could never be a playmate to a human being."

As soon as the frog had heard her promise, he disappeared into the well. Down, down, down, he sank; but he soon came up again, holding the golden ball in his mouth. He dropped it on the grass at the feet of the Princess, who was wild with joy when she saw her favorite plaything once more. She picked up the ball and skipped away with it, thinking no more about the little creature who had returned it to her.

"Wait! Wait!" cried the frog. "Take me with you, I can't run as fast as you."

But what good did it do him to scream his "quark! quark!" after her as loud as he could? She wouldn't listen to him but hurried home, where she soon forgot the poor frog, who now had to go back into his well again.

The next evening, the Princess was eating her dinner at the royal table when—plitch plotch, plitch plotch—something came climbing up the stairs. When it reached the door, it knocked at the door and cried:

> Youngest daughter of the King,
> Open the door for me!

The Princess rose from the table and ran to see who was calling her—when she opened the door, there sat the frog, wet and green and cold! Quickly she slammed the door and sat down at the table again, her heart beating loud and fast. The King could

 see well enough that she was frightened and worried, and he said, "My child, what are you afraid of? Is there a giant out there who wants to carry you away?"

"Oh no," said the Princess. "It's not a giant, but a horrid old frog!"

"And what does he want of you?" asked the King.

"Oh, dear father, as I was playing under the linden tree by the well, my golden ball fell into the water. And because I cried so hard, the frog brought it back to me; and because he insisted so much, I promised him that he could be my playmate. But I never, never thought that he would ever leave his well. Now he is out there and wants to come in and eat from my plate and drink from my cup and sleep in my little bed. But I couldn't bear that, papa, he's so wet and ugly and his eyes bulge out!"

While she was talking, the frog knocked at the door once more and said:

> Youngest daughter of the King,
>   Open the door for me.
> Mind your words at the old well spring;
>   Open the door for me!

At that the King said, "If we make promises, daughter, we must keep them; so you had better go and open the door."

The Princess still did not want to do it but she had to obey. When she opened the door, the frog hopped in and followed her until she reached her chair. Then he sat there and said, "Lift me up beside you."

She hesitated—the frog was so cold and clammy—but her father looked at her sternly and said, "You must keep your promise."

After the frog was on her chair, he wanted to be put on the table. When he was there, he said, "Now shove your plate a little closer, so we can eat together like real playmates."

The Princess shuddered, but she had to do it. The frog enjoyed the meal and ate heartily, but the poor girl could not swallow a single bite. At last the frog said, "Now I've eaten enough and I feel tired. Carry me to your room so I can go to sleep."

The Princess began to cry. It had been hard enough to touch the cold fat frog, and worse still to have him eat out of her plate, but to have him beside her in her little bed was more than she could bear.

"I want to go to bed," repeated the frog. "Take me there and tuck me in."

The Princess shuddered again and looked at her father, but he only said, "He helped you in your trouble. Is it fair to scorn him now?"

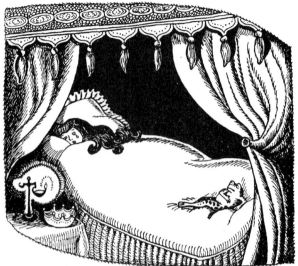

There was nothing for her to do but to pick up the creature—she did it with two fingers—and to carry him up into her room, where she dropped him in a corner on the floor, hoping he would be satisfied. But after she had gone to bed, she heard something she didn't like. *Ploppety plop! Ploppety plop!* It was the frog hopping across the floor, and when he reached her bed he said, "I'm tired and the floor is too hard. I have as much right as you to sleep in a good soft bed. Lift me up or I will tell your father."

At this the Princess was bitterly angry but she picked him up and put him at the foot-end of her bed. There he stayed all night but when the dark was graying into daylight, the frog jumped down from the bed, out of the door and away, she knew not where.

The next night it was the same. The frog came back, knocked at the door and said:

> *Youngest daughter of the King,*
> *Open the door for me.*
> *Mind your words at the old well spring;*
> *Open the door for me!*

There was nothing for her to do but let him in. Again he ate out of her golden plate, sipped out of her golden cup, and again he slept at the foot-end of her bed. In the morning he went away as before.

The third night he came again. This time he was not content to sleep at her feet.

"I want to sleep under your pillow," he said. "I think I'd like it better there."

The girl thought she would never be able to sleep with a horrid, damp, goggle-eyed frog under her pillow. She began to weep softly to herself and couldn't stop until at last she cried herself to sleep.

When the night was over and the morning sunlight burst in at the window, the frog crept out from under her pillow and hopped off the bed. But as soon as his feet touched the floor something happened to him. In that moment he was no longer a cold, fat, goggle-eyed frog, but a young Prince with handsome friendly eyes!

"You see," he said, "I wasn't what I seemed to be! A wicked old woman bewitched me. No one but you could break the spell, little Princess, and I waited and waited at the well for you to help me."

The Princess was speechless with surprise but her eyes sparkled.

"And will you let me be your playmate now?" said the Prince, laughing. *"Mind your words at the old well spring!"*

At this the Princess laughed too, and they both ran out to play with the golden ball.

For years they were the best of friends and the happiest of playmates, and it is not hard to guess, I'm sure, that when they were grown up they were married and lived happily ever after.

Hansel and Gretel
(A tale from the Brothers Grimm)

Once upon a time, near a deep, dark forest, there lived a poor woodcutter with his wife and two children. The boy was named Hansel, and the girl was named Gretel. The family never had very much to eat, and now, when times were hard and people around the land were starving, the poor woodcutter could not get enough food to feed even his family. As he lay in bed one night, tossing and turning with worry, he turned to his wife and said, "What is going to happen to us? How can we feed our poor children when we haven't got enough for ourselves?"

"Listen to me," said his wife, who was not the children's real mother. She was their stepmother, and she did not care for the children. "Early tomorrow morning," the cold-hearted woman said, "we'll take the children deep into the woods. We'll make a fire and give each of them a piece of bread. Then we'll leave them and go about our work. They will never find the way home, and we will be rid of them."

"No!" said the man. "I cannot do that. I cannot leave my children alone in the woods, where the wild animals would swallow them up."

"Then you are a fool," snapped the woman. "You might as well get four coffins ready, for we shall all starve." Then she nagged the poor man, and scolded him, and kept at him until at last he agreed. "But I feel so sorry for the poor children," he said quietly.

The two children were so hungry that they had not been able to sleep, and so they heard everything their stepmother said to their father. Gretel cried, but Hansel whispered, "Don't worry, I will think of something." And when the parents had gone to sleep, Hansel got up, put on his little coat, and sneaked outside. The moon was shining brightly, and the white pebbles that lay in front of the house glittered like silver coins. Hansel stooped and gathered as many pebbles as he could find. Then he tiptoed back to bed and said to Gretel, "Go to sleep, little sister."

At daybreak the woman came and woke the two children. "Get up, you lazybones! We're going to the forest to get some wood." She gave them each a piece of bread and said, "That's for dinner, and you must not eat it before then, because it's all you're going to get."

Gretel carried both pieces of bread in her apron, for Hansel's pockets were full of pebbles. They all started out on their way to the forest. As they walked, Hansel kept turning and looking back at the house, again and again. His father said, "Hansel, what are you looking at? You must watch where you're going."

"Oh," said Hansel, "I'm just looking at my little white kitten, who is sitting on the roof of the house to say good-bye."

The wife said, "You little fool, that's not your kitten. That's just the sun shining on the chimney. Now, come along!"

But Hansel stayed a few steps behind and kept turning, and each time he turned, he dropped a pebble from his pocket to mark the way.

When they were deep in the forest, the father said, "Gather some firewood, children. I'll start a fire so you won't get cold." Hansel and Gretel gathered a little mountain of twigs and sticks, and when the fire was burning, the wife said, "Stay by the fire, you two. We have to go and cut wood. When we're finished, we'll come back to get you."

So Hansel and Gretel sat by the fire. After a time, they ate their bread. And after a longer time, they got so tired that they closed their eyes and fell asleep. When they woke, it was dark, and they were all alone. Gretel began to cry, but Hansel comforted her. "Wait a little until the moon rises," he said.

And when the full moon had risen, Hansel took his little sister by the hand and followed the pebbles, which glittered like silver coins and showed them the way. They walked on through the night, and at last, at the break of day, they came to their father's house. They knocked on the door, and when the woman opened it, she was shocked. But she only said, "You naughty children, why did you stay so long in the forest? We thought you were never coming home again." But their father was glad, for it had broken his heart to leave them alone.

Not very long afterward, times were again hard, and there was little food to be eaten. Again the children heard their stepmother say to their father one night in bed, "There's nothing left but half a loaf of bread. After that, we're done for! We must get rid of the children. This time we'll take them so deep in the forest that they'll never find their way back."

"But wife," said the man, with a heavy heart, "it would be better to share our last bite of food with the children." But the wife would not listen to him. And, after all, once you've said yes, it's hard to say no. So she kept at him until once again he gave in to her and agreed with her plan.

When the parents were asleep, Hansel got up to collect pebbles. But he couldn't get out—the woman had locked the door! He got back in bed and tried to think of a different plan.

Early the next morning the woman pulled the children out of bed. She gave them a piece of bread, even smaller than before. As they walked into the wood, Hansel broke up the

bread in his pocket, and often stopped to throw a crumb on the ground.

"Hansel," said his father, "what do you keep stopping and looking back for?"

"I'm looking at my little pigeon that's sitting on the roof and wants to say good-bye to me," answered Hansel.

"Little fool," said the wife, "that's no pigeon. It's only the sun shining on the chimney." So they walked on, and Hansel dropped bread crumbs all along the way.

The woman led the children deep into the forest where they had never been before in all their lives. Again they gathered sticks for a fire, and the woman said, "Sit there, children, and when you are tired, go to sleep. We're going to cut wood, and when we're finished, we'll come get you."

Later, when it was noon, Gretel shared her small piece of bread with Hansel, since he had left his in crumbs along the road. Then they fell asleep, and as evening came, no one came to get them. When they woke, it was dark and they were alone. When the moon rose, they started for home, but they could not find the bread crumbs, for the birds had eaten them up. "Come, Gretel," said Hansel, "I know we can find our way." But they didn't find it. They went on all night, and the next day from morning until evening, but they could not find their way out of the forest. They were terribly hungry, for they had nothing to eat but a few berries. And when they were so tired that they could drag themselves no farther, they lay down under a tree and fell asleep.

It was now the third morning since they had left their father's house. They started on again, always looking for the way home, but instead only getting deeper into the forest. Unless help came soon, they would surely die of hunger.

About noon they saw a pretty snow-white bird sitting on a branch and singing so beautifully that they stopped to listen. Then the bird spread its wings and flew before them, as though to say "Follow me!" And so the children followed the bird until they came to a little house. The bird flew up and perched on the roof. And then the children saw that the walls of the house were made of gingerbread, and the roof was made of cake, and the windows of clear sugar candy.

"Let's eat!" cried Hansel. Hansel reached up and broke off a piece of the roof, while Gretel chewed on a wall.

Suddenly they heard a thin, screechy voice call out from inside the house:

> "Nibble, nibble, like a mouse,
>   Who is nibbling at my house?"

The children answered,

> "It's only the air heaving a sigh.
>   It's only the wind passing by."

And they were so hungry that they went on eating. But then the door opened, and a very old woman came out, leaning on a crutch. Hansel and Gretel were so frightened that they dropped the food from their hands. But the old woman just nodded her head and said, "My dear little children, what has brought you here? Come inside and stay with me. I'll take good care of you."

So she took them by the hand and led them into her little house. There they found a wonderful meal of hot pancakes, with honey, nuts, apples, and cold milk. After that, the old woman showed them two little white beds, and Hansel and Gretel lay down and wondered if they were in heaven.

Now, the old woman seemed kind, but in fact she was a wicked witch. She had built her house just to trap little children, and once she had them, she would cook them and eat them! She had bad eyes and could not see well, but she could smell as well as an animal, and earlier in the day she had sniffed Hansel and Gretel coming near.

The next morning, before the children were awake, the witch got up and looked at their rosy cheeks. "Mmm, what a fine meal I will have," she cackled. Then she dragged Hansel out of bed and locked him in a cage outside. Then she went back and shook Gretel awake, and shouted, "Get up, lazybones! Fetch water, and cook something nice for your brother. Feed him well, for once he's nice and fat, I will eat him!"

Gretel screamed and cried, but it was no use. She had to do what the wicked witch said. Day after day she cooked pots full of rich food for Hansel, while she herself ate nothing but crumbs. Every morning the wicked witch would creep to the cage and say, "Hansel, stick out your finger so I can tell if you are fat enough to cook." But clever Hansel held out a little bone, and the old woman, who had bad eyes, couldn't tell that it wasn't Hansel's finger. She wondered why he wasn't getting any fatter. And when four weeks had passed and Hansel seemed as thin as ever, she lost patience. "Hurry up and get some water," she snarled at Gretel. "Be he fat or thin, I'm going to cook him and eat him."

The tears ran down poor Gretel's cheeks as she fetched water and lit the fire. "First we will bake," said the old woman. "I've heated the oven, and the dough is ready." Then she pushed poor Gretel toward the oven, where the flames were burning brightly. "Stick your head in," the witch said to Gretel, "and tell me if it's hot enough for us to bake the bread." But Gretel knew what the witch had in mind: she knew that the witch meant to shut her in the oven, and bake her, and eat her! So Gretel said, "I don't know how to do it. Where do I look in? Could you show me how?"

"You stupid goose!" cried the old woman. "There's a big opening, don't you see? Why, I could fit in myself!" And she stuck her head in the oven. Then Gretel rushed up and, with all her might, pushed the witch into the oven. She shut the iron door and locked it tight. Gretel did not stay to hear the witch's howls and shrieks. She ran right to Hansel and let him out of the cage.

"Come, Hansel, we are free!" she cried. "The old witch is dead!" Hansel sprang out and hugged Gretel, and the children danced for joy. Then, since they had nothing to fear, they went back inside the witch's house. There they found chests full of pearls and precious jewels. "These are better than pebbles!" laughed Hansel as he filled his pockets, while Gretel filled her apron.

"Now, away we go," said Hansel. Then he said quietly, "If only we can find our way out of the witch's wood."

When they had walked a few hours, they came to a wide lake. "There's no bridge, and no stepping stones," said Hansel. "We can't get across."

"And there's no boat either," said Gretel. "But look," she said. "Here comes a duck. I will ask her for help." So she called out,

> *"Duck, duck, here we stand,*
> *Hansel and Gretel on the land.*
> *Stepping stones and bridge we lack,*
> *Carry us over on your nice soft back."*

And, lo and behold, the duck came over. Hansel got on her back and told Gretel to sit behind him. "No," said Gretel, "that would be too hard on the duck. Let us go across one at a time."

And so, that is how they did it. When they were on the other side, they walked on for a little while, and soon found a path. The forest began to look more and more familiar. At last, in the distance, they saw their father's house. They began to run as fast as they could. They burst through the door and cried out, "Father! We're home!" Then they threw themselves upon him.

Since he had left the children in the wood, the man had been worried sick. And as for his mean wife—well, she had died. Now he hugged his children as though he would never let them go. As he squeezed Gretel to him, the pearls and jewels fell from her apron. Then Hansel reached into his pockets and pulled out handful after handful of treasure.

They were together again, their troubles were over, and they lived in perfect happiness for a long, long time.

In Which Tigger Comes to the Forest and Has Breakfast
(A selection from *The House at Pooh Corner* by A. A. Milne)

PARENTS: *If your children have not yet met the bear named Winnie-the-Pooh and his friends in the Hundred Acre Wood, you might first want to read to them from the book called* Winnie-the-Pooh *by A. A. Milne (a chapter from which is included in* What Your Kindergartner Needs to Know).

Winnie-the-Pooh woke up suddenly in the middle of the night and listened. Then he got out of bed, and lit his candle, and stumped across the room to see if anybody was trying to get into his honey-cupboard, and they weren't, so he stumped back again, blew out his candle, and got into bed. Then he heard the noise again.

"Is that you, Piglet?" he said.

But it wasn't.

"Come in, Christopher Robin," he said.

But Christopher Robin didn't.

"Tell me about it tomorrow, Eeyore," said Pooh sleepily.

But the noise went on.

"*Worraworraworraworraworra,*" said Whatever-it-was, and Pooh found that he wasn't asleep after all.

"What can it be?" he thought. "There are lots of noises in the Forest, but this is a different one. It isn't a growl, and it isn't a purr, and it isn't a bark, and it isn't a noise-you-make-before-beginning-a-piece-of-poetry, but it's a noise of some kind, made by a strange animal. And he's making it outside my door. So I shall get up and ask him not to do it."

He got out of bed and opened his front door.

"Hallo!" said Pooh, in case there was anything outside.

"Hallo!" said Whatever-it-was.

"Oh!" said Pooh. "Hallo!"

"Hallo!"

"Oh, *there* you are!" said Pooh. "Hallo!"

"Hallo!" said the Strange Animal, wondering how long this was going on.

Pooh was just going to say "Hallo!" for the fourth time when he thought that he wouldn't so he said: "Who is it?" instead.

"Me," said a voice.

"Oh!" said Pooh. "Well, come here."

So Whatever-it-was came here, and in the light of the candle he and Pooh looked at each other.

"I'm Pooh," said Pooh.

"I'm Tigger," said Tigger.

"Oh!" said Pooh, for he had never seen an animal like this before. "Does Christopher Robin know about you?"

"Of course he does," said Tigger.

"Well," said Pooh, "it's the middle of the night, which is a good time for going to sleep. And tomorrow morning we'll have some honey for breakfast. Do Tiggers like honey?"

"They like everything," said Tigger cheerfully.

"Then if they like going to sleep on the floor, I'll go back to bed," said Pooh, "and we'll do things in the morning. Good night." And he got back into bed and went fast asleep.

When he awoke in the morning, the first thing he saw was Tigger, sitting in front of the glass and looking at himself.

"Hallo!" said Pooh.

"Hallo!" said Tigger. "I've found somebody just like me. I thought I was the only one of them."

Pooh got out of bed, and began to explain what a looking-glass was, but just as he was getting to the interesting part, Tigger said:

"Excuse me a moment, but there's something climbing up your table," and with one loud *Worraworraworraworraworra* he jumped at the end of the tablecloth, pulled it to the ground, wrapped himself up in it three times, rolled to the other end of the room, and, after a terrible struggle, got his head into the daylight again, and said cheerfully: "Have I won?"

"That's my tablecloth," said Pooh, as he began to unwind Tigger.

"I wondered what it was," said Tigger.

"It goes on the table and you put things on it."

"Then why did it try to bite me when I wasn't looking?"

"I don't *think* it did," said Pooh.

"It tried," said Tigger, "but I was too quick for it."

Pooh put the cloth back on the table, and he put a large honey-pot on the cloth, and they sat down to breakfast. And as soon as they sat down, Tigger took a large mouthful of honey . . . and he looked up at the ceiling with his head on one side, and made exploring noises with his tongue and considering noises, and what-have-we-got-*here* noises . . . and then he said in a very decided voice:

"Tiggers don't like honey."

"Oh!" said Pooh, and tried to make it sound Sad and Regretful. "I thought they liked everything."

"Everything except honey," said Tigger.

Pooh felt rather pleased about this, and said that, as soon as he had finished his own breakfast, he would take Tigger round to Piglet's house, and Tigger could try some of Piglet's haycorns.

"Thank you, Pooh," said Tigger, "because haycorns is really what Tiggers like best."

So after breakfast they went round to see Piglet, and Pooh explained as they went that Piglet was a Very Small Animal who didn't like bouncing, and asked Tigger not to be too Bouncy just at first. And Tigger, who had been hiding behind trees and jumping out on Pooh's shadow when it wasn't looking, said that Tiggers were only bouncy before breakfast, and that as soon as they had had a few haycorns they became Quiet and Refined. So by and by they knocked at the door of Piglet's house.

"Hallo, Pooh," said Piglet.

"Hallo, Piglet. This is Tigger."

"Oh, is it?" said Piglet, and he edged round to the other side of the table. "I thought Tiggers were smaller than that."

"Not the big ones," said Tigger.

"They like haycorns," said Pooh, "so that's what we've come for, because poor Tigger hasn't had any breakfast yet."

Piglet pushed the bowl of haycorns towards Tigger, and said: "Help yourself," and then he got close up to Pooh and felt much braver, and said, "So you're Tigger? Well,

well!" in a careless sort of voice. But Tigger said nothing because his mouth was full of haycorns. . . .

After a long munching noise he said:

"Ee-eers o i a-ors."

And when Pooh and Piglet said "What?" he said "Skoos ee," and went outside for a moment.

When he came back he said firmly:

"Tiggers don't like haycorns."

"But you said they liked everything except honey," said Pooh.

"Everything except honey and haycorns," explained Tigger.

When he heard this Pooh said, "Oh, I see!" and Piglet, who was rather glad that Tiggers didn't like haycorns, said, "What about thistles?"

"Thistles," said Tigger, "is what Tiggers like best."

"Then let's go along and see Eeyore," said Piglet.

So the three of them went; and after they had walked and walked and walked, they came to the part of the Forest where Eeyore was.

"Hallo, Eeyore!" said Pooh. "This is Tigger."

"What is?" said Eeyore.

"This," explained Pooh and Piglet together, and Tigger smiled his happiest smile and said nothing.

Eeyore walked all round Tigger one way, and then turned and walked all round him the other way.

"What did you say it was?" he asked.

"Tigger."

"Ah!" said Eeyore.

"He's just come," explained Piglet.

"Ah!" said Eeyore again.

He thought for a long time and then said:

"When is he going?"

Pooh explained to Eeyore that Tigger was a great friend of Christopher Robin's, who had come to stay in the Forest, and Piglet explained to Tigger that he mustn't mind what Eeyore said because he was *always* gloomy; and Eeyore explained to Piglet that, on the contrary, he was feeling particularly cheerful this morning; and Tigger explained to anybody who was listening that he hadn't had any breakfast yet.

"I knew there was something," said Pooh. "Tiggers always eat thistles, so that was why we came to see you, Eeyore."

"Don't mention it, Pooh."

"Oh, Eeyore, I didn't mean that I didn't *want* to see you—"

"Quite—quite. But your new stripy friend—naturally, he wants his breakfast. What did you say his name was?"

"Tigger."

"Then come this way, Tigger."

Eeyore led the way to the most thistly-looking patch of thistles that ever was, and waved a hoof at it.

"A little patch I was keeping for my birthday," he said; "but, after all, what are birthdays? Here today and gone tomorrow. Help yourself, Tigger."

Tigger thanked him and looked a little anxiously at Pooh.

"Are these really thistles?" he whispered.

"Yes," said Pooh.

"What Tiggers like best?"

"That's right," said Pooh.

"I see," said Tigger.

So he took a large mouthful, and he gave a large crunch.

"*Ow!*" said Tigger.

He sat down and put his paw in his mouth.

"What's the matter?" asked Pooh.

"*Hot!*" mumbled Tigger.

"Your friend," said Eeyore, "appears to have bitten on a bee."

Pooh's friend stopped shaking his head to get the prickles out, and explained that Tiggers didn't like thistles.

"Then why bend a perfectly good one?" asked Eeyore.

"But you said," began Pooh—"you *said* that Tiggers liked everything except honey and haycorns."

"*And* thistles," said Tigger, who was now running round in circles with his tongue hanging out.

Pooh looked at him sadly.

"What are we going to do?" he asked Piglet.

Piglet knew the answer to that, and he said at once that they must go and see Christopher Robin.

"You'll find him with Kanga," said Eeyore. He came close to Pooh, and said in a loud whisper:

"*Could* you ask your friend to do his exercises somewhere else? I shall be having lunch directly, and don't want it bounced on just before I begin. A trifling matter, and fussy of me, but we all have our little ways."

Pooh nodded solemnly and called to Tigger.

"Come along and we'll go and see Kanga. She's sure to have lots of breakfast for you."

Tigger finished his last circle and came up to Pooh and Piglet.

"Hot!" he explained with a large and friendly smile. "Come on!" and he rushed off.

Pooh and Piglet walked slowly after him. And as they walked Piglet said nothing, because he couldn't think of anything, and Pooh said nothing, because he was thinking of a poem. And when he had thought of it he began:

> *What shall we do about poor little Tigger?*
> *If he never eats nothing he'll never get bigger.*
> *He doesn't like honey and haycorns and thistles*
> *Because of the taste and because of the bristles.*
> *And all the good things which an animal likes*
> *Have the wrong sort of swallow or too many spikes.*

"He's quite big enough anyhow," said Piglet.

"He isn't *really* very big."

"Well, he *seems* so."

Pooh was thoughtful when he heard this, and then he murmured to himself:

> *But whatever his weight in pounds, shillings, and ounces,*
> *He always seems bigger because of his bounces.*

"And that's the whole poem," he said. "Do you like it, Piglet?"

"All except the shillings," said Piglet. "I don't think they ought to be there."

"They wanted to come in after the pounds," explained Pooh, "so I let them. It is the best way to write poetry, letting things come."

"Oh, I didn't know," said Piglet.

Tigger had been bouncing in front of them all this time, turning round every now and then to ask, "Is this the way?"—and now at last they came in sight of Kanga's house, and there was Christopher Robin. Tigger rushed up to him.

"Oh, there you are, Tigger!" said Christopher Robin. "I knew you'd be somewhere."

"I've been finding things in the Forest," said Tigger importantly. "I've found a pooh and a piglet and an eeyore, but I can't find any breakfast."

Pooh and Piglet came up and hugged Christopher Robin, and explained what had been happening.

"Don't *you* know what Tiggers like?" asked Pooh.

"I expect if I thought very hard I should," said Christopher Robin, "but I *thought* Tigger knew."

"I do," said Tigger. "Everything there is in the world except honey and haycorns and—what were those hot things called?"

"Thistles."

"Yes, and those."

"Oh, well then, Kanga can give you some breakfast."

So they went into Kanga's house, and when Roo had said, "Hallo, Pooh" and "Hallo, Piglet" once, and "Hallo, Tigger" twice, because he had never said it before and it sounded funny, they told Kanga what they wanted, and Kanga said very kindly, "Well, look in my cupboard, Tigger dear, and see what you'd like." Because she knew at once that, however big Tigger seemed to be, he wanted as much kindness as Roo.

"Shall I look, too?" said Pooh, who was beginning to feel a little eleven o'clockish. And he found a small tin of condensed milk, and something seemed to tell him that Tiggers didn't like this, so he took it into a corner by itself, and went with it to see that nobody interrupted it.

But the more Tigger put his nose into this and his paw into that, the more things he found which Tiggers didn't like. And when he found everything in the cupboard, and couldn't eat any of it, he said to Kanga, "What happens now?"

But Kanga and Christopher Robin and Piglet were all standing round Roo, watching him have his Extract of Malt. And Roo was saying, "Must I?" and Kanga was saying "Now, Roo dear, you remember what you promised."

"What is it?" whispered Tigger to Piglet.

"His Strengthening Medicine," said Piglet. "He hates it."

So Tigger came closer, and he leant over the back of Roo's chair, and suddenly he put out his tongue, and took one large golollop, and, with a sudden jump of surprise, Kanga said, "Oh!" and then clutched at the spoon again just as it was disappearing, and pulled it safely back out of Tigger's mouth. But the Extract of Malt had gone.

"Tigger *dear!*" said Kanga.

"He's taken my medicine, he's taken my medicine, he's taken my medi-cine!" sang Roo happily, thinking it was a tremendous joke.

Then Tigger looked up at the ceiling, and closed his eyes, and his tongue went round and round his chops, in case he had left any outside, and a peaceful smile came over his face as he said, "So *that's* what Tiggers like!"

Which explains why he always lived at Kanga's house afterwards, and had Extract of Malt for breakfast, dinner, and tea. And sometimes, when Kanga thought he wanted strengthening, he had a spoonful or two of Roo's breakfast after meals as medicine.

"But *I* think," said Piglet to Pooh, "that he's been strengthened quite enough."

Issun Boshi: One-Inch Boy

PARENTS: *"Issun Boshi" [IH-soon BOH-she] is a folktale from Japan. If you have access to a world map or globe, help your child locate Japan. Like the next story in this book, "Tom Thumb," this story is about the adventures of a very little person.*

Long ago in a village in Japan, there lived an old man and his wife who more than anything wanted a child. They hoped and they wished and they prayed. "May we be blessed with a child," they said, "even if it is no larger than a fingertip."

And then their prayers were answered. A fine baby boy was born to the old couple. They called him Issun Boshi, which means "One-Inch Boy," for he was no taller than his father's thumb.

Issun Boshi grew up strong, smart, and helpful, though he grew no bigger. When twelve years had passed, Issun Boshi came to his parents and said, "Father and Mother, please give me your permission to go to the capital city, for I wish to see the world, and learn many things, and make a name for myself."

His parents were very worried, but they knew their boy was smart and strong, so they agreed to let him go. They made for him a tiny sword out of a sewing needle. They also gave him a rice bowl and some chopsticks.

In the rice bowl he floated down the river, using one of the chopsticks as a paddle. In a few days he arrived at the city of Kyoto. "My, what a busy city this is!" he thought. "So many feet and legs!" He walked carefully through the streets, dodging feet and cart wheels. He kept walking until he came to a beautiful house, the largest in the city. At the foot of the steps sat a pair of shiny black wooden shoes. They belonged to the owner of the house, who was the wealthiest lord in the city.

The door of the great house opened. Out walked a man who slipped on the shiny black shoes. Issun Boshi called out, "Hello! Hello there!" The man looked around and, seeing no one, began to go back in. But Issun Boshi called out, "Down here, I'm down here, near your shoes! Please be careful you don't step on me." The man, who was the lord of the house, leaned down and was very surprised when he saw Issun Boshi. Issun Boshi bowed and politely introduced himself. "My name," he said, "is Issun Boshi. I am new here and I would like to work for you."

The lord picked up Issun Boshi in the palm of his hand. In a friendly voice he asked, "But what can a little fellow like you do?"

A fly was buzzing around and bothering the lord, so Issun Boshi drew out his sewing-needle sword. With a quick *swit-swat*, down went the fly. Then Issun Boshi did an energetic little dance on the lord's hand.

"You are quite an amazing little fellow," laughed the lord. "Come, you may work for me and live in my house."

And so Issun Boshi went to live in the big beautiful house. He made friends with everyone there, especially the princess, the lord's lovely daughter. It seemed that he was always at her side, helping her in whatever way he could, whether by holding down the paper when she wrote a letter or simply by riding on her shoulder and keeping her company while she walked through the beautiful gardens around the house.

In the spring Issun Boshi traveled with the princess and her companions to the cherry blossom festival. On their way home they began to hear strange noises behind them on the narrow road. They could see nothing in the shadows, when suddenly a huge monster leaped into their path. Everyone screamed and ran—everyone except Issun Boshi and the princess.

"Who are you, and what do you want?" cried Issun Boshi.

"I am an *oni* [OH-nee]," growled the monster. An *oni*! Everyone feared the *oni*, who were fierce and terrible creatures, like demons or goblins.

But Issun Boshi stepped forward and shouted, "Get out of the way, you demon! I am here to guard the princess, and if you try anything, you will regret it!"

"Ha! We'll see about that!" growled the *oni*. Then he snatched up Issun Boshi, popped him into his mouth, and, *gulp*, swallowed him whole. Down, down Issun Boshi slid until he landed, *plop*, in the *oni*'s stomach.

"This big oaf should be more careful about what he eats," said Issun Boshi. He pulled out his sewing-needle sword and began to jab it as hard as he could into the walls of the *oni*'s stomach.

"Ow! Ooh! Agh!" shouted the *oni*. Then he gave a loud "Burp!" and out popped Issun Boshi. In pain, the *oni* ran away whining and crying.

Issun Boshi ran over to the princess. She was bending down and picking up something from the ground. With great excitement she said, "Look, Issun Boshi, the *oni* was so scared that he dropped this magic hammer. If you make a wish on it, it will come true."

Issun Boshi bowed to the princess and said, "My lady, I would ask that you make a wish."

"No, Issun Boshi," said the princess. "You won this because of your bravery. You should be the first one to wish on it."

So Issun Boshi took the hammer and said, "I already have my greatest wish, which is to serve you. But if I could have another wish, I would wish to be as tall as other men."

Then he gave the hammer to the princess, who made a silent wish on it herself. Then and there, Issun Boshi began to grow taller . . . until beside the princess stood a handsome young man.

That night, when the princess told her father how brave Issun Boshi had been, and how he had risked his life to save her, the lord was so happy that he gave permission for Issun Boshi to marry the princess. And so, you see, the princess's wish came true, too.

Issun Boshi's brave deeds were celebrated throughout the land. He and the princess lived happily together, along with Issun Boshi's proud and happy parents, whom Issun Boshi had brought to the lord's house to be part of the family.

Tom Thumb

PARENTS: *People in many lands tell different stories about the little fellow called Tom Thumb. This version is from Germany, as collected by the Brothers Grimm. You might find it interesting to read this story to your child along with the story above, a folktale from Japan called "Issun Boshi" (One-Inch Boy). At the end of this story, you'll find suggestions for reading other similar stories from different lands.*

There was once a poor farmer who used to sit and poke at the fire while his wife sat at her spinning wheel. Night after night the man would let out a big sigh and say, "How sad it is that we have no children. Our house is so quiet, while other people's houses are so noisy and cheerful."

"Yes, it's true," said the wife. "If only we had a child. Why, I would be happy to have one no bigger than my thumb."

Some time after this, she had a little boy, who was strong and healthy in every way—

and, he was no bigger than a thumb. The man and woman said, "Small as he is, we will love him dearly." They named him Tom Thumb. And as Tom grew up, he proved to be a very clever lad.

One day, as Tom's father was getting ready to go to the forest to cut wood, he said, "I wish there was someone to bring the horse and cart to meet me."

"I'll do it!" said Tom.

"But how can you?" his father laughed. "You're much too small even to hold the reins."

"Never mind that, Father," said Tom. "Ask Mother to harness the horse, then I'll sit in the horse's ear and tell him which way to go." And so his mother harnessed the horse and put Tom in the horse's ear. Tom called out, "Giddy-up." The horse started walking.

Now it happened that as the horse and cart turned a corner, two strange men were walking by, and one of them heard Tom calling out directions to the horse.

"Look," he said to his friend, "there goes a wagon, and the driver is calling to his horse, but the driver is nowhere to be seen!"

"Let's follow and see where it goes," said his friend.

So they followed the horse and wagon to the place where Tom's father was chopping wood. When Tom Thumb caught sight of his father, he cried out, "Whoa, boy! Look, Father, here I am with the wagon. Now, help me down, please."

Tom's father lifted his son down out of the horse's ear and set him on a stump. When the two strangers saw this, one of them turned to the other and whispered, "Look here, that little fellow could make us rich! Let's take him to town and charge people money to see him." So they went up to Tom's father and said, "See here, how about selling the little man to us? We'll pay you well, and we'll take good care of him."

But Tom's father said, "No! He is the apple of my eye, and I would not part with him for all the money in the world."

Tom, however, crept up the folds of his father's coat to his shoulder, then whispered in his ear, "Go ahead, Father, sell me to them for a lot of money. Let them take me, and I'll be back in no time."

"But Tom," his father began.

"Trust me, Father," Tom broke in. "I'll take care of everything."

So his father sold Tom for a great deal of money. Off went Tom, riding on the brim of one man's hat. As evening fell, Tom asked to be put down, but the man refused. Tom insisted loudly, "I need to get down, now!" So the man set him down by the roadside. And as soon as he did, Tom scooted away and slipped into a mouse hole, crying out, "So long, my good fellows, have a good trip without me!" The men got down on their hands and knees and put their noses to the ground and poked sticks into mouse holes, but they never found Tom. So, angry and penniless, they made their way home.

When the men were gone, Tom came out of the mouse hole. He found an empty snail shell and said, "This looks like a safe place to spend the night." But just as he settled down to rest, he heard two men walking by. One said to the other, in a rough whispering voice, "Yes, the rich parson won't be back until tomorrow morning, so now is the time to rob his house. But how can we do it?"

Tom sprang out of his shell and shouted, "I can tell you!"

"Who was that?" asked one of the frightened robbers. "Come out and show yourself," he said.

"Take me with you and I'll help you," said Tom.

"Who's talking? Where are you?" asked the robbers.

"Down here!" cried Tom.

The robbers looked down, and there they saw Tom, waving and calling to them. One robber lifted him up and said, "Well, little elf, how are *you* going to help us rob the parson?"

"It will be easy," said Tom. "The parson keeps his money behind iron bars, right? I can slip between the bars and hand out to you as much money as you want."

"Hee-hee, that's a fine idea, little elf," said the robbers, and they snickered all the way to the parson's house. Then they fell quiet and whispered to Tom, "Speak softly, y'hear? We don't want to wake up anyone and get caught!"

"Of course!" said Tom. He sneaked into the parson's room, then slipped between the bars where the money was kept. Then he called out to the robbers, in just as big and loud a voice as he could manage, "HOW MUCH DO YOU WANT? DO YOU WANT IT ALL?"

"Shh, quiet!" hissed the robbers. "You'll wake the dead, you noisy little elf. We can hear you fine. Just start handing out the money."

But Tom pretended not to hear them, and once again he shouted, "WHAT'S THAT YOU SAY? YOU WANT TO TAKE ALL THE MONEY? I'LL GIVE YOU EVERY-THING, JUST HOLD OUT YOUR HANDS."

Tom's shouts were loud enough to wake the cook and the maid, who jumped out of bed and came running to see what was the matter. When they burst through the door, the robbers ran as though wild animals were after them. The maid went to get a light, but by the time she came back with it, Tom Thumb had slipped away to the barn.

Tom found a nice place to sleep in a big pile of hay. He settled down to rest but—poor Tom!—his troubles had just begun. Early the next morning the maid came to the barn and pitched a large bundle of hay to the cow for breakfast. And who should be in the middle of that bundle of hay but Tom! The cow ate up the hay and Tom with it. He was lucky not be crushed between her teeth. After she chewed awhile, she swallowed, and down went Tom to the cow's stomach.

"Goodness me," he said, "somebody forgot to put any windows in this house. It would be nice to have a candle, not to mention some fresh air!" Suddenly, *whump!*, something heavy fell on Tom's head. It was a lump of wet, sticky, chewed hay! The cow was eating again, and the more she ate, the more wet, sticky hay fell on Tom. He was almost squashed when he thought to call out, as loud as he could, "That's enough! No more hay! I'm quite full, thank you! I don't need any more food now!"

The maid happened to be milking the cow at this time, and when she heard the voice come out of the cow, she let out a scream and fell backward off her milking stool, knocking over the bucket of milk. She ran to the parson and said, "Oh, good sir, the cow—the cow has spoken!"

"What? Don't be silly," said the parson. He went to the barn to see for himself what was happening, and the maid walked fearfully behind him.

The parson looked at the cow and said, "So, this is the talking cow? Well, I don't hear anything." But just at that moment Tom shouted, "Thanks for the hay, but I'm quite full now. Perhaps I'll have dessert later!"

The parson jumped back. "Surely this animal is bewitched!" he cried. And so he ordered that the unlucky cow be made into steaks and ground beef. When the cow was cut up, the stomach, with Tom in it, was thrown onto a garbage heap. Tom struggled to get out, and he had just managed to poke out his head when, *zing*, a hungry wolf snapped up the stomach in his teeth and ran off with it.

As the wolf ran, Tom bounced along and thought, "Well, some days are better than others." Then he said to the wolf, "Mr. Wolf, why do you want to eat this nasty old cow stomach? I can tell you where to find some delicious treats."

"And where might that be?" growled the wolf.

"In a house near the forest," said Tom. "There you'll find sausages, ham, beef, cakes, as much as you can possibly eat." So the wolf, his mouth watering, went where Tom told him. And where do you think Tom was taking him? Back to his mother's and father's house!

When they got there, the wolf ate until he was stuffed. That's when Tom called out to his parents, "Help! Help! There's a big bad wolf in here! Help!"

Tom's father came running with a big stick. He whacked the wolf and sent him howling into to the woods. "Good work, Father," said Tom.

His father looked down and cried out, "Tom, where have you been? I've been so worried about you! Mother, come quick, our Tom is back!"

"Well," said Tom, "I've been in a mouse hole, and a snail's shell, and a cow's stomach. And I think that from now on I would rather stay with you!"

"Oh, my little Tom," said his father, "I never should have sold you, and I never will again!"

For Tom, there were plenty of hugs and kisses, and lots of food and drink, and even some new clothes, for, as you may well imagine, his old ones had been spoiled by his adventures.

PARENTS: You may want to talk with your child about how stories from different lands can be alike in many ways. After reading "Issun Boshi" and "Tom Thumb," you might begin by asking your child if she noticed some ways the two stories are alike.

For more similar stories from different lands, check your library for such titles as:

The Egyptian Cinderella and *The Korean Cinderella* by Shirley Climo, illustrated by Ruth Heller (Harper-Collins, 1989 and 1993).

Lon Po Po: A "Red Riding Hood" Story from China by Ed Young (Philomel Books, 1989; also available from Scholastic).

Mufaro's Beautiful Daughters: An African Tale by John Steptoe (Lothrop, Lee, & Shepard, 1987). A "Cinderella story" from Africa.

Sootface: An Ojibwa Cinderella Story by Robert D. San Souci (Doubleday Books for Young Readers, 1994).

Thumbelina by Amy Ehrlich (Penguin/Puffin, 1979). A Hans Christian Andersen story, here beautifully illustrated by Susan Jeffers.

Tom Thumb by Richard Jesse Watson (Harcourt Brace, 1989). A "Tom Thumb" story from England, different from the "Tom Thumb" in this book.

It Could Always Be Worse

Once there was a poor Jewish man who had come to the end of his rope. So he went to his rabbi, a holy teacher, for advice.

"Holy Rabbi!" he cried. "Things are in a bad way with me, and are getting worse all the time! We are poor, so poor, that my wife, my six children, my in-laws and I have to live in a one-room hut. We get in each other's way all the time. Our nerves are frayed and, because we have plenty of troubles, we quarrel. Believe me—my home is awful, and things could not possibly be worse!"

The rabbi pondered the matter gravely. "My son," he said, "promise to do as I tell you and your condition will improve."

"I promise, Rabbi," answered the troubled man. "I'll do anything you say."

"Tell me—what animals do you own?"

"I have a cow, a goat and some chickens."

"Very well! Go home now and take all these animals into your house to live with you."

The poor man was amazed, but since he had promised the rabbi, he went home and brought all the animals into his house.

The following day the poor man returned to the rabbi and cried, "Rabbi, what misfortune have you brought upon me! I did as you told me and brought the animals into the house. And now what have I got? Things are worse than ever! The house is turned into a barn! Save me, Rabbi—help me!"

"My son," replied the rabbi calmly, "go home and take the chickens out of your house. God will help you!"

So the poor man went home and took the chickens out of his house. But it was not long before he again came running to the rabbi.

"Holy Rabbi!" he wailed. "Help me, save me! The goat is

smashing everything in the house—she's turning my life into a nightmare."

"Go home," said the rabbi gently, "and take the goat out of the house. God will help you!"

The poor man returned to his house and removed the goat. But it wasn't long before he again came running to the rabbi, crying loudly, "What a misfortune you've brought upon my head, Rabbi! The cow has turned my house into a stable! How can you expect a human being to live side by side with an animal?"

"You're right—a hundred times right!" agreed the rabbi. "Go straight home and take the cow out of your house!"

And the poor unfortunate man hurried home and took the cow out of his house.

Not a day had passed before he came running again to the rabbi. "Rabbi!" cried the poor man, his face beaming. "You've made life sweet again for me. With all the animals out, the house is so quiet, so roomy and so clean! What a pleasure!"

PARENTS: After reading this story, you might want to ask your child, "What do you think the title means?"

Jack and the Beanstalk

Once upon a time there was a poor widow who had an only son named Jack and a cow named Milky-white. All they had to live on was the milk the cow gave every morning, which they carried to the market and sold. But one morning Milky-white gave no milk.

"Oh, Jack," said the poor widow, wringing her hands, "we have nothing to eat and no money. We must sell poor Milky-white."

"Cheer up, Mother," said Jack. "It's market day today. I'll sell Milky-white, then we'll be better off, you'll see."

So Jack took the cow and started down the road. He had not gone far when he met a strange-looking old man. The old man said, "Good morning, Jack."

"Good morning to you," said Jack, and wondered how the old man knew his name.

"Well, Jack, where are you off to?" said the man.

"I'm going to market to sell our cow here."

"Oh, yes, you look like just the sort of fellow to sell a cow," said the man. "Now I wonder," he asked Jack, "do you know how many beans make five?"

Jack thought this was a strange question, but he answered anyway. "Two beans in each hand, and one bean in your mouth—that makes five."

"Right you are!" said the old man. And then, pulling something out of his pocket, he said, "And here they are." He held out five very strange-looking beans. "Now, because you're such a smart fellow," he said to Jack, "I will trade you these beans for your cow."

"Well now," said Jack, "that would be a nice trade for *you!*"

"Ah, but you don't know what kind of beans these are," said the man. "If you plant them tonight, then by morning they grow right up to the sky."

"Really?" said Jack, who was beginning to get interested.

"Yes," said the man. "And if it doesn't turn out to be true, then you can have your cow back."

"All right, then," said Jack. He gave the man the cow, and took the beans, and went home.

"Jack, are you back already?" said his mother. "I see you've sold Milky-white. How much did you get for her?"

"Mother, you'll never guess," said Jack.

"Oh, you good boy!" said his mother. "Did you get five? Or ten? Maybe even—no, it can't be—twenty?"

"I told you you couldn't guess!" said Jack. Then, reaching in his pocket, he said, "See here, Mother. I got five . . . beans. You plant them and then overnight they . . ."

"What!" cried his mother. "Beans! You gave away my Milky-white for *beans?* How could you be such a fool? Off to bed with you, and no supper. And as for your precious beans, here they go, out the window!"

So Jack went to his little attic room, where he flopped down and finally fell asleep.

When he woke up, the room looked funny. The sun was shining into part of it, but all the rest was dark and shady. He jumped up and went to the window. And what do you think he saw? Why, the beans his mother had thrown out the window had landed in the garden, and overnight they had sprung up into a big beanstalk, which went up and up and up till it reached the sky. So the old man had been telling the truth!

The beanstalk grew up close to Jack's window. All he had to do was step out onto it and then start climbing it, like a ladder. So Jack climbed, and he climbed and he climbed and he climbed and he climbed and he climbed till at last he reached the sky. And when he got there, he saw a long straight road. He followed the road until he came to a great big tall house, and on the doorstep there was a great big tall woman.

"Good morning, ma'am," said Jack, quite politely. "Could you be so kind as to give me some breakfast?"

"Oh, so you want breakfast?" said the great big tall woman. "Well, you'll *be* breakfast if you don't get out of here. My husband is a fierce giant, and there's nothing he likes better than a nice cooked boy on buttered toast. You'd better get going, for he'll be coming soon."

"Oh, please, ma'am," said Jack, "I haven't eaten since yesterday, really and truly."

Well, the giant's wife wasn't so bad after all. So she took Jack into the kitchen and gave him a chunk of bread and cheese and a jug of milk. But Jack hadn't half finished these when—*thump! thump! thump!*—the whole house began to tremble with the noise of someone coming—someone big!

"Goodness gracious, it's my old man!" said the giant's wife. "What on earth shall I do? Quick, jump in here!" And Jack jumped into the oven just as the giant came in.

He was a big one, to be sure. He had three cows tied to his belt. He threw them down on the table and said rudely to his wife, "Here, woman, cook me a couple of these for breakfast. But wait—what's this I smell?

"Fee-fi-fo-fum,
I smell the blood of an Englishman.
Be he alive or be he dead
I'll grind his bones to make my bread!"

"Now, dear," said his wife, "it's nothing but the leftover smell of that little boy you had for dinner yesterday. Run along and wash up, and by the time you come back, I'll have breakfast ready."

So the giant went off, and Jack was about to jump out of the oven when the woman whispered, "Wait till he's asleep. He always has a nap after breakfast."

The giant gulped down his breakfast. Then he went to a big chest and took out two big bags. He sat down, and from the bags he took out piles of gold coins. He began counting them, very slowly—"One . . . two . . . uh, three . . . um, ah, four . . ."—then his head began to nod, and then he began to snore, so that the whole house shook.

Jack crept out of the oven, tiptoed past the giant, grabbed one of the bags of gold (which he could barely lift), and ran lickety-split back to the beanstalk. He threw down the bag of gold, which fell—*plump!*—into his mother's garden, then climbed down till at last he reached the ground.

"Well, Mother?" he said. "Wasn't I right about the beans? They really are magic!"

For a while Jack and his mother bought what they needed, and a little more, with the bag of gold. But at last the bag was empty, so Jack made up his mind to try his luck again at the top of the beanstalk. He climbed and he climbed and he climbed, and once again, sure enough, there was the great big tall woman standing on the doorstep. And once again he asked for something to eat.

"Go away, boy," said the woman, "or else my man will eat you up for breakfast. But, say—aren't you the youngster who came here once before? Do you know, on that very day my man lost one of his bags of gold?"

"Did he, now?" said Jack. "How very strange! Maybe I could help you find it, but I'm so hungry that first I must have something to eat."

So the great big tall woman gave him something to eat. But he had hardly taken a bite when—*thump! thump! thump!*—they heard the giant's footsteps. Once again the wife hid Jack in the oven.

And all happened as it had before. In came the giant, bellowing "Fee-fi-fo-fum!" Then, after gulping down three broiled oxen for breakfast, the giant said, "Wife, bring me my hen and my golden harp!"

The wife brought them. The giant looked at the hen and barked, "Lay!" And the hen laid an egg, all of gold. Then the giant looked at the golden harp and said, "Sing!" And the golden harp sang beautifully. And it went on singing until the giant fell asleep and started snoring like thunder.

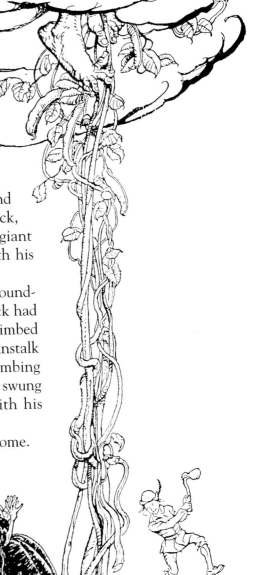

Jack sneaked out of the oven and crept like a mouse on his hands and knees. Then he crawled up the table, grabbed the hen and golden harp, and dashed toward the door. But the hen began to cluck, and the harp called out, "Master! Master!" The giant woke up just in time to see Jack running away with his treasures.

Jack ran as fast as he could, and the giant came bounding after him, and would have caught him, only Jack had a head start. When he got to the beanstalk, he climbed down as fast as he could. The giant reached the beanstalk and stopped short—he didn't like the idea of climbing down such a ladder. But, like it or not, the giant swung himself down on the beanstalk, which shook with his weight.

By this time, Jack had climbed down and run home. "Mother!" he cried. "Give me an axe, and hurry!" His mother came rushing out with an axe in her hand. She ran with Jack to the beanstalk, then she screamed with fright as she saw the giant's legs poking down through the clouds.

Jack swung the axe and gave a chop at the beanstalk. The giant felt the beanstalk shake, and he stopped to see what was the matter. Jack gave another chop, and another, and another, and the beanstalk began to topple over. Then the giant fell down and broke his crown, and the beanstalk came tumbling after.

From then on, Jack and his mother had all the money and music they wanted, for the hen gave them golden eggs, and the harp sang for them all day long. And so they lived happily ever after.

The Knee-High Man
(An African American folktale, retold by Julius Lester)

Once upon a time there was a knee-high man. He was no taller than a person's knees. Because he was so short, he was very unhappy. He wanted to be big like everybody else.

One day he decided to ask the biggest animal he could find how he could get big. So he went to see Mr. Horse. "Mr. Horse, how can I get big like you?"

Mr. Horse said, "Well, eat a whole lot of corn. Then run around a lot. After a while you'll be as big as me."

The knee-high man did just that. He ate so much corn that his stomach hurt. Then he ran and ran and ran until his legs hurt. But he didn't get any bigger. So he decided that Mr. Horse had told him something wrong. He decided to go ask Mr. Bull.

"Mr. Bull? How can I get big like you?"

Mr. Bull said, "Eat a whole lot of grass. Then bellow and bellow as loud as you can. The first thing you know, you'll be as big as me."

So the knee-high man ate a whole field of grass. That made his stomach hurt. He bellowed and bellowed and bellowed all day and all night. That made his throat hurt. But he didn't get any bigger. So he decided that Mr. Bull was all wrong too.

Now he didn't know anyone else to ask. One night he heard Mr. Hoot Owl hooting, and he remembered that Mr. Owl knew everything. "Mr. Owl? How can I get big like Mr. Horse and Mr. Bull?"

"What do you want to be big for?" Mr. Hoot Owl asked.

"I want to be big so that when I get into a fight, I can whip everybody," the knee-high man said.

Mr. Hoot Owl hooted. "Anybody ever try to pick a fight with you?"

The knee-high man thought a minute. "Well, now that you mention it, nobody ever did try to start a fight with me."

Mr. Owl said, "Well, you don't have any reason to fight. Therefore, you don't have any reason to be bigger than you are."

"But, Mr. Owl," the knee-high man said, "I want to be big so I can see far into the distance."

Mr. Hoot Owl hooted. "If you climb a tall tree, you can see into the distance from the top."

The knee-high man was quiet for a minute. "Well, I hadn't thought of that."

Mr. Hoot Owl hooted again. "And that's what's wrong, Mr. Knee-High Man. You hadn't done any thinking at all. I'm smaller than you, and you don't see me worrying about being big. Mr. Knee-High Man, you wanted something that you didn't need."

Medio Pollito
(A Hispanic folktale)

There was once a large black Spanish hen who had fine little chicks. All of them were ordinary chicks, except for one, who looked as if he had been cut right in half. All his brothers and sisters had two wings and two legs and two eyes, but he had only one of each. And he had only half a head and half a beak. So they called him Medio Pollito [MEH-dee-o poh-YEE-toh], which means "Half-Chick" in Spanish.

The brother and sister chicks did just what they were told to do, but Medio Pollito did not like to obey his mother. When mother hen called for him to come back to the chicken house, he pretended that he could not hear, because he had only one ear. And the older he became, the more he disobeyed his mother.

One day he said, "I am tired of life in the barnyard. I am going to the city to see the king."

His mother said, "You aren't old enough yet. When you get older, we will go to the city together."

But Medio Pollito would not listen to anyone. "I am going to visit the king, and I shall have a big house in the city, and become rich, and maybe I will invite you to visit me sometime." With that, he hopped down the road toward the city.

His mother called out, "Be sure to be nice to everyone you meet." But Medio did not listen, and off he went.

He first hopped to a little stream of water, choked with weeds. "Oh, Medio," it cried, "please help me clear away these weeds so I can flow."

"Do you think I have time to take from my travels?" said Medio. "I am off to the city to see the king." And away he hopped.

Later he came to some burning grass, and the fire said to him, "Medio, please put some sticks on me so I won't go out."

"Do you think I have time to take from my travels?" said Medio. "I am off to the city to see the king." And away he hopped.

As he got closer to the city, he came to a tree where the wind was caught in the branches and leaves, and the wind said to Medio, "Oh, please climb up here and get me out of these branches so I can fly away."

"Do you think I have time to take from my travels?" said Medio. "I am off to the city to see the king." And away he hopped.

As he entered the city, he saw the royal palace, and hopped right into the courtyard. Who should see Medio but the king's cook, who said, "I think I shall make the king a nice chicken soup for dinner." And he reached out, and caught Medio, and put him into a pot of water near the stove.

Medio felt very wet. "Oh, water," he cried, "don't wet me like this." But the water replied, "You would not help me when I was a little stream, so why should I help you?"

Then the fire on the stove began to heat the water. Medio felt very hot. "Oh, fire," he cried, "don't burn me like this." But the fire replied, "You would not help me when I was going out in the grass, so why should I help you?"

The pain was so bad that Medio thought he would die. Just then, the cook raised the lid of the pot to see if the soup was ready. But he saw the ugly little chick, and said, "I can't send such an ugly chick to the king." And he threw Medio out the window.

There the wind caught him and took him so fast he could hardly breathe. "Oh, wind," he cried, "don't carry me like this. Let me rest or I shall die." But the wind replied, "You would not help me when I was caught in the tree, so why should I help you?" And with that he lifted up Medio Pollito, up in the air to the top of the church tower, and left him stuck on the steeple.

There he is to this very day. If you look at the top of many a church steeple, you will see a weather vane in the form of half a chicken. It is Medio Pollito, the chick who would not help others. Now he must help everyone by showing them which way the wind is blowing.

The Pied Piper of Hamelin

Rats! Everywhere in the little town of Hamelin, there were rats, rats, and more rats. There were so many that no amount of traps could catch them, and no amount of poison could kill them. They fought the dogs and chased the cats. They made nests in the people's hats. They ate the food right off the tables. They ran up and down the streets in broad daylight, flicking their tails and twitching their whiskers. And they made such a squeaking and shrieking that you could not hear yourself speak, or get a wink of good sleep.

In the middle of Hamelin at the Town Hall, a crowd had gathered. The people were shaking their fists and shouting, "Mr. Mayor! Mr. Mayor! You must get rid of these rats, or we will get rid of you!"

"What do you expect me to do?" asked the mayor. He sat his big round body down in a big wooden chair. "I've racked my brain again and again, but all in vain." Then, giving his head a rap, he cried, "Oh for a trap, a trap, a trap!"

Just then at the door came a gentle tap. "It's a rat!" cried the mayor.

"Rats don't knock," said a townsman.

"Oh, yes, of course," said the mayor. Then, trying to sound brave, he called out, "Come in!" And in came the strangest-looking person you've ever seen.

He was tall and thin, with sharp blue eyes, each like a pin. His long coat, half of yellow and half of red, stretched from his heel to his head. From underneath a floppy hat flowed his hair, long and white, and in his hand he carried a silver pipe.

"Who are you?" asked the mayor.

And the strange-looking figure answered, "People call me the Pied Piper. On my pipe I play music that charms all things under the sun—all creatures that creep, or swim, or fly, or run. Whenever I play, they follow me, wherever I go. I can charm the birds of the air. I can charm the fishes of the sea. I can charm the wild beasts that live in the forests."

"And rats?" said the mayor. "What about rats? Can you charm them?"

"That I can," said the Pied Piper. "I can charm every last rat from your town. Give me a thousand gold pieces and I will set to it."

"A thousand?" said the mayor. "Why, you may have fifty thousand if you can do it!" And the townspeople cried, "Yes, yes, we will gladly give him fifty thousand. Just get rid of the rats!"

"As you wish," said the stranger. Then, with a strange smile, he stepped out into the street and put the pipe to his lips. And he had hardly played three notes when, from every direction, rats came running, tumbling, tripping, hurrying, scurrying.

Great rats, small rats, lean rats, brawny rats,
Brown rats, black rats, gray rats, tawny rats,
Grave old plodders, gay young friskers,
    Fathers, mothers, uncles, cousins,
Cocking tails, and prickling whiskers,
    Families by tens and dozens,
Brothers, sisters, husbands, wives—
Followed the Piper for their lives.
From street to street he piped advancing,
And step by step they followed dancing.

The Pied Piper walked slowly down the street, playing his merry tune. And when he came to the river, the rats jumped in and were carried under and away by the rushing water.

The townspeople hurrayed and hurrahed, and rang the bells till they rocked the steeples. But they fell quiet as the Pied Piper returned. He walked up to the mayor and said, "The rats are gone. It is time to pay the Piper. I will take my thousand gold pieces and go."

But the mayor hemmed and hawed and harrumphed, and said that really, he didn't see why the Piper should be paid so much for what was such an easy job. After all, what had he done but walk down the street and play on a pipe? And really, wouldn't the Piper think it fair to be paid, say, about ten gold pieces, yes, ten, didn't that seem about right for so easy a job?

And as the mayor spoke, the townspeople nodded and began to whisper among themselves that, indeed, this funny-looking man hardly deserved a thousand gold pieces just for playing a silly pipe—why, the very idea!

"You promised to pay a thousand," said the Piper. "You even offered me fifty thousand. Come now, I have no time to waste. I must be on my way. It's a thousand we've agreed on, and a thousand you must pay."

The mayor put ten gold pieces on the table and said with a huff, "Take it or leave it. Now, fellow, be off with you."

Once more the Pied Piper stepped into the street. Once more he began to play. And after only a few notes, there was a rustling, and a bustling, and a sound of small feet pattering, and little tongues chattering. Out came the children, all the children of Hamelin town, tripping and skipping and running merrily after the music with shouting and laughter.

The townspeople could not speak. They could not move. They stood as though they had been changed to blocks of wood. They could not shout or utter a cry as they

watched the children skipping by.

As the children danced merrily behind him, the Pied Piper played his tune. And the tune seemed to make a promise, a promise of a joyous land where the sun was shining and birds were singing, and children played in fields in which flowers bloomed brighter than rainbows. And on they danced, as the Piper led them far from town, until they came to a mountainside.

And there, in the rock, a door opened wide. The Piper walked in, and the children followed. And when all were in to the very last, the door in the mountainside shut fast.

The townspeople searched high and low, up and down. But they never again saw the Pied Piper or the children of Hamelin town.

Pinocchio

PARENTS: *Many children may already be familiar with one version of the story of Pinocchio as told in the Walt Disney film. The Disney film, a compelling animated classic, makes many changes from the original story, published in 1883 by an Italian author who used the pen name of C. Collodi. One big difference is that from the start Collodi's Pinocchio is a naughty, mischievous puppet. If your child knows the film, then it may be interesting to talk with him or her about how it differs from this story. Collodi's story fills a small book; here we retell a few episodes, rearranged in order to make this selection hold together on its own.*

Pinocchio Runs Away

There was once a poor woodcarver named Geppetto [jeh-PET-toe]. One day, Geppetto picked out an unusual block of wood and said, "I will carve a fine puppet out of this, one that can dance and jump when I pull the strings." And he thought that perhaps he could travel with the puppet and put on shows and earn a living.

"What shall I name my puppet?" thought Geppetto. "I know— Pinocchio. That sounds like a lucky name!" And so he started carving. First he worked on the head. He carved the eyes, and to his surprise, the eyes opened and stared at him! Then he carved the nose. Geppetto jumped back: the nose was growing longer and longer! "Stop, nose, stop!" Geppetto cried. Finally it stopped growing, but oh, it was long! Geppetto next worked on the mouth. As soon as he finished the mouth, the puppet began to laugh, and it kept on laughing. "Stop laughing, you!" said Geppetto. The puppet stopped laughing—but it stuck out its tongue!

"Pinocchio!" said Geppetto. "You're not even finished and already you're a bad boy."

Geppetto kept carving, and he finished the legs and feet. But as soon as he did, the puppet raised a foot and kicked him in the nose!

"Come, you mischief-maker," said Geppetto. "Let us see if you can use those legs." He put Pinocchio on the ground and held him up. At first Pinocchio's legs were so stiff that he could not walk. Geppetto showed him how to put one foot in front of another, and Pinocchio began to walk by himself. Then he began to run around the room. When he saw the door was open, he jumped out and ran away!

Pinocchio ran through the village until he came to the fields and meadows. He leaped over brambles and bushes, and across brooks and ponds. He heard the chirp-chirp-chirping sound of a cricket. Suddenly the cricket began to talk. "Pinocchio, listen to me," said the cricket. "Bad boys who run away and disobey their parents will never be happy."

"You silly cricket," said Pinocchio. "If I go back home, I know what will happen: I'll have to go to *school*, and whether I want to or not, I'll have to *study*. But it's much more fun to chase butterflies, and climb trees, and do just as I please."

"Then you are a silly wooden-head!" said the cricket. "If that's the way you spend your time, you'll grow up to be a big donkey, and everyone will make fun of you."

Pinocchio was angry. He picked up something heavy and threw it—and there was no more talking or chirping from the cricket.

As Pinocchio walked away, he felt a new feeling, a strange emptiness inside of him. Along with the emptiness came a loud growling sound. "Why, I'm hungry," the puppet said. "I'm hungry as a wolf."

He ran back to the village. It was dark. The shops were closed, and all the doors and windows were shut tight. "Oh, I'm so terribly hungry," he cried. He walked up to a house and rang the bell, again and again. "That's sure to wake someone up," he thought. And he was right. A window opened upstairs and a sleepy man stuck out his head. In an angry voice he said, "What do you want at this time of night?"

"I'm a poor hungry boy," said Pinocchio. "Please feed me."

"Wait a minute, I'll be right back," said the man.

The puppet looked up at the window and imagined the wonderful treats that the man might be bringing. Then—*splash!*—Pinocchio was hit in the face by a shower of ice-cold water!

"Maybe that cricket was right after all," Pinocchio grumbled. He found his way back to Geppetto's cottage. The old man was very glad to see him. "You must promise not to run away again," he said. "You must go to school, like a good boy."

"Yes, Father, I'll be good," said Pinocchio.

Pinocchio at the Puppet Show

The next morning Geppetto, who was very poor, sold his only coat in order to buy Pinocchio an A-B-C book. With his new book in hand, Pinocchio started for school.

"I *will* be a good boy," he said. But he had not gone very far when he saw a sign for a puppet show. "I can go to school any old day," he thought, "but I must see that show today!" So he sold his book for the price of a ticket and went to see the show.

The theater was full of people, laughing loudly at the puppets on the stage. Then a most unexpected thing happened: the puppets on stage cried out, "Look, it's Pinocchio, our fellow puppet! Pinocchio, come up here!" Pinocchio began leaping over people's heads to get to the stage. Well, you never saw anything like it, or heard such a great clattering, as the puppets knocked their wooden arms and legs together in their rush to hug Pinocchio.

The people in the audience were angry that the play had stopped. "The play! We want the play!" they shouted.

Suddenly the puppet master came out. He was a fierce-looking man, with a long black beard, sharp yellow teeth, and eyes like glowing red coals. "What's this? You don't belong here!" he roared as he grabbed Pinocchio. "So," he said, "you're made of wood. Then I will use you for firewood."

"No, please don't," pleaded Pinocchio. "Please spare me. My poor old father will miss me so much. Just this morning he sent me off to school, and he bought me an A-B-C book with the money he got from selling his only coat. It was an old coat, too, full of patches."

The puppet master looked fierce, but he wasn't all bad. With a loud sniff he said to Pinocchio, "I feel sorry for your poor father. Go back to him, and give him these five gold pieces to buy a new coat."

The Fox and the Cat

Pinocchio thanked the puppet master a thousand times and started on his way home. But he had not gone far when he met a fox who seemed to be lame and a cat who seemed to be blind.

"Good morning, Pinocchio," said the fox.

"How do you know my name?" asked the puppet.

"I know your father," said the sly fox. "I saw him yesterday morning, standing in the doorway of his house, wearing only a tattered shirt. He was cold and shivering."

"But he will be warm soon!" said Pinocchio. Then, holding out the five gold coins, he said, "See, I'm rich! I'm going to buy my father a fine new coat."

When he saw the gold pieces, the fox, who was supposed to be lame, jumped up; and the cat, who was supposed to be blind, stared with wide-open eyes that looked like two green lamps. But all this happened so quickly that Pinocchio didn't notice.

"My, my," said the fox, "so much money. And what exactly do you plan to do with it?"

"I'll buy Father a coat and myself a new A-B-C book," said Pinocchio.

"An A-B-C book?" asked the fox in a doubtful voice.

"Yes," said Pinocchio. "I'm going to school to study."

"*Study?!*" exclaimed the fox. "Do you know what happens when you study? I tried to study once, and now look at me—I am lame!"

"I also tried to study once," said the cat, "and now look at me—I am blind."

"You don't need to study or work," said the fox. "Just listen to me, my boy. How would you like to see those five gold coins turn into ten? Or twenty? Or a hundred? Or even a thousand?"

"Really?" said the puppet. "How?"

"Why, it's very easy," laughed the fox. "Do you know the place called the Field of Wonders? You just go there and dig a little hole in the ground. Then you cover the hole with a little dirt, water it, and go away. During the night your gold pieces will sprout and grow. And in the morning you'll find a tree loaded with gold pieces!"

"Oh, how wonderful!" cried Pinocchio. "How can I ever thank you? Oh, I know. When I have picked all the gold pieces, I will give you a hundred of them."

But the fox cried out, as though he were surprised and embarrassed, "A present! For us! No, really, we simply could not accept. Our greatest pleasure is to bring happiness and wealth to *others.*"

"Oh, yes," said the cat, "helping other people is all the reward we ask."

"Come on, then!" exclaimed Pinocchio. "Let's go to the Field of Wonders!"

"Certainly," said the fox. "But shall we stop for dinner on the way? I believe that one of your gold coins should be enough to feed us all."

The Return of the Cricket, and the Field of Wonders

At dinner the fox and cat stuffed themselves as though they were eating a meal to last a lifetime. Pinocchio was not very hungry, so he stepped outside to think about all the money he would soon have. He heard a small voice calling his name.

"Who is calling me?" asked Pinocchio.

"I am the spirit of the talking cricket," said the voice.

"What do you want?" asked the puppet.

"I want to give you a few words of advice," said the voice. "Return home and give the four gold pieces you have left to your father. Do not listen to those who promise to make you rich overnight. Either they are fools or they will make a fool out of you. Listen to me, Pinocchio, and go home."

"No," said the puppet. "I'm going to do what I want."

"It is very late," said the voice.

"I'm going to do what I want."

"The night is dark."

"I'm going to do what I want."

"There are dangers ahead."

"I'm going to do what I want."

"Remember that children who insist on doing what they want will be sorry for it, sooner or later."

"I've heard all that before," said the stubborn puppet.

Just then the fox and cat came out and joined him again. Together they walked on to the Field of Wonders. As they walked, Pinocchio kept thinking to himself, "I wonder how much gold the tree will grow? What if it's a thousand pieces? Or maybe two thousand? Or even five thousand? Oh, I will have a grand palace, and a thousand toys, and a kitchen filled with candy and cakes!"

They came at last to a large field. No one was in sight. "Here we are, my young friend," said the fox. "Now dig a hole and put your gold pieces in it."

Pinocchio dug a hole, placed the four remaining gold pieces in it, and carefully covered them with dirt. Then he went to a nearby well and filled his shoe with water, which he brought back and sprinkled on the ground where he had planted the coins.

"Is there anything else?" he asked the fox.

"Nothing else at all," said the fox. "Now, you simply have to leave this place for about twenty minutes. And when you return, you will find a tree covered with money."

"Thank you, thank you, a thousand times thank you," said Pinocchio as he jumped up and down for joy.

The fox and the cat went one way, and Pinocchio went another. He counted the minutes, one by one. When he thought it was time, he ran back to the Field of Wonders. He came to the field and looked for a tree but saw nothing. He turned around and looked in all directions—still nothing. Then he heard someone laughing. Looking up, he saw a big parrot siting in a tree.

In an angry voice Pinocchio asked, "Why are you laughing?"

"Oh," said the parrot, "only because I just tickled myself under the wing. And because I always laugh at silly people who believe everything they are told."

"Do you mean me?" snapped Pinocchio.

"Yes, indeed, I mean you," said the parrot. "You are foolish enough to think that money can grow like beans or peas. Don't you know that to earn money honestly, you have to work with your hands and with your head?"

"I—I don't understand what you mean," said Pinocchio in a trembling voice.

"Oh, I think you do," said the parrot. "Why don't you check where you planted the money?"

Pinocchio did not want to believe the parrot. Still, he bent down and began to dig the dirt out of the hole where he had planted the money. He dug and he dug and he dug until he had made a hole as big as himself. But the money was not there. Every piece of it was gone. And Pinocchio knew, as well as you know, who took it.

Sadly, Pinocchio walked back to the village. On his way he passed a small cottage, and there, standing in the door, was a beautiful blue-haired fairy. "Pinocchio," she called out. "What happened to your gold coins?"

"I, uh, you see, well, I lost them. Yes, that's it, I lost them," stammered Pinocchio.

No sooner had he said this than his nose grew longer, longer, and longer!

"Pinocchio," said the fairy, "I hope you've learned your lesson." Then she called in a flock of woodpeckers, who pecked on his nose until it was back to its old size. But from then on, you could always tell whenever Pinocchio was lying, for his nose would grow and grow.

Pinocchio has many more adventures. He meets a naughty boy named Lampwick. They sneak away from school to go to the Land of Toys. But when Pinocchio leaves the Land of Toys, he finds that he has grown the ears and tail of a donkey! The blue-haired fairy helps Pinocchio, and he decides that he wants to become a real boy. Before he does, he goes through some very hard trials—he is even swallowed by a giant shark! In the end, Pinocchio is reunited with Geppetto, and his wish comes true: he is no longer a puppet but a real boy.

The Princess and the Pea
(from the story by Hans Christian Andersen)

Once upon a time there was a prince, and he wanted to marry a princess. But not just any princess. He wanted to marry a *real* princess. So he traveled all over the world looking for a real princess.

He went from kingdom to kingdom and he met plenty of princesses. Of course, they were all beautiful, talented, graceful, and kind. But never did the prince feel that he had found an absolutely, totally, completely *real* princess. So, sad and disappointed, he returned home.

Back at the castle his mother, the queen, asked him, "Did you find a princess?"

"Oh, I found plenty of princesses," the prince replied, "but I never felt sure that I'd found a *real* princess."

That night there was a terrible storm. Lightning flashed, thunder crashed, the wind howled, and the rain pounded down. In the middle of the storm, there was a knock at the palace gates. The king opened them and there, standing in the rain, was a princess. And oh my, she was a mess! Her hair was dripping, her clothes were torn and muddy, and water poured out of her shoes.

"Who are you?" asked the queen.

"I am a princess," she said. "Really. A real princess."

"Humph!" said the queen, and she thought to herself, "We'll soon see about that!" The queen went into a bedroom and took all the sheets and blankets off the bed. Then she put one tiny pea on

the bed, and on top of that she piled twenty mattresses, and on top of those, twenty feather-filled pads. "Here is where you will sleep tonight," she said to the princess.

The next morning at the breakfast table, the queen asked the princess, "Did you have a good night's sleep?"

"No, not at all," said the princess. "I tossed and turned all night. Something in the bed was so hard and lumpy—why, I'm bruised black and blue all over."

So, she had felt the pea through the twenty mattresses and twenty feather-filled pads. The queen and her son smiled at each other. Surely, only a *real* princess could be so delicate and sensitive!

So the prince married her and felt happy that he had at last found a *real* princess. And as for the pea, it was placed in a museum, where it may still be seen, if nobody has taken it.

And that, children, is a *real* story!

Puss-in-Boots

Once upon a time there was an old miller, and when he died, he left his three sons all that he owned—which was not much. To the oldest son, he left his mill. To the middle son, he left his mule. And to the youngest son, he left only his cat.

With a sad sigh, the youngest son looked at the cat and said, "What can I do? My brothers can take care of themselves, but what can I do with only a cat? I suppose I could eat you and sell your skin, but then what?"

Now the cat heard all this, though of course, like all cats, he pretended to be paying no attention at all. And when the young man had finished speaking, the cat spoke up and said, "My good master, there's no need to worry. Just bring me a big bag and a pair of boots and I'll fix everything, you'll see."

"What can a cat do?" said the young man. But then he thought, "What have I got to lose?" After all, he had seen this cat play many clever tricks in order to catch mice. So he got the cat a bag and a pair of boots.

Puss pulled on the boots—and looking down at his booted paws, he had to admit that he did look rather handsome in them. Then he put some grain into the bag. He held the bag in his two front paws and went to a place where he knew there were many rabbits. He put the bag on the ground and left it wide open, with a little grain showing. Then he stretched himself out nearby and lay very still, as though he were dead. Soon a plump rabbit smelled the grain and hopped right into the bag. Quick as a wink, Puss jumped up and caught the rabbit.

Now Puss, bag in paws, went to the palace and asked to speak to His Majesty, the king. He was brought before the king, where he made a low bow and said, "Sire, I have brought you a fine plump rabbit, a gift from my noble master, the Marquis of Carabas." Puss purred with satisfaction at the fancy-sounding title that he had made up on the spot for his master.

"Tell your master," said the king, "that I accept his gift, and am well pleased with it."

"Yes, Your Majesty," said Puss, and after bowing low again, he walked out in his boots.

A few days later, Puss used his same trick to catch some partridges, and he brought the bag of birds to the king, who was again well pleased. And so things went on for some time. Every few days Puss brought something he had caught to the king, and each time Puss offered it as a gift from the grand and noble Marquis of Carabas. The king began to think of this marquis as a famous hunter and a generous man, though he was, as you and I know, only the poor miller's youngest son!

Now it happened one day that Puss heard about the king's plans to go for a ride in his coach along the riverbank. And with the king would be his daughter, who was, of course, the most beautiful princess in the land. When Puss heard this, he went to his master and said, "Master, if you will do just as I tell you, your fortune is made. All you must do is go and wash yourself in the river, in a spot that I shall show you, and leave the rest to me."

"Well, it seems strange, but all right," said the young man. He did as the cat told him, though he did not know why. While he was washing in the river, the king's coach passed by. And just at that moment Puss cried out, "Help! Help! My master, the Marquis of Carabas, is drowning! Save him, save him!"

The king heard the cries and looked out the window. When he saw it was the cat who had brought him so many gifts, he ordered his guards to run and help the Marquis of Carabas. While the guards pulled the young man out of the river, Puss ran up to the king's coach, his fur all puffed out. "Your Majesty!" he said in a breathless voice. "Thieves! Thieves! They robbed my master, and stole his clothes, and threw him into the deepest part of the river! He would have drowned if you had not come by with your men, just in time!"

The king told one of his guards to ride back to the palace and bring a fine suit of clothes for the Marquis of Carabas. When the young man had put on the clothes, he was dressed more finely than he had ever been in his life, and really did appear to be a handsome fellow. So the king invited him into his coach, where who should be waiting but the princess. The young man and the princess exchanged a few silent glances, and, as Puss had planned, this was all it took for them to fall in love.

Meanwhile, Puss hurried on ahead of the coach. He came to a field where some people were picking corn, and he spoke to them. "Good people," said Puss, "the king approaches. You will tell him that this field belongs to my master, the Marquis of Carabas. For if you do not," Puss hissed, "you'll be chopped up like vegetables for a pot of soup!" Then the cat ran on to an even larger field where people were working, and again ordered them to tell the king that the field belonged to the Marquis of Carabas, and again he hissed, "Or else you'll be chopped up like vegetables for a pot of soup!" And on and on Puss went, stopping at each field to give the same command and make the same warning.

As the king passed by the fields, he leaned out of his coach and said, "These are fine fields. Who owns them?" And the people, who had been greatly frightened by Puss, said, "The

Marquis of Carabas." The king was amazed and said to the marquis, "You own a great deal of very fine land!" And the marquis replied, in a somewhat sleepy voice, as though he had heard such comments all his life, "Yes, Sire, it is a lot, isn't it?" And the princess began to think even more of the handsome fellow.

Meanwhile, Puss had run ahead until he came to a grand castle. In this castle lived the real owner of all the fields. He was a mean, cruel ogre, and he had a most amazing power: he could change himself into any animal he wanted to be. Puss had learned of this power from some of the workers in the fields, who were scared of their cruel master. At the castle Puss said, "I have come to pay my respects to the owner of this great castle and all these lands, for I have heard that he is a man of great talents."

The ogre allowed Puss to come in. Puss bowed low before him and said, "I have been told that you have the power to change yourself into any kind of animal—even, they say, a lion or an elephant."

"That is true," the ogre grunted.

"Oh, is it?" said Puss.

"What? Do you not believe me?" the ogre roared. "Watch this!" And suddenly Puss saw before him a fierce lion. Filled with fear, Puss gave a loud "MEE-YOWL!" He leaped away and hid. When the lion changed back into an ogre, Puss came out of his hiding place and said, "That was most frightening. Truly, your powers are amazing! But I have heard that you can do something even more amazing. People say that you can turn yourself into a creature as small as a mouse. But surely that is impossible."

"Impossible!" cried the ogre. "Just you watch!" And with that he changed himself into a mouse and began to skitter around on the floor. Quicker than you can say "cheese," Puss jumped on the mouse and made a meal of him—and that was that!

By this time the king's coach had come to the gates of the castle. Puss scampered down, and as he opened the great doors, he announced, "Your Majesty is welcome to this castle, the home of my master, the Marquis of Carabas."

"What!" exclaimed the king. "Does this castle belong to you, too? I never saw anything so fine. I should really like to enter."

"Your Majesty is most welcome!" said the young man, bowing low. Then he gave his hand to the princess and they went up the steps, all following Puss, who danced along in his boots, with his tail twitching.

It will not surprise you, I am sure, if I tell you that the Marquis of Carabas married the princess, and that they were very happy together, and that Puss, the clever cat, lived in great comfort and never had to chase mice again—except, of course, when he wanted to.

Rapunzel
(A tale from the Brothers Grimm)

There once lived a man and his wife who, more than anything in the world, wished to have a baby. But so far, their wish had not come true.

Now, at the top of their house, in the very back, there was a little window. And from this window you could see a garden full of beautiful flowers and fresh vegetables. But around the garden was a high wall. And no one dared to enter the garden, because it belonged to a mean and powerful witch.

One day the wife stood at the little window and looked down into the witch's garden. There she saw fine-looking leaves of rapunzel, which is a kind of lettuce. And it looked so fresh and green that she felt that she simply must have some. Day after day she longed for it, and the more she wanted it, the more she became pale and sad.

Her husband saw her looking so sad and became worried. "Dear wife, what is the matter?" he asked.

"Oh," she answered, "I fear that I shall die unless I get some rapunzel to eat from the garden behind our house." Her husband loved her very much, and he thought, "I cannot let my wife die. I will get some of that rapunzel, no matter what."

That night he climbed over the wall into the witch's garden. He quickly picked a handful of rapunzel and brought it back to his wife. At once she ate it with delight. But she liked it so much and it tasted so good that the next day she longed for it twice as much as she had before. So, that night, the husband climbed the wall again and picked a handful of rapunzel. He turned around to go back when he saw before him the blazing eyes of the angry witch.

"How dare you climb into my garden, you thief," she hissed. "How dare you steal my rapunzel. You will pay dearly for this!"

"Oh, please," said the terrified man, "be merciful. I only did this because I had to. My wife was looking out our window and saw your rapunzel, and she would have died unless I got her some."

"Well then," the witch said, "you may have as much rapunzel as you want—*on one condition*. When your wife has a child, you must give it to me. I will take care of the child, like its very own mother."

The man was so scared that he said "Yes," and then tried to think nothing more of it. But later, at the very moment when his wife gave birth to a lovely baby girl, the witch appeared and took the child away.

She named the child Rapunzel, and she grew up to be a beautiful girl. When Rapunzel was twelve years old, the witch took her deep into a forest. There the witch locked her in a tower with no steps and no door, only a small window near the top. When the witch wanted to be let in, she would cry, "Rapunzel! Rapunzel! Let down your hair!"

Rapunzel had beautiful long hair that shone like gold. When she heard the voice of the witch, she would open the window and let her hair fall down, down, down to the ground far below. Then the witch would hold on to the hair and climb up to the tower window.

A few years passed like this when one day the king's son was riding through the forest, and he came upon the tower. As he came near, he heard a voice singing so sweetly that he stood still and listened. It was Rapunzel in her loneliness trying to

pass away the time with sweet songs. The prince wanted to go in to her, and he looked for a door in the tower but there was none. So he rode home, but the song had entered into his heart, and every day he went into the forest and listened to it.

Once, as he was standing nearby behind some trees, who should come up to the tower but the witch. The prince watched, amazed, as the witch called out, "Rapunzel! Rapunzel! Let down your hair!" Then he saw how Rapunzel let down her long hair, and how the witch climbed up by it and went into the tower. And he thought, "So that is the ladder. Well then, I too will climb it." And the next day, as dusk fell, he came to the tower and cried, "Rapunzel! Rapunzel! Let down your hair!" And she let down her hair, and the prince climbed up by it.

Rapunzel was greatly frightened when she saw the prince, for she had never seen a man before. But he spoke kindly to her, and told how her singing had entered his heart, and how he felt he could have no peace until he had seen her. Then Rapunzel forgot her fear, and when he asked her to be his wife, she put her hand in his hand and said, "I would gladly go with you, but I have no way to get out. Do this for me: every time you come, bring a bundle of silk, and I will make a ladder of it. When it is finished, I will use it to climb down from this tower, and then you will carry me away from here on your horse." They agreed that he would come to her every evening, since the witch came in the daytime.

So things went on this way until one day Rapunzel, without thinking, said to the witch, "Why do you climb up so slowly, while the king's son takes only a moment?"

"Oh, you wicked child!" screamed the witch. "I thought I had you hidden here from all the world. But you have betrayed me!" In a rage, the witch grabbed a pair of sharp scissors and cut off poor Rapunzel's hair. Then the witch took Rapunzel from the tower and left her to wander alone, poor and miserable.

Later that day, when evening fell, the prince came and called out, "Rapunzel! Rapunzel! Let down your hair!" The witch lowered the cut-off hair, and the prince climbed up. But instead of seeing his dear Rapunzel, he saw the glittering eyes of the witch. "Aha!" she cried, and laughed at him. "You came for your darling, but the sweet bird is no longer in its nest and sings no more. Rapunzel is lost forever. You will see her no more!" Filled with horror and grief, the prince fell from the tower. The fall did not kill him, but the thorns on which he fell cut his eyes and blinded him.

So, blind and alone, he wandered for several years, eating only roots and berries, and weeping over the loss of his dear Rapunzel. At last he came to a place where Rapunzel herself was wandering. He could not see her, but he heard a voice that he thought he knew; and when he went toward it, Rapunzel saw him, and knew him, and fell on his neck and wept. And when her tears touched his eyes, he could see again as well as ever.

And so he took her to his kingdom to be his bride, where she was welcomed with great joy, and where they lived happily ever after.

Rumpelstiltskin
(A tale from the Brothers Grimm)

Once upon a time there was a poor miller who had a beautiful daughter. She was so beautiful and clever that he could not help boasting about her. One day the miller happened to come before the king, and to impress the king, he began boasting about his daughter. And before he knew it, he found himself saying that his daughter was so amazing and so wonderful, why, she could even spin gold out of straw.

"That," said the king, "is a talent worth having. Bring your daughter to me, and let us see what she can do."

When the girl was brought to the palace, the king led her to a room that was almost full of straw. He pointed to a spinning wheel and said, "Get to work, and if by early morning you have not spun this straw into gold, you shall die."

The poor miller's daughter! Of course, she could not spin straw into gold. What could she do? She could think of nothing, and in the end she sat down and began to cry.

And that's when, all at once, *ka-lick,* the door opened and in walked a little man. "Good evening, miller's daughter," he said. "Why are you crying?"

"Because," she answered, "I must spin all this straw into gold before morning, and I don't know how."

Then the little man came close to her and whispered, "What will you give me if I spin it for you?"

"Why, I, I'll give you my necklace," she stammered.

The little man took the necklace, seated himself at the spinning wheel, and *whirr, whirr, whirr,* he spun and he spun, and by sunup all the straw had been spun into gold. And when the king arrived, he was amazed. But the sight of all that gold made the greed for more grow in him. So he took the miller's daughter to a larger room, filled with yet more straw, and told her that if she valued her life, she must spin all this into gold in one night. Again the girl did not know what to do and sat down to cry, when, *ka-lick,* the door opened and in walked the little man.

"Crying again, I see," he said. "So, I suppose you have to spin all this into gold, too. What will you give me if I do it for you?"

"The ring from my finger," answered the girl.

So the little man took the ring, seated himself at the spinning wheel, and *whirr, whirr, whirr,* he spun and he spun, and by sunup all the straw had been spun into gold. When the king arrived, he was overjoyed at the sight, but hungry for still more gold. So he took the miller's daughter to an even larger room filled with straw and said, "Spin all this in one night, and if you succeed—well then, you shall be my wife."

The king had hardly left the room when, *ka-lick,* the door opened and in came the little man, asking, "What will you give me if I spin all this straw for you one more time?"

"I have nothing left to give," the girl answered sadly.

"Then promise me this," said the little man. "Promise me that when you are queen, you will give me your first child."

The miller's daughter thought there was really very little chance that she would ever be queen, and so she promised, and the little man set to work at once. By morning the gold was piled so high that it reached the ceiling. When the king arrived, he was pleased to see all the gold he wanted. He married the miller's daughter and made her queen.

In a year's time, she brought a fine little baby into the world. She thought no more about the little man or her promise to him. Then one day, as she sat alone in her room rocking her baby, *ka-lick*, the door opened and in walked the little man, who said, "Now give me what you promised me."

The queen, filled with fear, clutched her baby tightly. "Please," she said, "I will give you all the riches of the kingdom, only leave me my child."

But the little man said, "No. I would rather have a living thing than all the treasures in the world." Then the queen began to weep and wail, and the little man felt pity for her. "I will give you this chance," he said. "In three days, if you can guess my name, then you may keep your child." Then he was gone as quickly as he had come.

The queen lay awake all night thinking of all the names she had ever heard. She sent a messenger to ride through the land and collect all the names that could be found. And when the little man came the next day, she tried all that she had been able to think of: Alexander, Balthazar, Casper, Doolittle, Eggleston, Ferdinand, and many more. But after each, the little man only said, "That is not my name."

The next day the queen sent servants all around the kingdom to find the most unusual names, and when the little man came, she tried them. "Are you called Sheepshanks? Roast-Ribs? Snickerdoodle? Groucho? Winklehopper?" But after each, the little man only said, "That is not my name."

On the third and last day, the queen was worried sick. She held her child tight and wondered what to do, when, *ka-lick*, the door opened and in walked—no, not the little man but the messenger the queen had sent in search of names. He bowed to the queen and said, "My lady, as I passed through the woods last night, I came to a high hill, and near it was a little house, and outside the house a fire was burning, and around the fire danced a funny little man, and as he hopped up and down he sang,

'Today I brew, tomorrow I bake,
And then the fair queen's child I'll take.
And no one can deny my claim,
For Rumpelstiltskin is my name.' "

The messenger left, and almost as soon as he had gone, the little man arrived. The queen greeted him by asking, "Is your name Jack?"

"That is not my name."

"Then are you called Harry?"

"That is not my name."

"Then perhaps," said the queen, "your name is—
Rumpelstiltskin!"

"The devil told you that! The devil told you that!" cried
the little man. And in his anger he stamped with his right
foot so hard that he went into the ground up to his waist.
Then he grabbed his other foot and pulled in such a fury that
he split in two. And the queen and her child never feared him
again.

Sleeping Beauty
(A tale from the Brothers Grimm)

Once upon a time there lived a king and queen who for many years were very sad because they had no child. At last a little daughter was born to them, and the king was so
happy that he gave a great feast in the palace, to which he invited all his friends and
relatives.

Now in his country there were thirteen fairies. Of course, the king wished to invite
all of the fairies to the feast, so that each might look kindly upon his child, and perhaps
give the baby a special fairy gift. But as the king had only twelve gold plates to eat
from, it was decided that one fairy had to be left out.

The feast was held, and what a wonderful celebration it was. And as it drew to an
end, the fairies stepped forth to give the child their special gifts. One
said to the child, "I give you virtue, so that you may be good." Another said, "I give you wisdom, so that you may be wise." A
third fairy gave her beauty. A fourth gave her riches.
And on it went, with each fairy giving everything
in the world that one could wish for.

Eleven of the fairies had given their gifts, and
the twelfth was just about to speak when suddenly,
in walked the thirteenth fairy—the one who had
been left out. She was very angry, and she cried out
in a loud voice, "When the princess is fifteen years of
age, she shall prick herself with a spindle and fall
down dead!"

Without another word, the angry fairy left
the hall. Everyone was terrified at what she had
said. Then the twelfth fairy stepped forward and said, "I

cannot undo the evil spell, but I can soften it. Here, then, is my gift to the child. The princess shall not die, but fall into a deep sleep for a hundred years."

The king was determined to protect his child. "Surely," he said, "my daughter cannot prick herself with a spindle if she never sees one." So he gave an order that every spindle in the kingdom should be burned.

The princess grew up, and all the fairies' gifts to the child were plain to see: she was good, wise, kind, and beautiful. Everyone who saw her loved her.

On the day that she turned fifteen, the king and queen happened to be away from the palace. The princess was left on her own, and she wandered about the palace, looking into all sorts of places, and peeking into rooms that she had never explored before. She climbed a narrow winding stair that led to a little door with a rusty key sticking out of the lock. She turned the key, and the door opened, and there in a little room sat an old woman with a spindle, busily spinning away.

"Good day," said the princess, entering the room. "What are you doing?" she asked, for she had never seen a spindle before.

"I am spinning," said the old woman.

The princess stretched forth her hand and asked, "What is this thing that spins around so merrily?" But hardly had she spoken when she pricked her finger on the spindle, and in that very moment she fell into a deep sleep.

And this sleep fell upon everyone in the palace. The king and queen, who had just come home and were in the great hall, fell fast asleep. The horses in their stalls, the dogs in the yard, the pigeons on the roof, the flies on the wall—all fell asleep. Even the fire that flickered on the hearth went out, and the wind stopped, and not a leaf fell from the trees.

Then around the castle there began to grow a hedge of thorns, which grew thicker and higher every year, until at last nothing could be seen of the castle, not even the flags on the highest towers.

As the years passed, stories spread throughout the land of a beautiful princess sleeping behind a wall of thorns. Many a young prince came, but none could break through the thorns. But at long last, after many many years, there came into the country a king's son who heard an old man tell that there was a castle standing behind the hedge of thorns, and that there a beautiful enchanted princess lay sleeping. The prince said, "I shall make my way through and see the lovely princess." The old man warned him that many had tried and failed, but the prince would not listen.

For now the hundred years were at an end, and the day had come for the sleeping princess to be awakened. When the prince drew near the hedge of thorns, it changed into a hedge of beautiful flowers, which bent aside to let him pass. When he reached the castle yard, he saw the horses and dogs lying asleep, and on the roof the pigeons were sitting with their heads under their wings. And as he entered the castle and mounted the steps, he saw everyone still asleep—the king, the queen, their councillors, the cook, the maids, everyone. All was so quiet that he could hear his own breathing.

At last the prince went up the narrow winding stair and came to the room where the princess was sleeping. When he saw her looking so lovely in her sleep, he could not turn away his eyes. He bent down and kissed her, and she opened her eyes and smiled at him. Together they went down, and they saw the king and queen waking up, and all the people in the castle waking up and looking at each other in great surprise. And the horses in the yard got up and shook themselves. The dogs sprang up and wagged their tails. The pigeons on the roof flew into the fields. The flies on the wall buzzed and crept a little farther. The kitchen fire leaped up and blazed.

Then the wedding of the prince and princess was held with great feasting and rejoicing, and they lived happily together for the rest of their days.

The Tale of Peter Rabbit

by Beatrix Potter

Once upon a time there were four little Rabbits, and their names were—Flopsy, Mopsy, Cotton-tail, and Peter.

They lived with their Mother in a sand-bank, underneath the root of a very big fir-tree.

"Now, my dears," said old Mrs. Rabbit one morning, "you may go into the fields or down the lane, but don't go into Mr. McGregor's garden: your Father had an accident there; he was put in a pie by Mrs. McGregor. Now run along, and don't get into mischief. I am going out."

Then old Mrs. Rabbit took a basket and her umbrella, and went through the wood to the baker's. She bought a loaf of brown bread and five currant buns.

Flopsy, Mopsy, and Cotton-tail, who were good little bunnies, went down the lane to gather blackberries. But Peter, who was very naughty, ran straight away to Mr. McGregor's garden, and squeezed under the gate!

First he ate some lettuces and some French beans; and then he ate some radishes; and then, feeling rather sick, he went to look for some parsley.

But round the end of a cucumber frame, whom should he meet but Mr. McGregor!

Mr. McGregor was on his hands and knees planting out young cabbages, but he jumped up and ran after Peter, waving a rake and calling out, "Stop thief!"

Peter was most dreadfully frightened; he rushed all over the garden, for he had forgotten the way back to the gate.

He lost one of his shoes among the cabbages, and the other shoe amongst the potatoes.

After losing them, he ran on four legs and went faster, so that I think he might have got away altogether if he had not unfortunately run into a gooseberry net, and got caught by the large buttons on his jacket. It was a blue jacket with brass buttons, quite new.

Peter gave himself up for lost, and shed big tears; but his sobs were overheard by some friendly sparrows, who flew to him in great excitement, and implored him to exert himself.

Mr. McGregor came up with a sieve, which he intended to pop upon the top of Peter; but Peter wriggled out just in time, leaving his jacket behind him. And rushed into the tool-shed, and jumped into a can. It would have been a beautiful thing to hide in, if it had not had so much water in it.

Mr. McGregor was quite sure that Peter was somewhere in the tool-shed, perhaps hidden underneath a flower-pot. He began to turn them over carefully, looking under each.

Presently Peter sneezed—"Kertyschoo!" Mr. McGregor was after him in no time. And tried to put his foot upon Peter, who jumped out of a window, upsetting three plants. The window was too small for Mr. McGregor, and he was tired of running after Peter. He went back to his work.

Peter sat down to rest; he was out of breath and trembling with fright, and he had not the least idea which way to go. Also he was very damp with sitting in that can.

After a time he began to wander about, going lippity—lippity—not very fast, and looking all round.

He found a door in a wall; but it was locked, and there was no room for a fat little rabbit to squeeze underneath.

An old mouse was running in and out over the stone doorstep, carrying peas and beans to her family in the wood. Peter asked her the way to the gate, but she had such a large pea in her mouth that she could not answer. She only shook her head at him. Peter began to cry.

Then he tried to find his way straight across the garden, but he became more and more puzzled. Presently, he came to a pond where Mr. McGregor filled his water-cans. A white cat was staring at some gold-fish, she sat very, very still, but now and then the tip of her tail twitched as if it were alive. Peter thought it best to go away without speaking to her; he had heard about cats from his cousin, little Benjamin Bunny.

He went back towards the tool-shed, but suddenly, quite close to him, he heard the noise of a hoe—scr-r-ritch, scratch, scratch, scritch. Peter scuttered underneath the bushes. But presently, as nothing happened, he came out, and climbed upon a wheel-barrow and peeped over. The first thing he saw was Mr. McGregor hoeing onions. His back was turned towards Peter, and beyond him was the gate!

Peter got down very quietly off the wheelbarrow, and started running as fast as he could go, along a straight walk behind some black-currant bushes.

Mr. McGregor caught sight of him at the corner, but Peter did not care. He slipped underneath the gate, and was safe at last in the wood outside the garden.

Mr. McGregor hung up the little jacket and the shoes for a scare-crow to frighten the blackbirds.

Peter never stopped running or looked behind him till he got home to the big fir-tree.

He was so tired that he flopped down upon the nice soft sand on the floor of the rabbit-hole and shut his eyes. His mother was busy cooking; she wondered what he had done with his clothes. It was the second little jacket and pair of shoes that Peter had lost in a fortnight!

I am sorry to say that Peter was not very well during the evening.

His mother put him to bed, and made some camomile tea; and she gave a dose of it to Peter!

"One table-spoonful to be taken at bed-time."

But Flopsy, Mopsy, and Cotton-tail had bread and milk and blackberries for supper.

Check your library for many more wonderful stories written and illustrated by Beatrix Potter, including *The Tale of Benjamin Bunny, The Tale of the Flopsy Bunnies, The Tale of Squirrel Nutkin, The Tale of Two Bad Mice, The Tale of Mrs. Tittlemouse,* and more.

Why the Owl Has Big Eyes
(An Iroquois legend)

PARENTS: *Like many Native American stories—indeed, like many folktales from different people around the world—this story tells how something came to be. (For an example of this kind of story from West Africa, see "All Stories Are Anansi's," page 38.)*

Raweno, the spirit who makes everything, was busy creating animals. This afternoon, he was working on Rabbit. "May I have nice long legs and long ears like Deer's?" Rabbit asked. "And sharp fangs and claws like Panther's?"

"Certainly," Raweno said. But he had gotten no further than shaping Rabbit's hind legs when he was interrupted by Owl.

"Whoo, whoo. I want a nice long neck like Swan's," Owl demanded. "And beautiful red feathers like Cardinal's, and a long beak like Egret's, and a royal crown of plumes like Heron's. I want you to make me into the swiftest and the most beautiful of all birds."

"Be quiet," Raweno said. "You know that no one is supposed to watch me at work. Turn around, and close your eyes!"

Raweno shaped Rabbit's ears, long and alert, just like Deer's.

"Whoo, whoo," Owl said. "Nobody can forbid me to watch. I won't turn around and I certainly won't close my eyes. I like watching, and watch I will."

Then Raweno became angry. Forgetting Rabbit's front legs, he grabbed Owl from his branch and shook him with all his might. Owl's eyes grew big and round with fright. Raweno pushed down on Owl's head and pulled up on his ears until they stood up on both sides of his head.

"There!" Raweno said. "Now you have ears that are big enough to listen when someone tells you what to do, and a short neck that won't let you crane your head to watch things you shouldn't watch. And your eyes are big, but you can use them only at night—not during the day, when I am working. And finally, as punishment for your disobedience, your feathers won't be red like Cardinal's, but ugly and gray, like this." And he rubbed Owl all over with mud.

Then he turned back to finish Rabbit. But where was he? Poor Rabbit had been so frightened by Raweno's anger that he had fled, unfinished. To this day, Rabbit must hop about on his uneven legs, and he has remained frightened, for he never received the fangs and claws he had requested. As for Owl, he remained as Raweno shaped him in his anger—with big eyes, a short neck, big ears, and the ability to see only at night, when Raweno isn't working.

Here are some more stories from different Native American peoples that tell how things came to be. Check your library for:

Coyote: A Trickster Tale from the American Southwest by Gerald McDermott (Harcourt Brace, 1994)

Crow Chief: A Plains Indian Story by Paul Goble (Orchard Books, 1992)

Quillworker: A Cheyenne Legend retold by Terri Cohlene (Watermill Press, 1990)

Drama

Do you like to pretend? Maybe sometimes you and your friends pretend to be knights and princesses, or space explorers, or cops and robbers. Maybe you like to play with dolls, and dress them up and speak for them.

When you do this, you are playacting. Another word for playacting is *drama*. Many television shows and movies are drama. Have you ever seen or been in a play, with actors in costume on a stage? That's drama, too.

You and some friends can perform your own drama. You can be the actors and actresses. You can put on costumes. You can decorate the stage with scenery, to show where your play is taking place. You will need to remember some words to speak; those words are called your *lines*. All the lines for the actors and actresses to say are written in the *script*. The script also gives some special directions, such as telling you when to come on the stage and when to go off.

Speak your lines in a big clear voice so that the people watching the play—the audience—can hear you. When you're acting onstage, people are watching you, but you have to act like they're not there!

Here is a script for a play called *The Boy Who Cried Wolf*. It's a drama based on one of Aesop's fables (which you can read in this book on page 33). What kind of costumes will you use? What kind of scenery will you make?

The Boy Who Cried Wolf: A Drama

Cast of Characters

Announcer
John the Shepherd Boy
Farmer Brown
Second Farmer
Third Farmer
The Wolf
Sheep

(*Note:* Boys or girls can play any of these parts. If a girl plays the shepherd, you can change the name if you want.)

The curtain opens. The Announcer comes onstage and talks directly to the audience.

ANNOUNCER: Hello. Our drama is called *The Boy Who Cried Wolf*. This play comes from a fable by Aesop. A fable is a story that teaches a lesson. We hope you enjoy the play. Thank you.

[*The Announcer leaves the stage. Enter from opposite sides of the stage Farmer Brown and John the Shepherd Boy. They meet in the middle.*]

FARMER BROWN: Good morning, John. What are you doing out so early?

JOHN: Good morning, Farmer Brown. I'm going to the pasture to watch the sheep for my father. I've been watching them all summer.

FARMER BROWN: That's a big job for a young boy! I'm sure your father is very grateful to you.

JOHN: Oh, yes, he is. But I wish that I had someone to talk to or play with. There's no one around but the sheep.

FARMER BROWN: Do you see that valley way over there? [*Points to one side of the stage*] I will be working there with my friends for a few weeks. We will be working very hard, so we cannot play. But if any trouble comes up, you can come get us.

JOHN: Thank you, Farmer Brown. Good-bye.

FARMER BROWN: Good-bye, John. Take good care of your sheep.

[*They exit on opposite sides of the stage. Now the Sheep come onstage.*]

SHEEP: We are a flock of fleecy sheep,
　　　　Baa! Baa! Baa!
　　　　We like to eat and play and sleep,
　　　　Baa! Baa! Baa!

The shepherd boy keeps watch all day,
Baa! Baa! Baa!
He keeps the big bad wolf away!
Baa! Baa! Baa!

[*John enters. He moves the Sheep toward a back corner of the stage. Meanwhile, Farmer Brown and the two other farmers enter and stay at the opposite end of the stage, where they "work" by pretending to dig, hoe, pick crops, etc.*]

JOHN: Oh, I'm so tired of watching sheep! I wish I had someone to talk to. Nothing exciting ever happens here, not even a wolf. [*He looks across to where the three farmers are working*] I wish Farmer Brown and his friends would come here. I know! I'll cry "Wolf!" and make them think a wolf is eating the sheep. Then they'll come running. [*He runs toward the farmers and cries loudly*] Wolf! Wolf!

[*The farmers drop their work and come running.*]

FARMER BROWN: Where is he? Where's the wolf?

SECOND FARMER: Where did he go? I don't see him.

THIRD FARMER: Has he gone already? Are we too late?

[*The farmers suddenly notice that John is laughing but trying to hide it.*]

FARMER BROWN: Why are you laughing, John? What's so funny about a wolf?

SECOND FARMER: Are you playing a joke on us, boy?

THIRD FARMER: If you are, I don't think it's very funny.

JOHN [*embarrassed*]: There wasn't any wolf. I was tired of staying here alone, so I cried "Wolf" just for fun.

FARMER BROWN: John, you had better not play any more jokes like that.

SECOND FARMER: That's right. You'll be sorry if a real wolf comes.

THIRD FARMER: Come on, friends. We have work to do!

[*The farmers leave the stage. John lets out a big sigh, hangs his head, and exits on the opposite side of the stage. The Announcer enters.*]

ANNOUNCER: Do you think that John learned his lesson? I am sorry to say he did not. A few days later, he played the same trick again. The farmers ran to help him, and when they found out there was no wolf, they were very angry. Now a few more days have passed. And once again John the Shepherd Boy is watching the sheep.

[*The Announcer exits. Enter the Sheep, followed by John, sighing loudly and looking very tired and bored. Also enter the farmers, who go to work in their field.*]

SHEEP: We are a flock of fleecy sheep,

> Baa! Baa! Baa!
>
> We like to eat and play and sleep . . .

JOHN [*interrupting the Sheep*]: Oh, blah, blah, blah! I don't think I can stand this anymore. Every day the same old thing. [*As John talks, the Wolf creeps onto the stage, looking very dangerous. The Sheep start baaing nervously but quietly, so that John can be heard*] I never get to see anyone, or talk to anyone, or play any games. I want to have fun. I want some excitement. I want a . . . [*The Wolf has pulled one sheep from the flock. As he does, that sheep lets out a loud "BAA!" just as John is speaking. John turns and sees the Wolf—and finishes his sentence*] wolf!

[*The Wolf pulls the sheep off the stage. All the sheep are baaing in fear. John runs toward the farmers, crying loudly*] Wolf! Wolf! Help, come quick!

FARMER BROWN: A wolf? Really and truly, John?

JOHN: Really and truly! Hurry, come quick!

[*Farmer Brown starts to walk toward John, but the Second Farmer stops him.*]

SECOND FARMER: Wait a minute. Don't let the boy make a fool of us again.

THIRD FARMER: That's right. He's already played the same trick twice.

FARMER BROWN: But what if it's a real wolf?

SECOND FARMER: Then that's the boy's fault. How can we trust him when he plays so many tricks on us?

FARMER BROWN: I guess you're right. Let's get back to work.

[*The farmers go back to their work. John runs back to the Sheep. He walks around the flock, looking as though he has lost something and can't find it.*]

JOHN: Oh, I have lost a poor little lamb. Why wouldn't they come to help me? What did I do to deserve this? Why didn't they believe me? Why? Why?!

SHEEP [*all turning to stare directly at John*]: BAAAAAAA!

JOHN: All right, I know, I know. I didn't tell the truth before, so they didn't believe me this time. I'll never do that again, I promise—really and *truly!*

[*John leads the Sheep, baaing, off the stage. Curtain closes.*]

One of the best parts of being in a play is hearing people applaud when it's over. That's when it's time for you to come out and take a bow. Usually only one actor at a time comes out on the stage. For this play, you would come out in this order: The Wolf, Sheep (all together), Third Farmer, Second Farmer, Farmer Brown, and John. When all of you are onstage, you can take one last bow together. And enjoy all the clapping—it's for you!

Familiar Sayings

PARENTS: *Every culture has phrases and proverbs that make no sense when carried over literally into another culture. To say, for example, that someone has "let the cat out of the bag" has nothing to do with setting free a trapped kitty. Nor—thank goodness—does it ever* literally *"rain cats and dogs"!*

The sayings and phrases in this section may be familiar to many children, who hear them at home. But the inclusion of these sayings and phrases in the Core Knowledge Sequence has been singled out for gratitude by many parents and teachers who work with children from home cultures that are different from the culture of literate American English.

For first graders, we have chosen to introduce a selection of sayings that are likely to have some connections to the child's world of experience.

An apple a day keeps the doctor away.

People use this saying to mean that eating apples helps keep you healthy.

When she unpacked her lunch, Janet groaned, "An apple again!"
"But that's good," said her friend Mae. "An apple a day keeps the doctor away."

Do unto others as you would have them do unto you.

This saying is called the Golden Rule. People use it to mean: treat people as you would like to be treated yourself. It comes from the Bible.

"Molly, stop drawing on Becky's picture," said the baby-sitter. "Would you like Becky to mess up *your* picture? Remember: Do unto others as you would have them do unto you."

Hit the nail on the head.

When you use a hammer, you have to hit the nail right on its head to make it go in straight. So, when someone says that you "hit the nail on the head," they mean that you have said or done something just right.

Caitlin was frustrated with her costume for the play. "There's just something wrong with it, and I can't figure it out," she said.
"Why don't you take off the crown and use this feather instead?" suggested Sara.
"That's it!" cried Caitlin. "Thanks, Sara. You hit the nail right on the head!"

If at first you don't succeed, try, try again.

People use this saying to mean: don't give up; keep trying.

Peter fell every time he tried the skateboard. "You'll get the hang of it, Pete," said his brother. "If at first you don't succeed, try, try again."

Land of Nod.

To be in the "land of Nod" means to be asleep.

"I can't sleep!" Cassie said to her big sister, Anne. Both girls had been in bed for half an hour. The room was dark and cool, and they could hear crickets chirping outside.

"Close you eyes, Cassie," said Anne, "and I'll sing you a lullaby." She began to hum a tune to her little sister, and it was not long before Cassie drifted off to the Land of Nod.

Let the cat out of the bag.

If you "let the cat out of the bag," you tell something that was meant to be a secret.

"Jake let the cat out of the bag: he told Hannah about her surprise party."

The more the merrier.

People use this saying to welcome newcomers to a group. They say this because it means: the more people who take part, the more fun it can be.

The house was full of kids playing. Still, when the doorbell rang, Mr. DeNiro opened the door and waved in more children, saying, "Come in, come in, the more the merrier."

Never leave till tomorrow what you can do today.

People use this saying to mean: don't put off things you have to do.

"Let's clean up in the morning," said Heidi.

"No," said Tina, "let's clean up now. You know what Grandma always says: 'Never leave till tomorrow what you can do today.'"

Practice makes perfect.

People use this saying to mean: doing something over and over makes you good at it.

"Mrs. Kim," asked Jennie, "we wrote capital letters yesterday. Do we have to do it again today?"

"Yes, Jennie. We'll write them again today and every day this week. Practice makes perfect!"

There's no place like home.

People use this saying to mean that travel may be pleasant, but home is the best place of all.

"What a great trip!" said Yoshiko. "We saw the Statue of Liberty and went to the beach and visited great museums!"

"Yes," said her mother, "we did have a wonderful time, but I'm glad to be back. There's no place like home."

See the Aesop fables in this book (pages 33–37) for more sayings:

- "A wolf in sheep's clothing."
- "Don't count your chickens before they hatch."
- "Sour grapes."

II.
History and
Geography

INTRODUCTION

For many years American elementary schools (especially in kindergarten through third grade) have taught "social studies" rather than history. Social studies have typically been made up of lessons about the family, neighborhood, and community. This focus on the personal and the local can be of value, but it is only a beginning.

As anyone knows who has witnessed children's fascination with dinosaurs, knights in armor, or pioneers on the prairie, young children are interested not just in themselves and their immediate surroundings but also in other people, places, and times. In first grade, we can take advantage of children's natural curiosity and begin to broaden their horizons. An early introduction to history and geography can foster an understanding of the broad world beyond the child's locality, and make her aware of varied people and ways of life. Such historical study can also begin to develop our children's sense of our nation's past and its significance.

In the following pages, we introduce—let us emphasize, *introduce*—a variety of people and events, most of which will be treated more fully in the Core Knowledge books for the later grades. The idea in first grade is to plant seeds of knowledge that can grow later. The purpose for the child is not to achieve deep historical knowledge but, rather, to become familiar with people, terms, and ideas in such a way that, in later years, when the child hears them mentioned or reads about them, she enjoys the satisfying sense that "I know something about that."

Learning history is not simply a matter of being able to recall names and dates, though the value of getting a firm mental grip on *a few* names and dates—such as 1607 and 1776—should not be discounted. First graders have not of course developed a sophisticated sense of chronology that allows them to appreciate the vast expanses of years between, say, the American Revolution, ancient Egypt, and the Ice Age—all of which, to the first grader, happened long, longer, or *really long* ago. Nevertheless, the development of a chronological sense is aided by having at least a few dates fixed in mind and associated with specific events, so that later, as the child grows, he can begin to place these dates and events into a more fully developed sense of what happened when.

While it's good to help children grasp a few important facts, for young children the best history teaching emphasizes the "story" in history. By appealing to children's naturally active imaginations, we can ask them to "visit" people and places in the past (for example, we take children on a trip down the Nile River with King Tut in ancient Egypt). We encourage parents and teachers to go beyond these pages to help children learn about history through art projects, drama, music, and discussions.

Suggested Resources

World History and Geography

Bill and Pete Go Down the Nile, written and illustrated by Tomie dePaola (Putnam, 1987)

The Hundredth Name by Shulamith Levy Oppenheim (Boyds Mills Press, 1995)

I Wonder Why Pyramids Were Built and Other Questions About Ancient Egypt by Philip Steele (Kingfisher, 1995)

The Nativity, illustrated by Ruth Sanderson (Little, Brown, 1993)

New Puffin Children's World Atlas by Jacqueline Tivers and Michael Day (Puffin, 1994)

The Story of Hanukkah by Amy Ehrlich (Dial, 1989)

Tales from the Old Testament (cassette tape), retold by Jim Weiss (Greathall Productions; phone 800-477-6234)

Tut's Mummy Lost—And Found by Judy Donnelly (Random House, 1988)

American History and Geography

Across the Wide Dark Sea: The Mayflower Journey by Jean Van Leeuwen (Dial, 1995)

The Flame of Peace (a story about the Aztecs), by Deborah Nourse Lattimore (Harper-Collins, 1987)

The Inca and *The Maya* by Patricia McKissack (Childrens Press, revised, 1992 and 1993)

Lewis and Clark: Explorers of the American West by Steven Kroll (Holiday House, 1994)

Sam the Minuteman by Nathaniel Benchley (HarperCollins, 1969)

Yankee Doodle: A Revolutionary Tail by Gary Chalk (Dorling Kindersley, 1993)

World History and Geography

History: Everyone's Story

History. Listen closely to the word: *history.* Do you hear another word in it? Do you hear the word *story?*

History is a story. It's the story of all the people who have lived before us. It helps us remember who we are and what we've done.

When you study history, you learn stories of great men and women who have done extraordinary things. You'll meet a Chinese emperor who—long, long ago—built a wall so large that astronauts today can see it all the way from outer space. You'll find out—if you don't already know—why our nation's capital city is named Washington, D.C. You'll meet a woman who risked her life again and again to help slaves escape to freedom.

History is not just the story of emperors and presidents. It's also the story of ordinary people, of farmers, builders, artists, sailors, soldiers, teachers, and children. Their stories are worth knowing. They are our stories. History is about how we have changed and how we've stayed the same. And so history is everyone's story.

The Ice Age: Humans on the Move

Our story begins a long, long time ago, before your parents or grandparents or even their parents or grandparents were born—in fact, way before their parents or grandparents or even their great-grandparents were born. How long ago? Well, take a deep breath and say "long, long, long, long . . ." over and over until your breath gives out—and that's about how long ago our story begins.

In this long-ago time, the earth was colder than it is now, and life was harder in many ways. To stay alive, people hunted and gathered plants. At night they huddled around fires in damp caves to keep warm. They couldn't buy their clothes or food. They had to make or find everything. They made tools out of sticks and stones. They made needles

out of bones, which they used to sew robes out of pieces of animal skin.

But their most important task was finding food. Just like you, they got hungry and they had to eat. Of course, way back then they couldn't go shopping at a grocery store! To get food, they sometimes picked the wild plants growing around them, but most of all they hunted for animals to eat.

Because the early humans were hunters, they were always on the move from place to place. Why did they have to keep moving? Can you think of a reason? They kept moving because they were following the animals they hunted. In those long-ago days, great herds of woolly mammoths, wild bison, and reindeer roamed the land. As the animal herds moved on, the human beings followed because those animals were their breakfast, lunch, and dinner!

The animals kept moving because they were looking for food, too, for greener grass and a warmer climate. Back then, the earth was colder than it is now. It was so cold that much of the earth was covered by huge sheets of ice, called glaciers—which is why we call that long-long-ago time the Ice Age.

We know only a little about how people lived way back in the Ice Age. Why don't we know more? Because one of the ways that we know about people who lived long ago is by looking at clues they left behind, and those clues aren't always easy to find. Modern scientists who are called *archaeologists* [ar-key-AHL-oh-jists] study the things that were left behind by people who lived long ago. They study things like tools, weapons, jewelry, cups and bowls, and pieces of old houses. But the Ice Age people didn't leave much behind. Compared with you and me, the Ice Age people lived very

Archaeologists can also learn a lot from something else people leave behind: writing. Think of all the writing that you can see today: books, magazines, newspapers, and a lot more. But writing had not been invented back in the Ice Age. The Ice Age people talked and told stories, but they did not have a way to write messages to each other.

Still, these early people did draw. In caves all around the world, scientists and explorers have discovered ancient paintings made by the Ice Age people. What do you think those wandering hunters drew? Was it something they needed to stay alive? If you said "Wild animals" you're right!

simply. They didn't want to have to carry a lot of things with them as they moved from place to place.

We've come a long way since the Ice Age. Today most people don't have to hunt to survive. Most of us don't have to wander around, but can settle in one place for a while. People have learned how to farm and grow food, so we don't have to follow animals. We have built towns and cities, and we know how to write.

You can see that, since the time of the early humans, there have been a lot of big changes in the way people live—changes like settling down in one place, learning how to farm, building cities, and communicating by writing. These changes are all part of what we mean by *civilization*. That's a big word: try saying it a few times. And as you say it, think of some of the things that make civilized people different from those Ice Age hunters long ago: things like living in one place, farming, building cities, and writing messages.

The first civilizations began in Africa and Asia. Can you find those continents on a globe or world map? Now let's learn about two of the earliest civilizations, both in Africa. Let's go first to ancient Egypt.

WHY ARE THEY CALLED *ANCIENT*?

When you hear the Egyptians or other people in this book described as *ancient*, it doesn't mean that they grew to be very old. It means that the people were part of a civilization that existed a long, long, long time ago. Ancient Egypt is the civilization in Egypt thousands and thousands of years ago.

Egypt: Gift of the Nile

Egypt is in Africa. It's in the middle of a giant desert. Do you know what the weather is usually like in a desert? It's dry. It doesn't rain much at all.

Even though they lived in a desert, the ancient Egyptians were among the first people to learn to farm. Now wait a minute: how could that be? To grow crops, you need enough water. But what about Egypt, with all that burning sun and so little rain?

In fact, the Egyptian soil wasn't as dry as you might think. Egypt had very little rain, but she had a great treasure—a fantastic flooding river called the Nile.

The Nile is the lo-o-o-o-ngest river in the world. Do you see it on the map? It begins high in the rain-soaked mountains of central Africa and trips down the mountainsides. It twists and splashes into calm lakes and beautiful waterfalls. The Nile travels north

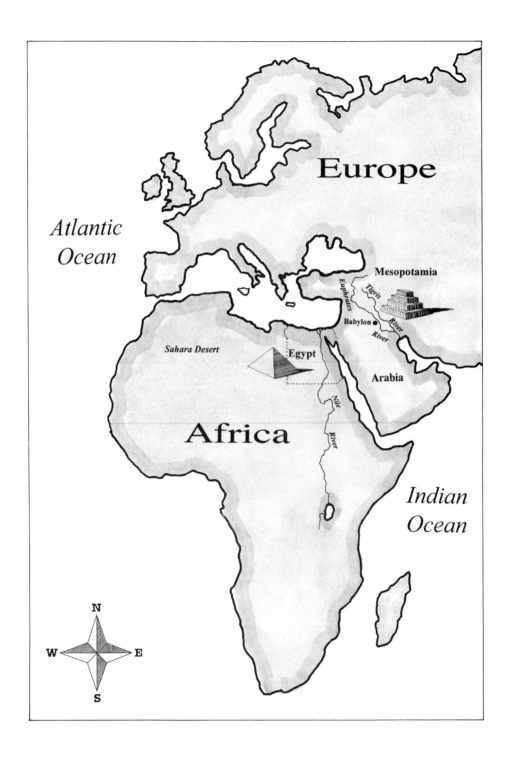

for thousands of miles, and when it finally reaches the desert, this river does more than flow. It floods!

Once a year the Nile overflows its banks. The river's yearly flood turns one of the driest parts of the world into fertile ground ("fertile" means that plants can grow there very easily). After the Nile floods, for about ten miles along either side of the river the soil turns a rich black color. It's full of minerals and other good things that help crops grow.

Five thousand years ago, the Nile's gift of rich black soil meant so much to the early Egyptians that they named their country "Black Land." We call such moist, rich soil "silt." If you mix silt, sunshine, and seeds together, plants will grow. Along the banks of the Nile, warm breezes blew wild barley seeds into the soil, and food crops sprang from the ground.

This is how the Nile River looks today.

The Egyptians didn't just wait for nature to blow the seeds into the soil. They began planting seeds on purpose along the banks of the Nile. They grew big crops of grains like barley and wheat, whose seeds can be ground up into flour. You still eat these grains in foods like cereal and bread.

When the Egyptians began to grow crops they could eat, then they didn't have to hunt as much. They began to stay in one place in order to be near their fields and take care of their crops. They began to build villages and cities. They began to build a civilization.

Fantastic Pharaohs and Marvelous Monuments

What a civilization! In the next two thousand years, the Egyptians built enormous buildings and monuments that are still among the biggest ever made. They built huge stone temples and pyramids (you'll learn more about pyramids soon). Why did they do it?

Well, one reason was that the pharaohs [FAIR-ohs] ordered them to do it. Who were the pharaohs? They were the rulers of ancient Egypt. The pharaohs had wonderful names that are fun to say—Rameses [RAM-uh-sees], Amenhotep [ah-men-HOE-tep], Tutankhamen [Toot-angk-AH-men], and Hatshepsut [hat-SHEP-soot]. They were like kings, but in some ways they were even more powerful than kings. The people of ancient Egypt thought the pharaoh was *divine*—which means the people thought he wasn't just a powerful person but also a *god*. This belief in the pharaoh as a living god-king made his commands very powerful indeed!

The pharaohs wanted to inspire and amaze people with their greatness. Each pharaoh wanted to show his people that he was even more powerful and important than the god-king who had come before him.

Imagine for a moment that you're the pharaoh. You are very proud and boastful. To show everyone how powerful and important you are, what would you do? Would you have someone write a story about the great things you've done? Would you make a huge statue of yourself for everyone to see? Those ideas occurred to the pharaohs, too.

The pharaohs ordered thousands of slaves to build great monuments to themselves and to the gods they worshiped.

A statue of Rameses II.

A giant carving of Rameses II and his family.

They ordered workers to carve large images of their faces in stone. Now, imagine for a moment that you're one of the workers: you sweat and strain in the sun as you drag huge, heavy stones across the hot sand. Maybe you don't think as highly of the pharaoh as he does of himself!

One very important pharaoh, Rameses II, thought he was so great that he even erased from the monuments the names of many pharaohs who had come before him. He made sure only *his* stories were written on the walls of the buildings!

Hieroglyphics: Picture Writing

Do you remember the reason we know only a little about the early humans in the Ice Age? It's because those early humans did not have a way to write anything about themselves. But we know a lot more about the ancient Egyptians. Why do you think we know more?

Did you say that the Egyptians knew how to write? Yes, the Egyptians did have a form of writing. Instead of writing with letters, as you're learning to do, they used picture writing. This picture writing is called *hieroglyphics*. Archaeologists have figured out what many of the hieroglyphics mean, so we can learn a lot about the Egyptians from what they wrote.

When Rameses II ordered his workers to tell his stories, they carved hieroglyphics in stone. Each picture—whether of a falcon, a snake, or a shepherd's staff—had a meaning. One of the reasons we know so much about Rameses is that he wrote a lot about himself!

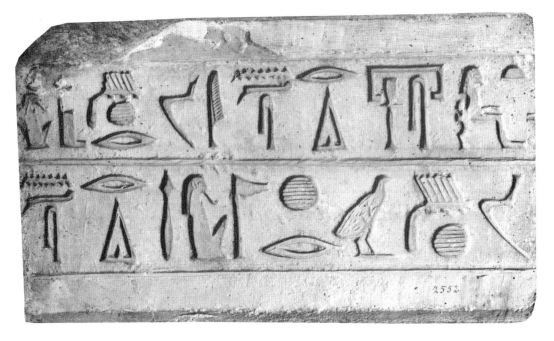

Hieroglyphics from ancient Egypt.

A Journey Down the Nile

Are you ready for an adventure? Imagine you can travel back thousands of years to ancient Egypt. We're going for a sail down the Nile!

There's a boat floating on the river. And look, there's a young man wearing a fancy headdress. He's nodding to you. You're lucky to have him as your host. Although he's young—only a teenager—he is very important. In fact, he's the pharaoh!

His name is Tutankhamen. Let's call him "King Tut" for short. Come on, hurry up—pharaohs aren't used to waiting for anyone.

In a very dignified voice, King Tut says, "Welcome aboard. I am so pleased that you can join us for the crocodile hunt."

"Crocodile hunt?!" you sputter. "But I don't even know how to fish!"

"Do not worry about a thing," King Tut responds. "My servants will spear the creatures for you." You look around and see that there are many people on the boat who are ready to wait on the young pharaoh's every need. They bow very low before him. You wonder what their lives are like: Are they afraid of this young pharaoh? Do they get tired of having to wait on him and do whatever he asks?

A Woman Pharaoh

Were all the pharaohs of Egypt men? Most were, but once there was a woman pharaoh named Hatshepsut. She didn't want to be called "queen." She wanted to be known as "pharaoh." She did the work of a pharaoh, too! She led armies into battle, and she ordered the building of great monuments.

A servant brings King Tut a fruit drink and offers you one, too. You sip your drink and enjoy the sights as the boat floats along the Nile. "Look over there," says King Tut. "Do you see that enormous statue—that huge figure with the body of a lion and the head of a human? That is the Great Sphinx. The Sphinx is like the pharaoh: the pharaoh rules as a man, and he is powerful as a lion.

"And look there," says Tut, "near the Sphinx. Do you see the pyramids?"

The Great Sphinx. (Its nose was accidentally knocked off about 200 years ago.)

How could you miss them? They're huge! The biggest pyramid covers a space on the ground as big as *thirteen* football fields (of course, they didn't play football way back in Tut's time)! You look at the young pharaoh and ask, "Why did you build the pyramids, King Tut? What are they for?"

Tut laughs and says, "Oh, *I* did not build them! Those pyramids have been around for a thousand years. They are the sacred tombs of the god-kings before me. They are the burial places of ancestor pharaohs from long ago."

"But King Tut," you ask, "why do you go to all that trouble to bury someone?"

"For us," the young pharaoh explains, "it is not a simple matter of just putting a pharaoh in the ground after he dies. No, what is important to us is the way the pharaoh lives *after* he dies."

Tut can tell that you're puzzled, so he goes on. "You know," he says, "that Egyptian pharaohs are god-kings. After our bodies die, we believe that our spirits keep on living if we make the necessary preparations. First, our bodies must be well preserved, because the body provides a home for the spirit after death. So our priests prepare the bodies of dead pharaohs in a special way. They do many things, such as wash and clean the body with fragrant spices, and rub it with special oils. One of the last things they do is wrap the body in rolls of white cloth, to make a mummy."

"Did you say *Mommy?*"

"No, *mummy*." Tut goes on: "The mummy is very important. It's a home for the pharaoh's ever-living spirit. If the mummy is damaged, the spirit cannot live. So the

These ancient Egyptian priests are preparing a mummy. As part of their work, they wrapped the body tightly in long strips of linen cloth. Each finger and toe was wrapped separately!

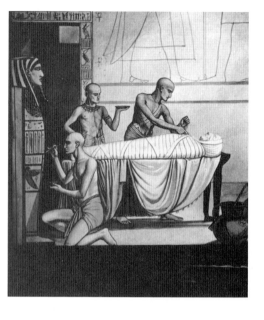

mummy must be kept safe. That is why the pyramids were built. The pyramids are very safe places to protect the pharaoh's mummy."

"Still," you ask, "why do the pyramids have to be so big?"

"Oh, there is much more in the pyramid than just a mummy," Tut answers. "The pyramids are filled with different chambers and passageways. The room where the mummy lies contains everything the pharaoh needs in the afterlife."

"What does he need?" you ask.

"Why," says Tut, "his spirit needs almost everything he needed in his earthly life—food, furniture, jewelry, games, and much more."

Tut leans over and motions for you to come very close. Then he whispers to you, "If you can keep a secret, I'll tell you where *I* am to be buried."

"You can trust me," you whisper back. "Where?"

"There," he says as he points to the distant hills.

"Is that where you'll have your pyramid built?" you ask.

"No, no," says Tut with a frown. Then he explains that pharaohs don't use pyramids anymore, because too many robbers, who have no respect for

Animal Gods

The ancient Egyptians believed in many gods. They often pictured their gods as having human bodies with the heads of animals, such as lions, rams, or crocodiles!

The god of the sun, called Amon (sometimes Amon Ra), had a ram's head. Here you can see a picture of the god of the sky, Horus, who had the head of a bird called a falcon.

the dead, have broken into the monuments of the great pharaohs and stolen all the treasures. So, when Tut dies, he will be buried in a tomb hidden underground in this place, called the Valley of the Kings.

Thinking about tombs has made Tut very serious. In a friendly but firm voice he tells you, "It is time for you to go now." You're just about to speak up and point out that you haven't caught a crocodile yet, but then you remember: it's not a good idea to talk back to a pharaoh!

The Treasures of King Tut

King Tut was a real pharaoh who lived thousands of years ago. He did a very good job hiding his tomb. It wasn't so very long ago—in 1922—that a hardworking archaeologist, after searching for five years, finally found Tut's tomb in the Valley of the Kings. As he entered the tomb, his eyes opened wide in amazement: it was in almost perfect condition! The tomb was full of decorated chairs, shining jewelry, fancy clothes, and thousands of other objects that had been buried with the pharaoh.

Here you can see some of the treasures buried with Tut, including a beautiful gold mask that shows what he looked like. (To see a color picture of Tut's magnificent mummy case, turn to page 180 in this book.)

A golden collar.

King Tut's golden mask.

Mesopotamia—Another Gift

In Egypt the Nile flooded every year. East of Egypt, on the continent of Asia, *two* other rivers flooded yearly. These neighboring rivers are called the Euphrates [yoo-FRAY-teez] and the Tigris [TIE-gris]. Like the Nile, when these rivers flooded, they gave the gift of rich soil. That meant people who lived beside or between the rivers could farm, grow plenty of food, and build their homes.

This warm and pleasant region has a long name, Mesopotamia [MESS-uh-puh-TAY-me-uh]. Mesopotamia means "the place between two rivers." (Look at the map on page 114.) What happened between the Tigris and Euphrates rivers? *A lot!*

Mesopotamia is known as "the cradle of civilization" because history was born here. Remember, history is a story: so, when we say history was born in Mesopotamia, we mean that it's the place where people first began to write down the story of human lives. Even *before* the ancient Egyptians started writing with hieroglyphics, the early people of Mesopotamia had begun to write. We call their kind of writing *cuneiform* [KYOO-nee-uh-form]. It's a strange-sounding word, and it means "wedge-shaped," which is exactly what cuneiform was: a thin, triangular, wedge-shaped kind of writing.

This cuneiform writing describes medicines used by a doctor long ago.

A Great Mesopotamian Story

Not so long ago, archaeologists were digging in this cradle of civilization. They found twelve clay tablets covered with cuneiform. The tablets were over five thousand years old! They told an exciting story—perhaps the world's oldest story. We do not know what the people of Mesopotamia called it, but we call it the *Epic of Gilgamesh* [GILL-guh-mesh].

An epic is a long story filled with the adventures of heroes. The *Epic of Gilgamesh* tells the story of a mighty king named Gilgamesh, who rules harshly over his people.

He forces them to build high walls and tall monuments and never lets them rest. But another hero, named Enkidu, fights Gilgamesh. Although they begin as enemies, Enkidu and Gilgamesh eventually become friends. Enkidu teaches Gilgamesh what it means to rule wisely.

Because the *Epic of Gilgamesh* was written down, we can learn a lot from it about how the people in long-ago Mesopotamia saw the world. It tells us what they admired in a hero, what gods they worshiped, and how they thought the gods wanted them to behave.

What's a Ziggurat?

Like the ancient Egyptians, the Mesopotamian people worshiped many gods. They prayed to a sky god, a sun god, a water god, a storm god, and many more. From what you know about ancient peoples and the importance of growing crops, why do you think weather gods were so important to them?

To honor their gods the people of Mesopotamia built temples called ziggurats [ZIG-uh-rats]. Ziggurats were enormous monuments with sides that looked like stair steps. They were not quite as tall as the pyramids, but if you saw one today, you'd feel very tiny standing next to

A huge statue
of Gilgamesh.

it! You can still see the remains of a very large ziggurat in a city called Ur.

The Mesopotamian people believed in a powerful goddess they called Ishtar. To honor Ishtar, they built a wall around their largest and most important city, Babylon. The wall had a beautiful blue gate called the

This ancient ziggurat is being rebuilt today.

The Gate of Ishtar.

Gate of Ishtar. This blue-tile gate was decorated with golden bulls and lions, the favorite animals of Ishtar. In this way the people of Babylon warned their enemies, "Do not mess with us, for we are protected by Ishtar!"

A Leader and the Laws

In early Mesopotamia the people did not have pharaohs as rulers. They had kings. One very important king was named Hammurabi [ha-muh-RAH-bee]. He ruled over Babylon. He also ruled the land around the city, because he had sent his armies out to conquer it. He was known for miles around as a strong and fair king.

Hammurabi decided that to make Babylon strong, the kingdom needed to have good laws. Do you know what laws are? Laws are the rules we obey. Today, for example, we have laws that say that all cars have to stop when a school bus is loading or unloading children. Do you know of any other laws?

Of course, Hammurabi lived a very, very long time before school buses. In fact, he lived in a time when people were first beginning to understand why it's important to have laws.

Hammurabi collected laws from as many kingdoms as he could, and then he put to-

Think about it: Why do people need
laws? What would happen without
them?

gether the Code of Hammurabi. This was
a very long list of laws, and some of them
seem strange or cruel to us today. For example, one law said that if a doctor oper-
ated on a patient and the patient died,
then the doctor's hand should be
chopped off!

This is *definitely* not the way we would
do things today. But not all of Hammurabi's laws were so harsh. In fact,
many of his laws protected those who
could not protect themselves. For example, one law said that if a man was poor, a
doctor should charge him less than a rich
man for the same operation.

The Code of Hammurabi is carved
in this stone.

Justice: An Important Idea

Hammurabi was one of the first people to recognize how important laws are.
Although we would not agree with some of the harsh laws he made, we share
today Hammurabi's concern with an idea called *justice*. Justice is a big and
important idea. When we think about justice, we think about what is fair for everyone.
And we ask, what can we do to make life in our communities more just—better
and fairer—for everyone?

Religions:
What Different People Believe

PARENTS: *In the World History and Geography section, we introduce children not only to ancient civilizations but also to topics in the history of world religions. As the many people who contributed to the development of the Core Knowledge Sequence agreed (see pages xix–xxi), religion is a shaping force in the history of civilization and thus should be part of what our children know about. The pages on religion have benefited from the critiques of religious scholars and representatives of various faiths, whom we wish to thank for their advice and suggestions. In introducing children to the history of world religions, we focus on major symbols, figures, and stories. Our goal is to be descriptive, not prescriptive, and to maintain a sense of respect and balance.*

Have you noticed that when we talk about early civilizations, we keep mentioning "the gods"? When we talk about the gods, or God, that people believe in, we are talking about their *religion*.

For thousands of years, different religions have helped many different people try to answer some big questions. These are not just questions that people asked long ago in ancient times. People still ask these questions today, questions like: How did the world begin? Where did people and animals come from? Why is the world the way it is? How should people behave?

Today there are many religions in the world. Let's find out more about three religions that have been important to many people for thousands of years. These three religions are called Judaism, Christianity, and Islam.* Today these religions have millions of followers. But thousands of years ago, each of these religions was just getting started. We're going to look back to these long-ago times and learn about how Judaism, Christianity, and Islam began.

But first, think about this: do you remember that people in ancient Mesopotamia and ancient Egypt believed in *many* gods? They believed in gods of nature, such as a sun god and an earth god. They believed in many other gods, such as a god of the dead and a god to protect the city. Well, there's a big difference in the religions you're going to learn about now. Judaism, Christianity, and Islam do *not* believe in many gods. Instead, all of these religions believe in just *one* God. (When you refer to just one God, you spell the name with a capital "G," because that's how you begin a name, right?— with a capital letter.) Thousands of years ago, this belief in just one God was a new idea. And this new idea came first from the religion called Judaism.

---

*Later books in the Core Knowledge Series discuss other religions. In *What Your Second Grader Needs to Know* (Revised Edition, forthcoming), children are introduced to Hinduism and Buddhism.

Judaism

The followers of Judaism today are called Jews. The Jewish people believe in one God. To worship God, they go to a place called a synagogue. The holy book of the Jewish people is called the Bible, or sometimes the Hebrew Bible. It was written in Hebrew, a language that is still spoken by many Jews today. The first part of the Hebrew Bible is called the Torah: it tells the history of the Jewish people and their God. Many Jewish people believe that the Torah was written by a man named Moses.

The Star of David, an important symbol of the Jewish religion.

The Story of Moses

Moses was a great leader of the Jewish people. Way back in the time of Moses, the Jewish people were known by another name: they were called Hebrews. Sometimes the Bible also calls them Israelites or the Children of Israel. Here is some of the story of Moses, as told in the Hebrew Bible.

The story of Moses begins in Egypt more than three thousand years ago. It was an awful time for the Hebrews because they were forced by the Egyptians to work as slaves. The Hebrews had to work long and hard in the hot sun, carrying the heavy rocks used to build the big monuments.

Now, the pharaoh of Egypt noticed something that bothered him. He saw that among the Hebrews more and more children were being born every day. He began to worry that one day there might be so many Hebrews that they would rise up and fight against their Egyptian masters. And so Pharaoh gave a cruel command. He ordered that all boy children born to the Hebrew people should be drowned in the Nile River!

Just at this time a Hebrew woman gave birth to baby boy. She knew of Pharaoh's awful command. She decided she must do something to save her boy, but what? What could she do?

For a few months she did her best to hide him, but she could not keep him hidden forever. And so this is what she did. She wove a basket out of a long grass called bulrushes. She put tar on the bottom of the basket so that it would float. Then she carried her baby down to the Nile River and put him in the basket. She left the basket, with the baby in it, floating among the long grass by the riverbank. Hidden in the distance, the baby's older sister, named Miriam, watched the basket and waited to see what would happen.

Soon a group of women came walking along the riverbank. It was Pharaoh's daughter, along with the maidens who served her, coming to bathe in the river. Pharaoh's daughter saw the basket in the bulrushes, and she sent a maid to fetch it. When she looked inside, she saw a crying baby boy! "He must be one of the Hebrew children," she said. She felt sorry for the little child, all alone. She named him Moses, which, it is said, means "drawn out of the water."

Just then the baby's older sister, Miriam, came out of her hiding place. She approached Pharaoh's daughter and asked, "Shall I go and find a Hebrew woman to help you take care of the child?"

"Yes, do," said Pharaoh's daughter. Now, who do you think Miriam went to get? Moses's own mother! So, with two mothers to take care of him, Moses was raised as a prince in the palace of his people's enemies!

When Moses grew up, he saw something that upset him. He saw an Egyptian beating a Hebrew slave. Moses fought the Egyptian, and he killed him. And now Moses was in very big trouble. He had to leave Pharaoh's palace. He left behind his comfortable life and went far away and began to live as a shepherd.

The Hebrew Bible tells us that one day, as Moses was keeping watch over the sheep, he saw an amazing sight: it was a bush covered with flames, yet the bush itself was not burned by the flames. Then a voice spoke from the burning bush and said to Moses, "I am the God of your fathers. I have seen the suffering of my people who are in Egypt. I will send you to Pharaoh that you may bring forth my people out of Egypt to a good and broad land, a land flowing with milk and honey."

Moses was afraid. He said, "O Lord, who am I to do this? Pharaoh will not listen to me. I am not a man of words. I do not speak well." Then God became angry and asked Moses who had given him the power to speak in the first place; and God told Moses, "I will teach you what to say."

So Moses, together with his brother, named Aaron, went to Pharaoh and said, "God has commanded you: 'Let my people go.'" But Pharaoh said, "I do not know your God, and I will not let your people go." And Pharaoh made the Hebrews work even harder.

Then, says the Hebrew Bible, God punished the Egyptians. He sent a plague of frogs: the Nile River was filled with frogs, and the people found frogs in their beds and in their food bowls. Still, Pharaoh refused to let the Hebrews go. So God sent more punishments. The land was covered with gnats, and flies, and locusts. The crops died, and the cattle died. The people of Egypt found their skin covered with terrible sores. Thunder crashed in the sky as a terrible hail battered the earth.

Finally, Pharaoh had had enough. He let the Hebrews leave Egypt. They gathered their few belongings and set off to the land that God had promised to Moses and his people, the promised land "flowing with milk and honey."

The journey of the Hebrews out of Egypt is called the Exodus. It was a long, hard journey. Soon after they started, the Hebrews came to the shore of a sea, where they stopped to rest. They didn't know, however, that Pharaoh had changed his mind about letting the Hebrews leave. He wanted them back to work as slaves. So he sent his soldiers after them.

When the Hebrews saw Pharaoh's mighty troops approaching, they were terrified. The soldiers, riding fast in their horse-drawn chariots, were coming at them from one side. On the other side was the sea. What could they do? They turned to Moses and cried out, "Have you brought us out of Egypt only to die here in the desert?"

But Moses raised his staff and a great wind began to blow. It blew so hard and so strong that the waters of the sea parted in two. The Hebrews were amazed to see a dry path between two walls of water! Moses led his people across this path through the sea. Not far behind came the soldiers of Pharaoh. But as they came across, the walls of water came crashing down, and all of Pharaoh's men were drowned.

The Hebrews were safe. Moses led them to their promised homeland, which is now called Israel. The escape of the Hebrews from Egypt is still celebrated by Jewish people today as an important holiday in the Jewish religion. It is called Passover.

 Another popular holiday in the Jewish religion is called Hanukkah [HAH-nuh-kuh; sometimes spelled Chanukah]. It is usually celebrated in December, and is sometimes called the Festival of Lights. On each night for eight nights, a candle is lit in a special holder called a menorah.

Christianity

The religion called Christianity began about two thousand years ago. It grew out of the religion you've just learned about, Judaism. It happened like this.

As you know, Moses led the Hebrews to their promised homeland, called Israel. But there were still many hard times ahead. More than once, the Jewish people were conquered and ruled over, as they had been by the Egyptians.

The Jewish people, as well as many other people, were conquered by the powerful Romans. The Romans had strong armies with thousands and thousands of soldiers. It was hard for the Jewish people to be ruled by the Romans. Many people in Israel hoped for a savior—a person who would come and save them. The Jewish people called this savior they hoped for the Messiah. Many Jewish people thought that when the Messiah came, he would lead the Jews against their Roman conquerors and make them free.

Into this world was born Jesus of Nazareth. Many people believe that Jesus was the Messiah the Jewish people were waiting for. These people are called Christians because Jesus was also called the Christ (which means something like "the chosen one").

Jesus was not the son of a king or a powerful warrior. His parents, named Mary and Joseph, were humble people. The story of Mary, Joseph, and the birth of Jesus is told in the holy book of Christians, called the Bible.

> The Bible is a holy book for both Christians and Jewish people. But the Hebrew Bible of the Jewish people does not include a part of the Christian Bible—the part that tells the story of Jesus.

The First Christmas

Christians celebrate the birthday of Jesus on the day called Christmas. Here, from the Bible, is the story of the first Christmas.

In the city of Nazareth, there lived a young woman named Mary. She did not know that something amazing was going to happen to her.

The Bible tells us that one day Mary was visited by an angel sent by God, an angel named Gabriel. "Hail, O favored one!" Gabriel said to Mary ("Hail" means "Hello"). Mary was amazed and scared. "Do not be afraid," said the angel. But what Gabriel told her made her more afraid and very excited. The angel said that Mary would have a son, and that this son would be the Messiah, the promised one, the savior of Israel.

Then Mary asked the angel, "How can I have a son? I do not even have a husband." The angel told her that the baby would be sent from God, and that her child would be called the Son of God.

Months later, Mary prepared to go on a trip with her new husband, Joseph. It was a hard time to travel, for indeed, Mary was now expecting a child. But they had to make the trip. The ruler of the Romans, called the emperor, had sent out an order. The Roman emperor wanted to tax all the people he ruled (that means he wanted to get money from them). He ordered them to return to the town of their ancestors to pay their taxes.

So Mary and Joseph went to the town of Joseph's ancestors, the little town of Bethlehem. It was a hard journey. When they arrived, Mary could feel that it was time for her baby to be born, that very night.

This painting shows how an artist imagined the first Christmas.

But they could find nowhere to stay: there was no room at the inn. The innkeeper told them they could stay in the stable where the animals were kept. In there they would at least find some straw to rest on.

And there in the stable, with the cattle and other animals moving softly about, Mary gave birth to her baby son. And since there was no crib or bed, she placed him in a manger, which held the feed for the animals to eat.

Nearby there were shepherds in the field, keeping watch over their flock by night. An angel appeared to them and said, "Fear not: for, behold, I bring you good tidings of great joy. For unto you is born this day a Savior, which is Christ the Lord."

The shepherds were amazed. For so many years their people had waited for a savior, a mighty leader. Could it be that their savior was born *here*, among such plain and humble people?

The shepherds hurried to Bethlehem to see the child. They found Mary, and Joseph, and the babe, who was lying in a manger. The shepherds told Mary what the angel had said. Then they went to tell everyone the good news. But Mary remained quiet and thought deeply about all that had happened.

And that is what the Bible tells us of the first Christmas. Christians today remember and celebrate the first Christmas each year on the twenty-fifth of December by putting on special plays, by giving gifts, and by singing songs about Bethlehem, the angels, the shepherds, and the baby Jesus.

Jesus the Teacher: The Parable of the Good Samaritan

When Jesus grew to be a man, he started teaching. People flocked to listen and Jesus soon had many followers. When Jesus taught people, he often told parables. A parable is a story that teaches a lesson.

Jesus taught that you should love your neighbor as you love yourself. Once a lawyer asked Jesus, "Just exactly who is my neighbor?" To answer this question, Jesus told the parable of the Good Samaritan. (A Samaritan is a person from the region called Samaria.)

Once, said Jesus, a man was traveling along a road. Suddenly he was attacked by thieves. They robbed the man and beat him. He lay half-dead by the side of the road. Soon a priest came along. He saw the man lying in pain, but did not stop to help him. Then another man came down the road; he, too, walked right on by without helping. Then along came a Samaritan. When the Samaritan saw the half-dead man, he went to him and took care of his wounds. He took the man to a nearby inn. He told the innkeeper that he would pay whatever it cost to take care of the man.

When Jesus had told this story, he turned and asked the lawyer, "Which now of these three was neighbor unto him that fell among the thieves?"

And that, from the Bible, is the story of the Good Samaritan. What do you think? Who was most like a neighbor to the man who was robbed and beaten? Why?

Today, people sometimes call anyone who goes out of his or her way to help someone in need a "good Samaritan."

Easter

Many people listened to Jesus and believed him. But many others got angry with Jesus. They expected a savior who would lead them in a great fight against the Romans. Instead, Jesus said that people should forgive their enemies.

Although many people began to follow Jesus, other people became his enemies. His words made them angry and scared. And so they hurt Jesus, and eventually they killed him. He was put to death on a cross, so the cross has become the main symbol of Christianity. Christians believe that on the third day after Jesus died, he rose from the dead; Christians celebrate his rising from the dead at Easter. Easter and Christmas are the two most important holidays and celebrations for Christians.

Islam

A long time after Jesus lived—in fact, more than five hundred years later—a man named Muhammad was born in the land then called Arabia (look at the map on page 114).

The religion of Islam began in the time of Muhammad. Followers of Islam are called Muslims (sometimes spelled Moslems).

Muhammad was a merchant, a person who buys and sells things for a living. He was a respected man in his hometown of Mecca (sometimes spelled Makkah). Many people called him al-Amin, which means "the Trustworthy."

Because he was a merchant, Muhammad traveled a lot to buy and sell his goods. In his travels he met many different people. Some of them were followers of the two religions you've already learned about: Judaism and Christianity. From these Jews and Christians, Muhammad learned about the idea of one God. And from the Christians he learned about the teachings of Jesus.

Muhammad thought about what he learned during his life and travels. When he returned home, he looked around at what he saw in his own land and he became troubled. He saw that many of the people still worshiped many gods. He felt that too many people in the city of Mecca had become proud and greedy. He did not like the rich rulers of the city. He believed they fought too much and were too concerned with money.

Here is the story that Muslims tell about how their religion began. Muhammad liked to go off to sit alone in a quiet cave, where he could think about things that were worrying him. One day, when he was forty years old, he went to the cave and there he had a vision (a vision is like a dream, except you're awake). Muhammad saw an angel, the angel Gabriel. Is that name familiar to you? Gabriel is the *same* angel that, the Bible says, came to Mary to tell her that she would give birth to the baby Jesus.

Muslims believe that God spoke to Muhammad through the angel Gabriel. The angel told Muhammad to tell everyone in Arabia that there was only one God, whose name is Allah. "Allah" is the Arabic word for the English word "God." So, you see, Muslims worship the same God that Jewish people and Christians worship.

Muhammad set out to tell people that they should worship only the one God, Allah. Some people listened to Muhammad's teachings and believed him. But most people were not very happy to hear what he said. He told them that their ideas about religion were wrong and that they should change what they believed and how they behaved. Some people got so mad at Muhammad that they even killed some of his followers and forced him to leave Mecca, the city that was his home.

But Muhammad was determined to spread his message. He continued to teach about Allah, and more people began to follow him. The people liked Muhammad's lessons about being kind to each other and about helping the poor. They prayed many times every day. They tried hard to live better lives.

The rulers of Mecca were still angry at Muhammad, and they were worried as more people began to follow him. More than once the rulers of Mecca sent soldiers to attack the Muslims. But the Muslims fought back, and in the end they beat the soldiers of Mecca. Muhammad returned to his home city, and his many followers came with him.

Soon all of Arabia accepted Muhammad as the mes-

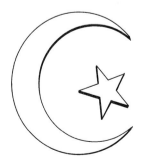

The star and crescent have become an important symbol of Islam.

This mosque is the Islamic Center in Washington, D.C.

A page from a 600-year-old Qur'an.

senger of God. Since the time of Muhammad, the religion of Islam has spread from Arabia to many parts of the world. Muslims everywhere study the Qur'an (sometimes spelled Koran), which is the holy book of Islam. They worship Allah in buildings called mosques [MOSKS].

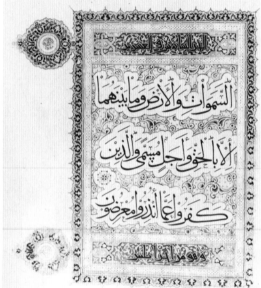

Today Judaism, Christianity, and Islam are three of the world's biggest religions. Jews, Christians, and Muslims have much in common. All the followers of these religions believe in the same God, though they call this one God by different names. The holy books of the three religions tell some of the same stories. In the Qur'an there are many stories that are also told in the Torah and the Bible, such as the story of Noah and the flood, and the story of Moses.

In later books in this series, you'll learn more about the place of these religions in the story of world history, and you'll learn about other religions, too.

American History and Geography

PARENTS: *Please read the World History and Geography section of this book with your child first, as the following section assumes some familiarity with terms introduced in World History and Geography.*

Crossing the Land Bridge

Do you know the seven continents? Can you name them and point to them on the map? (If you want to read about the continents, you can look back at the World History and Geography section of *What Your Kindergartner Needs to Know.*)

Can you find North America and Asia on this map? Look way up to what is now the state of Alaska. Do you see how close Alaska is to Asia? They are separated by only a small body of water.

But that water wasn't always there. Many, many thousands of years ago, way back in the Ice Age, there was a narrow strip of land that connected Asia and North America. It was like a bridge across the water: and that's why it's called the *land bridge*.

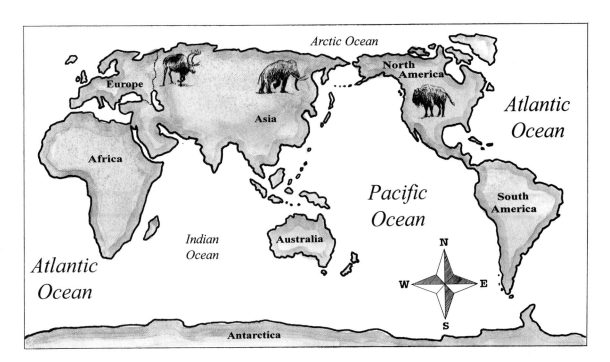

On this map or a globe, locate the four major oceans (Atlantic, Pacific, Indian, Arctic), and the seven continents.

Do you remember learning about the Ice Age earlier in this book (see pages 111–13)? What do you remember about that long-ago time? Yes, it was cold! Do you remember how people lived then? They spent most of their time just trying to stay warm and trying get enough to eat. Do you remember how the people back then got their food? They hunted big animals like reindeer and woolly mammoths.

Well, those big animals didn't just sit around and say, "Come get us, Ice Age hunters!" No, those animals kept on the move. Just like people, the reindeer, woolly mammoths, and other animals needed to eat, too. So they kept moving, looking for food.

From Asia, big herds of animals moved east and south. They moved right across that land bridge and came to what is now North America. And who else do you think was

"Stop! It's dinnertime."

hurrying across the land bridge, following the animals? That's right, the people! Why did they follow the animals? They were following their food!

As the years passed—in fact, thousands of years—more and more people came across the land bridge, and they spread all over North and South America. These people from Asia were the ancestors of the people we now call Native Americans, or American Indians.

For a long time, these early people kept alive by hunting, fishing, and gathering wild

---

EVERYONE'S ANCESTORS

If people from Asia were the ancestors of Native Americans, who were the ancestors of the people in Asia? Many scientists believe that the first humans came from Africa, over *half a million* years ago. If those scientists are right, then all of us have ancestors who lived in Africa!

berries, nuts, and fruit. As time passed, the earliest Americans began to grow their food, especially the people who lived farther south, where it was warmer and easier to grow crops. These crops, such as corn and beans, gave them plenty to eat. When people can grow enough food to eat, they don't have to keep moving around and chasing their dinner. They can stay put and make their homes in one place.

Little by little, the first Americans did what people in ancient Egypt and Mesopotamia had done thousands of years before. As they learned to farm and built their homes, the first Americans built *civilizations*. They settled down, they built towns and cities, they made works of art, and some of them learned to write.

Let's look back in history to some of those first American civilizations.

Cities in the Jungle: The Maya

First you're going to meet a civilization that developed in Central America. You know where North America and South America are, but where is *Central* America? If you don't know, you can probably figure it out. Look at the map on page 135. You can find the continents of North and South America, right? Well, do you see how the land gets narrower as you move down from North America to South America? That area, which is kind of in the center of two big continents, is called Central America.

> You can learn more about rainforests on page 279 in the Science section of this book.

Deep in the rainforests of Central America, the Mayan people made their home. In the moist jungle soil, the Maya grew corn, squash, and beans. And there, thousands of years ago, the Maya built their cities.

And what amazing cities they were, with big stone palaces and—what's this? Take a look: here's a tall stone building, with stairs going up the slanted sides. Does this remind you of some-

The Temple of the Giant Jaguar as it appears today.

thing? Something Egyptian? Like a pyramid?

Well, the Egyptians built their pyramids a *long* time before the Maya, and in a different part of the world. So the Maya never knew about the Egyptians. Still, like the Egyptians, the Maya buried their kings in big stone buildings that reach way above the tallest trees in the jungle. The stairs on the Mayan pyramids were for the priests, who would climb to the top to worship their gods.

Like other ancient people you've learned about, the Maya worshiped nature gods, such as gods of the wind and the rain. They also worshiped animal gods. They made pictures showing some of their gods as partly human and partly

This Mayan animal god is part opossum.

in the form of a big, fierce jungle cat, the jaguar. The big pyramid you see in the picture here is the Temple of the Giant Jaguar.

The Maya knew how to write. You remember Egyptian hieroglyphics, don't you? The Maya had their own form of picture writing. They used their picture writing to make a kind of calendar. And they used it to tell stories of the lives, battles, and triumphs of the Mayan leaders. Sometimes they wrote in books made from the bark of trees. Sometimes they carved their stories on big stone pillars. Just imagine if *you* had to write by carving letters in hard stone! Aren't you glad you have pencil and paper?

You're learning to write in school, along with your friends

A stone pillar with Mayan writing on it.

and with children in schools all across the country, and in other countries, too. But did you know that the idea that everyone should be able to write is a pretty new idea in human history? In long-ago times, only a very few people learned to write. Only a few of the Mayan people knew how to write, and these few were called the scribes.

An Unsolved Mystery

Sometimes history is a mystery. We don't know about some very important things that happened in the past. We know that the Maya built great cities, and we know they lived in these cities for hundreds of years. But then, they left. And that's the mystery: we don't know *why* the Maya left their cities. Not even the Maya who still live in Central America today know the answers to these questions:

Why, long ago, did the ancient

Grass has grown over much of this Mayan palace in Mexico.

Maya allow the jungle to spread over their buildings and monuments? What happened to their civilization? Was there a drought—a long time without rain—that killed the crops? Did they catch some awful disease? Was there a terrible war?

We don't know the answers, but historians and archaeologists are working to find out. Maybe someday you can help solve this mystery!

City in the Lake: The Aztecs

Now let's meet another early American civilization. Like the Maya, these people also built great cities, but not until hundreds of years after the Maya. These people were called the Aztecs.

The Aztecs built a great city in what is now the country of Mexico, at the place where you can now find one of the biggest modern cities in the world: Mexico City. The Aztecs called their city Tenochtitlán [tay-nosh-tee-TLAHN].

The Aztecs chose an unusual location to build their city: in a lake! Actually, they built their city on islands in the lake, and then, to connect the islands, they built bridges, as well as waterways called canals. They built huge stone temples devoted to the worship of their many gods, such as a god of rain, a god of corn, and—most important of all to the Aztecs—the sun god.

The Aztecs told a legend about why they picked such an unusual location for Tenochtitlán. They said their sun god had commanded them to keep moving until they saw an eagle sitting on a prickly pear cactus while eating a snake. There, they should build their city. According to the legend, the Aztecs traveled until they saw this strange sight at Tenochtitlán. In fact, Tenochtitlán means "place of the prickly pear

This drawing shows how Tenochtitlán looked when it was a busy city.

cactus." If you look at a flag of Mexico, you'll see that modern-day Mexicans still remember this legend.

See pages 148–50 to learn more about Mexico.

After the Aztecs built their great city, they set out to conquer the people around them. "To conquer" means to defeat someone in a war and to take them over. The Aztecs believed in fighting and conquering other people. All boys had to serve in the army, and the army's job was to conquer. Other people feared and hated the Aztecs because they were always making war and taking prisoners and killing people.

Can you find the eagle and the cactus in this old Aztec drawing?

Aztec Artistry

The Aztecs were not just fierce warriors. They were also very good craftsmen. They made wonderful sculptures. They made many beautiful things using turquoise stones, jade, gold, and other precious materials.

An Aztec artist made this two-headed snake of turquoise stones.

Cities in the Clouds: The Incredible Inca

On the continent of South America, there's a big, long mountain range. Look on the map on page 140. Run your finger up and down the Andes Mountains on the map.

High up in the Andes, the air is thin and cold. The mountains are steep, rough, and rocky, so it's not easy to get around—unless you're a sure-footed llama, or maybe a condor soaring above the mountain ledges.

Does this seem like a place to start building a civilization?

Maybe not, but that's just what the Inca people did. In the country now called Peru, the Inca built their cities high in the mountains. How did they do it? They used something the Andes Mountains have plenty of—rock!

The Inca were very skillful masons (masons are people who cut stone). They cut and hauled huge blocks of

A llama in the Andes Mountains.

Here is one of the Inca's incredible
stone walls.

This "city in the clouds" is
Machu Picchu, high in the
Andes Mountains.

stone. They put the big stone blocks together so exactly that you couldn't even slide a piece of paper between them! After they built beautiful stone walls and fortresses, they decorated the insides with gold and silver, which they found plenty of in the mountains.

The Arrival of the Europeans

For many hundreds of years, the Mayan, Aztec, and Incan civilizations were strong. What happened to them?

As you've already learned, we don't know what happened to the Maya. We know that they left their great cities, but we don't know why. It's a mystery.

What happened to the Aztecs and the Inca is not a mystery. What happened was the arrival of new people. These people dressed differently, and they spoke a different language. They came on ships, across the Atlantic Ocean, from the faraway continent of Europe.

One of the first Europeans to arrive was Christopher Columbus. In three small ships, he and his sailors made a bold and daring voyage from Europe to "the New World." At least it was a new world for Columbus and other Europeans. For the Maya, Aztecs, Inca, and many other Native American peoples, it was home!

Do you remember the story of Columbus's voyage? If you've learned about Columbus in the Kindergarten book in this series, or in other books, let's see what you remember. (Don't worry if you can't remember everything; most of us have to hear a story more than once before we can remember much about it!) Ready? Here goes.

Think back. In what year did Columbus make his voyage? (Remember? "In fourteen-hundred and ninety-two, Columbus sailed the ocean blue.")

It was hard for Columbus to find someone who would help pay for his voyage. He finally got help from a king and queen. Do you remember what country they were king and queen of? (The King and Queen of Spain helped Columbus. Their names were King Ferdinand and Queen Isabella.)

Columbus set sail from Europe in three ships: do you remember any of their names? (They were the *Niña*, the *Pinta*, and the *Santa María*.) The voyage across the Atlantic Ocean was hard and sometimes stormy. Some of the sailors grew scared; they wanted Columbus to turn back. But he kept on, and finally, they reached land.

They landed on a little island in a group of islands now called the Bahamas. They were greeted by the friendly people who lived there. The people were part of the Taino [TIE-no] tribe. But Columbus and others called them "Indians." Do you remember why? Because Columbus thought he had landed near Asia, which the Europeans also called "the Indies." Columbus thought he was in "the Indies," so he called the people he met there "Indians." Even though that name was a mistake, it is still used today. Many descendants of these early people in America still call themselves American Indians, and they

> PARENTS: If you have access to a world map or a globe, help your child use his finger to trace Columbus's route and identify significant locations. Have him move his finger from Spain across the Atlantic Ocean to the Bahama Islands (between what are now Florida and Cuba). Have him find the continent of Asia so that he can appreciate just how far away Columbus landed from his intended destination.

are also called Native Americans. ("Descendants" are people who come from other people: you are a descendant of your parents, your grandparents, your great-grandparents, your great-great grandparents, and so on.)

So Columbus thought he was in Asia (or "the Indies"). He didn't know that he had bumped into land near North America and South America. He and other Europeans didn't know that these continents existed!

Columbus wasn't interested in finding any new continents. Neither were Queen Isabella and King Ferdinand. Well then, what *did* they want from this voyage? Mainly two things. They wanted to spread their religion: they wanted the people Columbus met to become Christians. And, even more, they wanted to find valuable stuff like gold and spices.

You know that gold is valuable, but *spices?* Yes, spices were valuable back then— even spices like pepper, which you may have in your kitchen today. In those days the people in Europe did not have many spices, and they were willing to pay lots of money to get them. Remember, people long ago didn't have refrigerators to keep their meat from rotting. They wanted the pepper because they thought that it and other spices would help keep the meat fresh, and would certainly make their meals taste better!

When Columbus landed on the island, he put up a Spanish flag and claimed the land for Spain. If you say, "I claim this," you are saying, "This belongs to me." Did the land belong to Spain? No. The Taino people already lived there. And not too far away, in parts of Central America and South America, there were already great civilizations (though Columbus never saw them), such as those of the Aztec and Inca peoples.

But Europeans like Columbus didn't think much about the people already living in the lands they found. Back then the Europeans thought that everything was "finders-keepers." When Columbus arrived in the New World, he thought, "I've found it. I am sailing for the King and Queen of Spain. So, I claim this land for Spain." Do you think the Native Americans would have agreed with this? Why not?

This painting shows Columbus claiming the land for Spain.

The Spanish Conquerors

Soon after Columbus, more and more people from Spain came to North and South America. Many of them came hoping to find gold and other riches. Both the Aztecs and the Inca had a lot of gold and other riches that the Spaniards wanted. And the Spaniards would fight to get them.

Do you remember what it means to "conquer" someone? Not long ago you learned that the Aztecs went to war against many people around them and conquered them. But now the Aztecs themselves would be conquered by the Spanish.

The Spanish word for "conqueror" is *conquistador* [kon-kee-stah-DOR]. That is what we call the Spanish explorers who conquered the Native Americans. One *conquistador*,

The Aztecs drew this picture of a battle with Cortés's soldiers.

named Hernando Cortés [core-TEZ], led the Spanish against the Aztecs.

The leader of the Aztecs at this time was named Montezuma [mon-teh-ZOO-mah]. You may also see Montezuma spelled Moctezuma. Have you ever heard the song that begins, "From the halls of Montezuma"? It's the song of the United States Marines. Montezuma had terrible dreams that something bad was going to happen to his people. That something bad was Cortés. Cortés and his soldiers captured the city of Tenochti-tlán, and took the gold and other riches.

Not many years later, the Inca people were defeated by another Spanish *conquistador*. His name was Francisco Pizarro. He forced the people he conquered to work as slaves, digging silver from mines in the ground.

Why Did the Spanish Win?

The Aztecs were fierce warriors; they had conquered many people around them. The Inca, too, were a strong people. And there were many more Aztec and Inca people than there were Spanish soldiers. So, why did the Spanish win?

The Spanish soldiers won because they had much stronger weapons. They had swords, guns, and cannons. The Spanish soldiers wore armor, which is a helmet and coat made of strong metal. The armor protected them from the spears and arrows of the Native Americans.

The Spanish soldiers rode horses, too. The Native Americans had never seen a horse before. At first they thought the horse and rider were one animal. Think how frightened you would be to see such a strange creature!

But something even more powerful worked against the Native Americans. They caught diseases from the Spaniards.

The Spanish soldiers wore armor and rode horses.

The Native Americans had never been exposed to the terrible diseases, such as smallpox, that had killed so many people in Europe. So, many of the Native Americans never had a chance to fight the Spanish soldiers, because they died from diseases like smallpox.

Because of Columbus, Cortés, Pizarro, and other explorers, Spain claimed a lot of land in North and South America. Some of this land is now part of the United States, including the states of California and Texas. Spain also claimed almost all of the land south of our country—and that's why, even today, most people in these countries south of the United States still speak Spanish.

Mexico Today

Do you know the names of the three biggest countries on the continent of North America? Take a look at a globe or map. Find the United States of America. What country is to the north? Canada. What country is to the south? Mexico.

Mexico is south of the United States, and north of the area called Central America. The capital of Mexico is Mexico City. Do you remember the Aztec city, Tenochtitlán? Today it's called Mexico City, and it's one of the largest cities in the world, with more than 15 million people.

Look at the map below: can you find the river called the Rio [REE-oh] Grande? The name means "Large River." The Rio Grande is so large that it forms the border (the di-

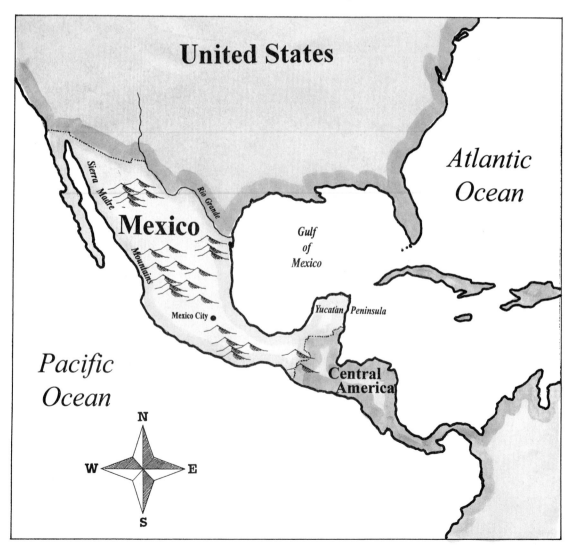

viding line) that separates the state of Texas from Mexico. The Rio Grande flows into a body of warm water called the Gulf of Mexico: can you find this on the map? Look at the map again: what ocean is on the other side (to the west) of Mexico? (The Pacific Ocean.)

If you were to take a trip from the Rio Grande and go south through Mexico today, you'd see a mix of land, people, and customs. You would drive by the giant Sierra Madre [see-AIR-ah MAH-dray] Mountains, through dry deserts, and even through humid rainforests. You would meet a variety of people living everywhere from big cities to small villages.

On the map, look at the southern part of Mexico. If you use your imagination, can you see the part that looks kind of like the tail of a whale? This area is called the Yucatán [yoo-kah-TAHN] Peninsula. What is a "peninsula"? It's a piece of land surrounded by water on three sides. Do you see the water on three sides of the "whale's tail"? The Yucatán Peninsula is a big rainforest. The ancient Maya lived there, and descendants of the Maya still live there today.

Many people who live in Mexico today are the descendants of both Spanish and Indian people. Most Mexicans speak Spanish. Many Mexicans enjoy foods that came from the Indians, such as *tortillas* [tor-TEE-yahs]. Tortillas are thin, round, flat breads made from ground-up maize ("maize" is another word for corn flour). Tortillas are the bread for most Mexicans, and they can be eaten alone or filled with *carne* [CAR-neh] (meat) or *frijoles* [free-HO-less] (beans).

Children dancing at a Mexican festival.

Many Mexicans celebrate holidays with *fiestas* [fee-ES-tahs] (festivals), which include singing, dancing, fireworks, parades, and a variety of food. Also, Mexican children love to play a game in which they put on a blindfold and swing a stick at a *piñata* [peen-YAH-tah], a colorful shape usually made out of papier-mâché. When someone hits the piñata, it breaks open and surprises like toys and candy fall out! (See page 189 in this book for a painting called *Piñata*, by the Mexican artist Diego Rivera.)

The flag of Mexico.

One of the most important holidays in Mexico is *el diez y seis de septiembre* [dee-ess-ee-SAYS de sep-tee-EM-bre]. That means the sixteenth of September, and it is Mexico's Independence Day. Now, you may know that the United States fought to gain its independence from England—but which European country do you think Mexico wanted to be independent of? If you said Spain, you're right.

Check your library for more books about Mexico, such as:

Count Your Way Through Mexico by James Haskins (Carolrhoda, 1989)
Mexico by Karen Jacobsen (Childrens Press, 1982)

And Then Came England

Let's go back in history again, almost five hundred years ago, to the time of the Spanish explorers and conquistadors. While Cortés, Pizarro, and others were claiming lands in the New World for Spain, back in Europe people were starting to tell stories. They said that the Spanish were finding incredible treasure in the New World, whole cities full of gold and silver. Now, this wasn't true, but people still told such stories. And the stories made people stop and ask themselves, "Why should the Spanish have all the gold and silver? Let's get some for ourselves, too!"

Some people in England began to think of sending English settlers to the New World. Maybe they would find treasure, too. So the Queen of England, Queen Elizabeth, turned to one of her favorite people, the bold and handsome Sir Walter Raleigh. She asked Sir Walter to get together a group of Englishmen and send them to start a colony in North America. (Do you remember what a "colony" is? A colony is a place ruled by people living in another, often faraway, part of the world.)

There's a famous story about Sir Walter Raleigh and Queen Elizabeth. The story says that one day when the queen was out taking a walk, she came to a big puddle. Would you expect a queen to walk through a puddle and get her feet wet and dirty? Certainly not! What should be done? Sir Walter Raleigh did not hesitate. He took off his fine cloak and spread it out over the puddle for the queen to walk across. Now, that's good manners!

Sir Walter Raleigh sent about a hundred Englishmen in several ships on a trip across the stormy Atlantic Ocean. They landed on an island off the coast of what is now North Carolina. They did not bother to grow food for the coming winter. Instead, they spent much of their time digging for gold—which they didn't find. To get food, they had to trade for it with the Indians. But then the English colonists—who thought they were so much better than the Indians—started bragging about their cities and their religion. Soon the Indians refused to give them any food. So, tired and disappointed, the colonists went back home to England.

The Lost Colony

Still, Sir Walter Raleigh was not ready to give up. He brought together another group of people to go to the New World. This group included not just men but women and children, too. On a fine June day, they set sail for America. But things went wrong from the start. They were supposed to land on the continent of North America, but the ship's captain refused to go any farther than the little island of Roanoke—the same island that the English colonists had left behind only a year before. Would these new-comers have better luck?

The colonists had been in the New World only a few weeks when a happy event occurred: one of the women had a baby. The baby, named Virginia Dare, was the first English child born in the New World. As Virginia grew up, did she like her new home? Did she have a happy childhood? We don't know! Why not? Because we don't know what happened to the colonists on Roanoke Island.

Here is what we *do* know. The ship that brought the colonists to the little island turned around and went back to England for more supplies. The ship was supposed to come back to the colonists within a year. But when the ship got back to England, England was in a war with Spain. So no English ship was able to return to Roanoke for three years! When a ship finally did get back to the island, the crew found no one there. Everyone in the colony was gone. Roanoke was a "lost colony."

The English sailors found nothing but some letters carved into a tree: "CRO." What did "CRO" mean? There was an Indian tribe called the Croatan on a nearby island.

Had the Croatan people attacked the colonists? Or had the colonists gone to live with the Croatan people? Some American Indians who live in North Carolina today say that they are descendants of both the Croatan Indians and the lost colonists. So maybe the colonists did find a new life after all. Or maybe something else happened. It's a mystery in our history!

The letters "CRO" were all that remained of the Lost Colony.

A Lasting English Colony: Jamestown

After these hard times, you might think the English would give up trying to start a colony in the New World. But the English did not want to let Spain take all the riches of the New World. They wanted to find gold. And they wanted some useful things as well.

They wanted to cut trees so that they could get wood to build ships. They wanted to catch the fish that swam in the waters off North America. So the English kept on trying.

Look at the map on page 159. Can you find the area that is now the state of Virginia? Here, in 1607, the English set up their first successful settlement. They named it Jamestown after the English king at the time, James I.

About a hundred men came to Jamestown in 1607—no women came on this trip (they would not arrive until twelve months later). Most of the men came because they wanted to get rich. They expected to find lots of gold. They had heard stories that in the New World you could walk around and pick up diamonds, rubies, and other riches just lying on the ground!

What they found was quite different. The settlers didn't know they had picked a dangerous place to build their fort. The ground was swampy. There were many mosquitoes, which carried a

This is what the fort at Jamestown probably looked like in 1607.

Captain John Smith.

deadly disease called malaria. Even the water was unhealthy, and many of the settlers would get sick from drinking it. Eight months later, only thirty-eight of the original hundred colonists remained alive.

The Jamestown settlers had a strict leader: Captain John Smith. John Smith helped them get through some very hard times. He ordered them to stop looking for gold and instead begin planting corn. Gold may be valuable, but you can't eat it!

Still, the settlers did not have enough food at first. Sometimes they took food from the Indians who lived in the area. Sometimes John Smith was able to trade with the Indians: he traded copper kettles and tools in exchange for corn and other food.

The most powerful Indian leader in the area was called Powhatan by the English settlers (though his real name was Wahunsonacock). He had brought thirty tribes together under his leadership.

The settlers and the Indians didn't trust each other. They each suspected the other of wanting to do something bad. Sometimes they managed to get along peacefully. John Smith said that Powhatan once asked him, "Why should you take by force from us that which you can obtain by love?" Still, sometimes the settlers and Indians fought fiercely.

Jamestown Uncovered

Some very exciting things have been happening at Jamestown lately. For many years, historians thought that the land on which the settlers built their fort had been washed away by the James River. But in 1996 archaeologists discovered the remains of the original fort built in 1607! They found holes and stains in the ground left by decaying logs that formed one of the high walls of the triangle-shaped fort. By carefully digging through layers of ground, the archaeologists also found thousands of objects from the days of the early settlers, including jewelry, coins, tools, swords, and armor. They found sheets of copper metal, which the settlers traded with the Indians for food. And do you know what else they found? A skeleton from those long-ago days! The bones, scientists say, are from a man about five feet six inches tall, who may have died from being shot in the leg.

Pocahontas

Once, John Smith was captured by the people of Powhatan. Nobody knows for sure exactly what happened next. But years later John Smith wrote a book in which he said he was saved by a courageous Indian girl. This girl was Powhatan's daughter. You may know her name—Pocahontas.

In his book, John Smith said that he was about to be killed by the Indians when Pocahontas begged that his life be spared. But no one would listen to the young girl. Heavy clubs were about to come down on Smith's head when suddenly Pocahontas rushed forward. She took Smith's head in her arms, and forced the Indians to choose between hurting her or saving Smith. Pocahontas's father chose to release John Smith.

John Smith might have made up this story. But it has been told over and over, and it became so popular in England that people wrote poems and plays about Pocahontas. The story of Pocahontas is still popular today.

The Pilgrims

Jamestown was the first important English settlement in our country. But only thirteen years after the founding of Jamestown, another important English settlement was started in the north, in what is now the state of Massachusetts (see the map on page 159). It was started by the Pilgrims.

You may already know some things about the Pilgrims (if you've learned about them from the Kindergarten book in this series, or from other books). You might remember their hard voyage in 1620 on the *Mayflower*, as well as the story of the first Thanksgiving. Let's learn more now about who the Pilgrims were and why they came to this country.

The Pilgrims were Christians who believed strongly in living the way they thought the Bible said they should live. But the Pilgrims wanted to worship God in a way that was not allowed in England. Back in those days, many people did not have religious freedom. If you have religious freedom—which you do today—then you are free to make up your own mind about what you believe and how you want to worship. But the Pilgrims did not have this freedom. No: back then, in many places all over the world, kings and other rulers had the power to say, "You must worship my way or leave!"

Well, the Pilgrims left. In fact, that's why we call them "pilgrims." Pilgrims are people who go on a journey—often a religious journey. When the Pilgrims left England,

This painting shows the Pilgrims of Plymouth on their way to church.

they first went to the nearby country of Holland. They went there because the people in Holland had more religious freedom than the people in England.

But the Pilgrims, who were English, didn't feel at home in Holland, where the people spoke a different language. Then some of the Pilgrim leaders had a new idea—more than an idea, really, almost a dream! Maybe, they thought, just maybe, they could begin a new life in the New World—in America! Maybe in America they could make a new home and be free to worship the way they wanted to.

> Here's something to think and talk about. The first English people who came to America came here for different reasons. Why did people come to Jamestown? Why did the Pilgrims come to Plymouth?

In the year 1620 the Pilgrims boarded a tiny ship. (Remember the name? The *Mayflower*.) They crossed the rough Atlantic Ocean. You may already know that when they arrived in America, their lives were terribly hard, and many of them died. But they were courageous. They worked hard and started a small village called Plymouth Plantation. Here they could worship in their own way. For this, they were thankful.

The Puritans

Other English colonists followed the Pilgrims. They also set up their homes in the area called New England. These people were called Puritans. Like the Pilgrims, the Puritans were a deeply religious group of Christians. But even people of the same religion can disagree, and the Puritans did not agree with all the beliefs of the Pilgrims.

The Puritans settled in the area around what is now the city of Boston, in Massachusetts (look at the map on page 159). (Of course, there was no big city back then!) The Puritans worked hard and their colony grew quickly. It was called the Massachusetts Bay Colony. Soon many more Puritans came to America and started other colonies.

What was it like to grow up as a Puritan child? Puritan parents could be strict: they expected children to behave properly at all times. They knew their children couldn't always be perfect, but they expected them to constantly try to be their best. They also placed a great value on learning to read because they felt it was very important to be able to read the Bible.

Puritan children would often learn their letters from a little book called a primer (which rhymes with "swimmer"). You may still hear that word used today: a "primer" is a first book for a beginning reader. One primer that many Puritan children used was named *The New England Primer*. It taught a little rhyme to go along with each letter of the alphabet. Often the rhymes tried to teach a lesson. For example, for the letter "F," children read:

> The idle Fool
> Is whipped at school.

You wouldn't want to be caught daydreaming in a Puritan school!

A page from *The New England Primer*.

Slavery Comes to the Colonies

The Pilgrims and Puritans, as well as the first settlers of Jamestown, came to America because they wanted to. But one group of people came to America because they were forced to.

What do you know about slavery? (Have you learned about slavery from the Kindergarten book in this series, or from other books?)

The first black people who came to Jamestown were not exactly slaves. In 1619 a ship arrived at Jamestown carrying people from Africa. These people had been taken from their homes and forced to get on a ship that brought them to America. They were sold to the Virginia settlers, and they were made to work, usually on farms. But after they worked for a number of years, they were allowed to go free. When they were free, some of them bought land where they could farm and make their homes.

But soon the white people of Virginia decided they would not let their black workers go free. As the years went on, big farms were started in Virginia and other Southern colonies. These farms were called plantations. The owners of these big farms needed lots of workers to grow their crops of tobacco, rice, and (later) cotton. And

Slaves working on a sugarcane plantation.

so, more and more people were taken from Africa and brought to America. Here, they were forced to work as slaves on the big farms.

Many of these people did not survive the terrible voyage across the Atlantic Ocean. This voyage was called the Middle Passage. Africans were jammed into ships that were dirty and unhealthy, and many died along the way.

If you've read the World History and Geography section of this book, then you may remember hearing about slaves in ancient civilizations, thousands of years before Jamestown and thousands of miles from America. Many civilizations have forced some

This picture shows the terrible crowding on a ship carrying slaves.

people to work as slaves. The Egyptians forced the Jewish people to work as slaves. The Aztecs made slaves of the people they conquered. In Africa, too, some people forced others to be slaves. But just because slavery happened often, that doesn't make it right. Slaves have no freedom. They have no rights. To take away someone's freedom is to treat someone like a thing, not a human being—and that is absolutely wrong.

In America some people did believe that slavery was wrong. But from the time that the first Africans were brought to Jamestown in 1619, it would take more than two hundred years before slavery was ended in America. And it would take a terrible war to do this. (You'll learn about this war in the next book in this series.)

Thirteen Colonies

Do you remember when the first English settlers arrived at Jamestown? (In 1607.) How about Plymouth? (In 1620.) Over the next century—that's one hundred years— more and more people moved from Europe to America. Most came from England, but others came from France, Holland, Germany, and other countries. Some people came to the Virginia and the Massachusetts Bay colonies. Other people started new colonies: the Dutch (who came from Holland) started a colony in what is now New York.

As the years passed, thirteen colonies grew up in the eastern part of the country near the Atlantic Ocean. Later these thirteen colonies would become the first states of the United States. Use the map on page 159 to locate and name the thirteen colonies.

A colony, you may remember, is an area ruled by the government of a faraway country. The thirteen colonies in America were ruled by the king of faraway England. How did

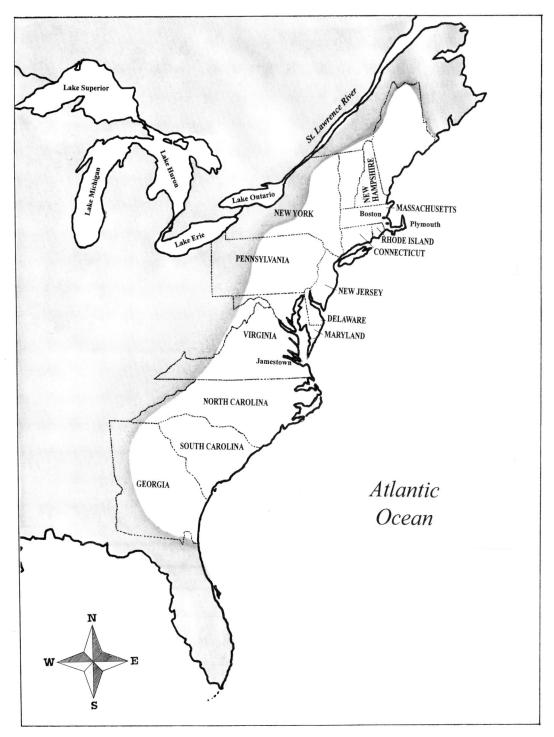

The thirteen colonies.

these thirteen colonies break away from England and become the first thirteen states of a new country called the United States of America? That's what you're about to find out!

The Colonists and the King

Let's move ahead many years to the 1760s: that's about 150 years after the first settlers arrived at Jamestown. In the 1760s the thirteen English colonies in America were growing. The colonists were happy. They were proud to be English and proud to be ruled by King George III. They were so proud that they even named towns and colleges after the king, like Georgetown and King's College.

But then things started to change. King George started to do things that worried the colonists. He made laws the colonists did not like. And he ordered them to pay taxes on things like sugar, stamps, and paper—which meant that when the colonists bought some paper, they had to pay whatever the paper cost, of course, but then they had to pay some *extra* money. This extra money was a tax.

A tax is money that a government charges people to pay for things the government does—things like build roads, or pay for soldiers and what the soldiers need to fight a war. The taxes the American colonists paid went straight to the British government. At this time King George needed lots of money because England had just fought a very expensive war against France.

The Boston Tea Party

As King George made more laws and charged more taxes, many colonists got worried and upset. Some colonists spoke out: "The king is way across the ocean in England," they said. "He doesn't really know what's good for us here in the American colonies." But many colonists still liked the king. They said, "If we just explain our worries to the king, he will understand."

WHAT'S "BRITISH"?

Sometimes people use the word "British" the same way they use the word "English." Are "British" and "English" the same? Not quite, but they're close. "British" comes from the name Great Britain. A long time ago, the little country of England took over some other lands. The English used the name Great Britain for their own country of England and for the lands nearby that England took over. That's why people who come from England are called "English" but also "British."

So the colonists tried to explain. And they kept on explaining, but things didn't change. The colonists got more worried. They thought, "If we have to keep paying taxes, and if the king keeps sending us laws we don't like, then pretty soon we won't have any money left and we won't be free to do anything!"

Then King George placed a new tax on something that almost every colonist bought a lot of—tea. Well, that was the last straw! The colonists said, "The king just doesn't get it! He needs to be shown that we colonists are not kidding!" And so they planned a "tea party"—but, as you'll see, it was a very strange party!

On a cold day in December, a ship arrived in Boston harbor. It was carrying a load of tea. Many colonists were angry. They did not want to pay taxes on this tea. So, that night, a group of colonists dressed like Mohawk Indians tiptoed onto the docks at Boston harbor. They quietly boarded the ship that brought the tea. They worked quickly. What did they do? They dumped 250 chests of tea into Boston harbor! They would show the king what they thought of his taxes!

That was the Boston Tea Party—and nobody drank any tea!

A Fight with Mother?

When the British heard about the Boston Tea Party, they were mad—no, they were furious! King George decided to punish the colonists. He closed the port of Boston, and that hurt the colonists. Many people depended on the ships going in and out of Boston. The ships carried away things that the colonists wanted to sell to other countries. And the ships brought in things that the colonists needed or wanted from other countries. So, closing the port meant that the colonists lost money and jobs. And that made them mad.

The Boston Tea Party.

A Redcoat and a Minuteman.

The British government did other things that made the colonists mad. The people in Boston were not allowed to come together in town meetings. British soldiers were sent to keep order. Soon British soldiers were everywhere. They wore uniforms that were bright red, and many colonists began to refer to them angrily as "the Redcoats."

Americans started to think things they had never thought before. Some even began to say that maybe they would have to *fight England*, their own mother country, to be free! Maybe they would have to do battle with the Redcoats!

This was a scary idea, but more and more people began to think it was a good idea. In Massachusetts the colonists formed groups of men to fight the British, if it came to that. They were called Minutemen because they could be ready to fight in a minute. The colonists also gathered weapons and ammunition. They hid them outside Boston in Concord, Massachusetts.

While many colonists wanted to break free of England, others did not. These people were called Tories. The Tories were colonists who were still on the side of King George and the government of England.

Of course, the British soldiers didn't like this at all. They decided to find the colonists' weapons and take them away. But the colonists were ready. They had spies keeping watch to see when the Redcoats would make their move.

The Midnight Ride of Paul Revere

Well, the British did make their move. But one colonist, a silversmith named Paul Revere, knew they were coming. How did he know? He had already made plans with a friend in Boston who was keeping an eye on the British soldiers. If and when the Redcoats started to move toward Concord, then Paul Revere's friend was to send a signal from high in the steeple of a church tower. The signal was: "One if by land, two if by sea." That meant: "Light one lamp if the British troops are marching by land from Boston to Concord. But light two lamps if the British are coming in boats or across the bay."

On a clear spring evening, two lamps shone in the steeple of the Old North Church.

Paul Revere knew the British were coming by sea. He got into a small boat and rowed silently past a large British warship in Boston harbor. Although it was a bright night, he made it safely to the other side. There he leapt onto a fine horse and galloped off.

It was near midnight. Most people in the towns of Lexington and Concord were in bed. Paul Revere had to wake them up. He had to warn them that the British soldiers were coming. So he rode through the towns, shouting his warning, "The Redcoats are coming! The Redcoats are coming!"

Now, you may find this hard to believe, but as Paul Revere shouted his warning, someone actually shouted back, "Quiet down! You're making too much noise!" "Noise!" said Paul Revere; "you'll have noise enough before long!" And Paul Revere was right. Following his warning, American Minutemen were getting dressed and grabbing their muskets.

Paul Revere warns the colonists.

A Nation Is Born—July 4, 1776

The very next day, at Lexington and Concord, the Minutemen were waiting for the Redcoats. The Redcoats came. A shot was fired; more shots rang out. A famous poem says that first shot was "the shot heard round the world." No, not because it was loud but because it was important, *very* important. It was the beginning of a war that would lead to a new nation.

We call that war the American Revolution, or sometimes the Revolutionary War, or sometimes just the Revolution. One meaning of the word "revolution" is "a really big change." The American Revolution was certainly a big change. It turned out to be more than just a little fight between the colonists and their mother country over weapons and taxes. It became a big fight about being free, about being our own country and ruling ourselves.

In 1776—a year after the first shots were fired at Lexington and Concord—the colonists took a very big step. They told King George that Americans wanted to be free and start their own country—a country called the United States of America.

On the fourth of July, in the year 1776, many American leaders signed the Declaration of Independence. That's why we still celebrate every fourth of July as Independence Day, the birthday of our nation. Do you remember (from the Kindergarten book in this series) who wrote the Declaration of Independence? His face is on the nickel: his name is Thomas Jefferson.

The Declaration of Independence said:

> **We hold these truths to be self-evident;**
> **that all men are created equal;**
> **that they are endowed by their Creator**
> **with certain unalienable rights.**

Those are important words: see if you can memorize them.

Think about what they mean. What did Jefferson mean when he said that some "truths" are "self-evident"? He meant: "Anyone can plainly see that this is true." What is true? "That all men are created equal" (back then, people sometimes used "men" to mean "everyone"). Well, that was a bold statement: no one had ever started a country before with the idea that "all men are created equal." Do you think King George agreed? Would he accept the idea that a king and his subjects "are created equal"? No!

And the king definitely wouldn't like the idea that all people have "certain unalienable rights." "Unalienable" means that nobody—not even a king—can take away those rights. Jefferson said that people have the right to be free and decide how to rule themselves. He said, "King George, we are not going to listen to you anymore. We have the right to decide for ourselves how to rule our own country!"

Thomas Jefferson and his fellow Americans knew they were doing something new, something big, something *revolutionary*. They were starting a new nation. They were making a new government. Could they make it work? Were they ready for a democracy—a government by the people, not by a king?

Jefferson thought Americans were ready. He said other people around the world would look to America to see if we could make democracy work. But first, the United States had to win the war against England.

Let Freedom Ring! The Liberty Bell

If you had been in the city of Philadelphia on July 4, 1776, you would have heard the ringing of a big bell, the Liberty Bell. From the town hall, the Liberty Bell rang out news of American independence.

Why would people use a bell to announce important news? Do you think they had radio, telephones, or television back then?

When the bell rang, the people of Philadelphia gathered to hear the first reading of the Declaration of Independence. After independence was won, the bell was rung on special occasions. Almost sixty years later, it cracked. But it still remains a symbol of our country. You can see the Liberty Bell if you go to Philadelphia.

The Liberty Bell.

Some Revolutionary Lives

Our war for independence from England was a long and hard war. Often our soldiers didn't have enough to eat. They didn't get paid. Their clothes were in tatters. Sometimes they had to march through snow with no shoes. They wrapped their feet in rags.

The British had more soldiers and more guns, but still the Americans did not give up. They fought hard for what they believed in. They fought for their dream of a free country where the people could rule themselves. And in the end, after years of fighting, during which many soldiers died, that dream came true. The Americans won, and we became a free and independent country.

Let's meet some of these Americans who helped our country. Some were soldiers, and some helped in other ways.

During a thunderstorm, Ben Franklin flew a kite. No, he wasn't being silly! He was conducting an experiment in which he proved that lightning is electricity. In fact, it's *very powerful* electricity, so *don't try this at home!*

An Inventive Man: Ben Franklin

A little lightbulb should go off in your head when you think of Benjamin Franklin. Why? Because he was so bright! And because he was one of the first people to make some important discoveries about electricity.

Benjamin Franklin was born into a family with many children and very little money. But that didn't bother young Ben. He loved learning, he liked to experiment, and he was willing to work very hard. When he was still a young man, he started a printing business, published a newspaper, and taught himself to read four different languages.

Ben Franklin's Wisdom

Ben Franklin wrote a lot, including a book called *Poor Richard's Almanac*. An "almanac" is a book that comes out every year and is filled with lots of information about the weather, about growing crops, and about all sorts of other things. In *Poor Richard's Almanac*, Ben Franklin included many bits of advice on how to live a successful and happy life. Some of these bits of advice have become famous sayings. See if you have heard any of these, and think about what they mean:

Early to bed and early to rise, makes a man healthy, wealthy, and wise.

Little strokes fell great oaks.

Lost time is never found again.

Ben Franklin was one of the American leaders who signed the Declaration of Independence. During the Revolutionary War, he was sent to France. Why so far away? Because Americans hoped that Franklin could get the French to help us in our fight against the British. And Ben Franklin did just that: he convinced the French to send soldiers to America, and those French troops helped us win the war.

A Courageous Woman: Deborah Sampson

Deborah Sampson was a young woman with big dreams. When the Revolution started, she helped on her family's farm and worked to get food to the American soldiers. But Deborah wanted to do more. She wanted to fight the British and help the Americans win the war.

In those days, women weren't allowed to fight in the army. People wanted to protect women from the dangers of war, and some people thought women were too weak to fight. But not Deborah Sampson.

So Deborah thought of a plan. She dressed up like a man. She called herself "Robert Shurtleff," and she joined the American army!

Deborah (or "Robert") was well liked by her fellow soldiers, and nobody suspected she was a woman. She fought bravely in several battles, and once she was wounded in the leg. Deborah hid her wound so that no doctor could treat her and find out she wasn't a man! Her leg wound got better, but later she was wounded again and ran a high fever. Her captain put her in the hospital in Philadelphia. When the doctors discovered she was a woman, they said, "Really, Miss Sampson, we think you should go home now."

Deborah did go home. But for almost a year, she had managed to fool everyone—and to serve her country.

Deborah Sampson fought bravely for her country.

A Poet for Freedom: Phillis Wheatley

Phillis Wheatley came to America on a slave ship when she was only eight years old. She was sold to a merchant in Boston named John Wheatley. Mr. Wheatley and his wife did something very unusual. They taught Phillis to read and write—which was something that almost no slaves were taught to do.

Phillis studied hard. She used her knowledge and talents to write poetry. She wrote very good poetry, and people began to notice her. In 1773, before the Revolution started, Phillis published her first book of poems.

In some of her poems, Phillis Wheatley asked the colonists to think. How could they demand freedom from England, Phillis asked, but at the same time make people like herself live as slaves? How, Phillis wondered, could people say, "We have a right to be free!" and then say, "You people from Africa must continue to be slaves"?

Phillis was not a slave for her whole life. The Wheatleys freed her, and she married a free black man and kept on writing.

A Father to His Country: George Washington

What do you already know about George Washington? Have you learned about "the father of our country" in other books? (You can find out about him in the Kindergarten book in this series.)

George Washington may have done more than anyone

The poet Phillis Wheatley.

else to help win the American Revolution. When our war for independence started, there was no American army. Each colony sent men who wanted to help fight for liberty, but these men were not soldiers. They were farmers, blacksmiths, shoemakers, carpenters, and shopkeepers. Who would turn them into an army and lead them in battle?

George Washington. He taught them how to fight together. He stayed with them through terrible hardships. For eight years General Washington commanded the American soldiers against the mighty British army, and he led them to victory.

There's a story about George Washington that says a lot about the kind of leader he was. The story goes like this:

One day during the Revolutionary War, some soldiers were struggling to lift a huge log into place. One of the soldiers was giving orders to the others. Now, in the army, people have different

George Washington leads the American soldiers.

ranks, such as sergeant, captain, and, at the top, general. People of higher rank are in charge and can give orders to people of lower rank. So, on this day, a man with the rank of corporal—which is not a very high rank—was giving orders to the soldiers trying to lift the heavy log. "Heave-ho, men!" the corporal shouted. "Come on! Put your backs into it!"

Just then a stranger rode up on a horse. The stranger was not wearing a military uniform. The stranger asked the corporal, "Why don't you help your men?" The corporal looked at the stranger with amazement. Then he said, in a very proud voice, as though he were a great king or emperor, "Sir, I am a *corporal!*"

"You are?" replied the stranger. Then he got down from his horse, took off his hat, and bowed to the corporal. "I beg your pardon, Mr. Corporal," he said. The stranger helped the soldiers lift the heavy log. He pushed and pulled and sweated with the soldiers until finally they got the log in place.

Then the stranger turned to the corporal and said, "Mr. Corporal, when you have another job and do not have enough men to do it, send for your general and I will come again to help you." The corporal's mouth fell open: it was General Washington!

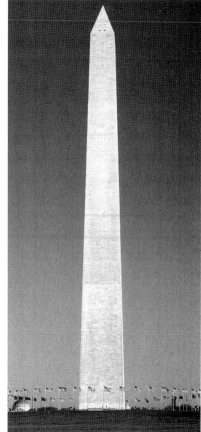

When the Revolutionary War was over, some people thought George Washington was so great a leader that he should be crowned King of America! But Washington said he didn't fight the British just so the United States could have another King George! After the war he went back home to his farm.

But a little while later, Americans decided their new country needed a strong leader—not a king but a president. They wanted George Washington because they felt he was "first in war, first in peace and first in the hearts of his countrymen." Now, part of George Washington wanted to stay at Mount Vernon, his home in Virginia, with his wife, Martha. But another part of him knew that he had to do what was right for his country. And so, George Washington became our first President.

Because he did so much for America, George Washington is called "the father of our country." Our nation's capital, Washington, D.C., is named after him.

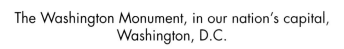

The Washington Monument, in our nation's capital, Washington, D.C.

HOW DOES A PERSON BECOME PRESIDENT?

Do you remember? Is it like a king, who is born into a royal family?

No: the American people *choose* the President. We *vote* for the person we want to lead our country.

"And called it macaroni"!

Here's part of a song you may know.

> *Yankee Doodle went to town,*
> *A-riding on a pony.*
> *Stuck a feather in his cap*
> *And called it macaroni.*

Have you ever sung "Yankee Doodle"? Did you know that it comes from the American Revolution? Here's some more of the song:

> *Father and I went down to camp*
> *Along with Captain Gooding,*
> *And there we saw both men and boys*
> *As thick as hasty pudding.*
>
> *And there was Captain Washington*
> *Upon a slapping stallion,*
> *A-giving orders to his men,*
> *There must have been a million.*
>
> *Yankee Doodle, keep it up,*
> *Yankee Doodle dandy,*
> *Mind the music and the step,*
> *And with the girls be handy.*

It was the British who came up with the name Yankee Doodle. They used it to insult the Americans. But the Americans said, "Fine, call us Yankees! We like the name, and we'll sing the song, too!" And "Yankee Doodle" has been a favorite song of the American people ever since. (By the way, "hasty pudding" is a thick pudding made of cornmeal or oatmeal.)

Freedom for All?

The American Revolution brought on big changes, but it didn't change everything. Did the Declaration of Independence make women as free as men? No. Did it free the slaves? No. Even after the Revolution, women did not have the same rights as men— for example, women could not vote. And slaves had no rights at all.

Sometimes the hardest thing to change is the way people think and act. People don't change all at once. It would take time for Americans to understand the ideals—that means the most important goals—behind the American Revolution, especially the ideal that "all men are created equal . . . with certain unalienable rights."

Still, with the Revolution, Americans took a big and daring step. We said, "We won't have a king. We, the people, will vote and decide!" That was a new idea—it was downright revolutionary!

America Grows

Look on page 159 at the map of the original thirteen colonies. After the Revolution, these became the first thirteen states of the United States of America.

Do you see how all those states are on the coast of the Atlantic Ocean? But the United States is now a country that stretches "from sea to shining sea"—from the Atlantic Ocean to what other ocean? That's right, the Pacific. So how did this happen? How did this country grow from east to west, "from sea to shining sea"?

It happened in many ways, over many years. It began even before the Revolutionary War, when Americans were still under British rule. More and more Americans kept moving away from the Atlantic Ocean. In what direction were they going? To the west. They were going into the "frontier"—into places without settlements or towns, places that were new and strange to them. They didn't know where they were going, but they were helped by trailblazers like Daniel Boone.

Do you know what it means to "blaze a trail"? A trail is a path through the wilderness. To make a path, sometimes you have to cut your way through a forest thick with trees and bushes and briers. "Blazing a trail" means marking trees with paint or small cuts so that others can follow where you have gone.

Daniel Boone was a trailblazer. He set out to find a path through the Appalachian Mountains that would lead him to the good farmland in Kentucky. (Look at the map on page 173; can you find the Appalachian Mountains?) At first Daniel Boone couldn't find a way through the mountains: they just stood there, big and high and hard to get over. But then he found an Indian trail that led through a gap—a space—in the mountains.

Later, in 1775 (just a year before the signing of—remember?—the Declaration of Independence), Daniel Boone and some helpers set to work. They cut down trees and

Daniel Boone.

moved big rocks and turned the Indian trail into a road wide enough for families to travel on. This road was called the Wilderness Road. In just a few years, thousands of frontiersmen and frontierswomen were heading west on the Wilderness Road. They were looking for land they could farm and build their homes on.

Daniel Boone and the settlers who followed him often fought with the American Indians. For the Indians, these settlers meant trouble because they were making their farms and homes on the land where the Indians hunted. How would the Indians live if the settlers scared away the animals the Indians needed for food and many other uses? But the settlers were not concerned with what the Indians needed. The settlers knew what they wanted: land, and lots of it. And so they kept coming, thousands of them. They built homes, forts, and towns, including Boonesboro, named after the trailblazer who opened the way west.

What a Bargain! The Louisiana Purchase

Have you ever heard your parents or a friend say, "I got a bargain"? Which means, "I got a great deal! I bought something and paid a lot less money than it's worth!"

The United States got a really great bargain in the year 1803. At the time, Thomas Jefferson was President—our country's third President, by the way. (Do you remember what he wrote at the beginning of the American Revolution?) President Jefferson wanted to buy some land that was claimed by France. The land was on the Mississippi River and included the small city of New Orleans (which is now a *big* city).

France did not want to sell just the little bit of land that Jefferson wanted. Instead, France wanted to sell *all* the land she claimed. It was so much land, and for such a low price, that Jefferson said, "Yes!"

This bargain is called the Louisiana Purchase ("to purchase" means the same thing as "to buy"). Louisiana is the name the French gave to the land, in honor of the King of France, King Louis [LOO-ee]. Overnight, the Louisiana Purchase made our country more than twice as big! Take a look at the map below and see.

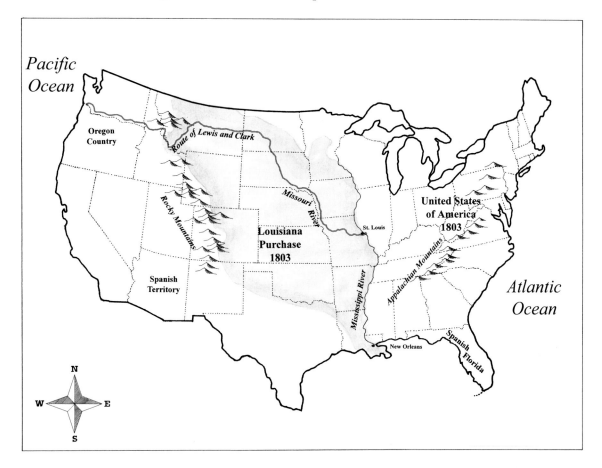

Thomas Jefferson wanted to know more about all the land out west that he'd bought for the United States. He wanted to know how far west the land went. He wanted to know what Native American people lived there, and what kinds of animals and plants there were. So he sent a group of men to explore it. They were led by Lewis and Clark. That's two men, Meriwether Lewis and William Clark. With their men and supplies, they set off on boats, heading west on the Missouri River. (Find this river on the map shown above.)

Lewis and Clark didn't have modern equipment like cameras or tape recorders. So, to collect the information that President Jefferson wanted, every day they wrote descriptions of what they saw. They drew lots of pictures and made many maps.

A painting of Sacajawea pointing the way for Lewis and Clark.

They saw animals they had never seen before, including huge herds of buffalo, and poisonous rattlesnakes. Once, a grizzly bear chased Lewis up a tree!

Lewis and Clark met many American Indians along the way. They traveled through the lands of the Cheyenne, Crow, Nez Perce, Chinook, and others. They met a young woman named Sacajawea, of the Shoshone tribe. She helped guide them on part of their journey through the rough Rocky Mountains, and she spoke for them when they met other Native Americans.

Sacajawea did not go with Lewis and Clark to the end of their journey, which finally took them all the way to the Pacific Ocean. But when they reached the Pacific, Lewis and Clark knew that without the skill and help of Sacajawea they might not have made it.

Looking Ahead

You know how some books have chapters? Well, if you imagine American history as a big book, then what you've learned so far is like the first chapters. You've learned about the early Indian civilizations, the Spanish conquerors, and the English settlers. You've seen how thirteen colonies of England declared their independence and fought to become a new country, the United States of America. And you've seen how that country started to grow "from sea to shining sea."

There are many more exciting chapters ahead in the story of American history. In the Second Grade book in this series, you'll learn about how the new nation, the United States, decided—after lots of arguments!—to make laws and govern itself. You'll find out about how the Americans got into *another* war with England—a war that gave us our national anthem ("Oh, say, can you see by the dawn's early light . . ."). You'll follow more settlers as they move west, and learn about how this affected the Native Americans. You'll read the story of a terrible war with a good result. It was terrible because Americans fought against Americans, and many people died; but it led to the end of slavery in this country. And you'll learn how America has grown and changed as many people from countries all over the world have become part of this country.

III.

Visual Arts

INTRODUCTION

For the first grader, art should mostly take the form of *doing:* drawing, painting, cutting and pasting, working with clay and other materials. In this section, we suggest many activities your child can do, sometimes with your help. You can also find good art activities in some of the books recommended below.

By reading this section aloud with your child, you can also help him or her learn some of the ways that we talk about art, and introduce some wonderful works of art. In this way, your child will come to understand that, while art is *doing,* it is also *seeing and thinking.* By looking closely at art, and talking about it, your child will begin to develop a love of art and a habit of enjoying it in thoughtful, active ways.

But let us repeat: Beyond looking at art and talking about it, do try to provide your child with materials and opportunities to be a practicing artist!

Suggested Resources

Activity Books
Kids Create! Art and Craft Experiences for 3- to 9-Year-Olds by Laurie Carlson; and *The Kids' Multicultural Art Book: Art and Craft Experiences from Around the World* by Alexandra M. Terzian (Williamson Publishing, 1990 and 1993)

Mudworks: Creative Clay, Dough, and Modeling Experiences and *Scribble Cookies and Other Independent Creative Art Experiences for Children* by MaryAnn F. Krohl (Bright Ring Publishing, 1985 and 1989)

Books That Reprint Artworks for Children
A Child's Book of Art: Great Pictures, First Words by Lucy Micklethwait (Dorling Kindersley, 1993)

The *Come Look with Me* series by Gladys Blizzard (Thomasson-Grant), including *Come Look with Me: Enjoying Art with Children* (1990); *Come Look with Me: Animals in Art* (1992); *Come Look with Me: World of Play* (1993); *Come Look with Me: Exploring Landscape Art with Children* (1992)

Pictures Tell Stories: A Collections for Young Scholars Book by John Grandits (Open Court, 1995)

People Have Been Making Art for a *Very* Long Time

Pretend that you're exploring a mountainside. You come upon a big, dark hole in the rock: it's a cave! You take out a flashlight and use it to light your way as you go inside. It's cool, damp, and dark. The ground is rough and slippery. Whoops—you almost fall! As you throw out your hands to steady yourself, the flashlight shines on the wall of the cave, and that's when you notice something. It's a picture—a small drawing. You shine your light and look closely. You see the figures of some animals. Who drew these pictures? What artist would use the wall of a cave instead of a piece of paper?

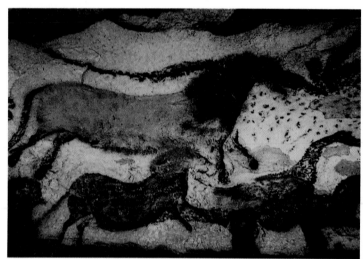

Well, how about an artist who lived long before paper was invented? These pictures on a cave wall were drawn by a person so many thousands of years ago that it's hard to imagine—almost thirty thousand years ago!

Drawings by the world's earliest artists have been found on the walls of caves in France, Spain, and right here in the United States. Why do you think these early people drew pictures of animals? Were the animals important to these early people? (You can find out more about these long-long-ago people in the World History and Geography section of this book; see pages 111–13.)

As the cave paintings show, people have been making art for a *very* long time. Long after the cave people, but still thousands of years before you were born, the people in ancient Egypt made beautiful and amazing works of art. For the ancient Egyptians, art was an important part of their religion. If you have read the World History and Geography section of

This is one of the decorated mummy cases made for King Tut's mummy.

A sculpture of the Egyptian queen Nefertiti.

this book, then you know about some of the wonderful works of the ancient Egyptians, such as the pyramids, or the Great Sphinx, or the mummy cases.

Activity: If you can find a *really big* cardboard box that no one is using, like the kind of carton a refrigerator comes in, you can pretend to make your own cave art, using the box for a cave. What animals will you draw on the inside? Bear and deer? Buffalo and horses?

A World of Color

Do you have a favorite color? Let's look at color in a painting by the French artist Claude Monet [moe-NAY]. Monet loved light and color. He liked to go

outside and set up his easel and paint in the bright sunlight. What is the first color you notice in Monet's painting called *Tulips in Holland?* Do you see how Monet was not worried about giving each object a sharp outline? For example, look at the windmill: it looks a little blurred. Monet was more interested in creating the impression of a field of brightly colored tulips.

Do you remember (from the Kindergarten book in this series) how some colors seem "warm," such as yellow, orange, and red, while others seem "cool," such as blue, green, and violet? Do you see how Monet has balanced the cool colors of the sky with the warm colors of the flowers? Which color seems to stand out more? (Warm colors like red seem to jump forward, while cool colors like blue seem to be farther away.)

Here are three colors:

red   yellow   blue

Red, yellow, and blue are sometimes called the *primary colors.** You cannot make them by mixing any other colors together. But you can make other colors when you mix together red, yellow, and blue. Here's what you get:

Not all paintings are filled with bright colors. Some artists express themselves by leaving bright colors out of their paintings. Look at this painting by the American painter James McNeill Whistler. Many people know this painting by its popular nickname, *Whistler's Mother*.

Though many people call this painting *Whistler's Mother*, Whistler himself gave it a different title. Before you find out that title, here's a question: does Whistler use any bright colors in this picture? Whistler called this painting *Arrangement in Gray and Black*. When you look at the painting, what kind of person do you think Whistler's mother was? Does she look like a happy, fun-loving person, ready to get up and dance around the room? Do you see how the white of her cap, cuffs, and handkerchief attracts your attention to her face and hands? How would you describe the expression on her face?

Activity: Different colors can make us feel different ways. Try drawing two pictures of the same object, such as a house, bird, car, or person. Color one with lots of bright colors, like red, yellow, and orange. Color the other with dark colors, like brown, dark gray, and dark green. Which do you like better?

Get in Line!

Take a pencil and make a dot on a sheet of paper. Now, put your pencil on the dot and let it wander away from it. Now you have a *line*.

A line starts with a dot and then goes somewhere. Lines come in all types—straight, curved, zigzag, wavy, and spiral.

Lines can be fat or skinny, rough or fine, depending on how they are made. Use a sharp pencil and you can make a fine line. With a big piece of chalk you can make a rough line.

Activity: Gather together some drawing materials: pencils, fine-point markers, ink pens, chalk, and crayons. Use them to fill a page with different lines: straight, curved, wavy, zigzag, and spiral. Experiment with how hard you press down on the paper. Does this change how the lines look?

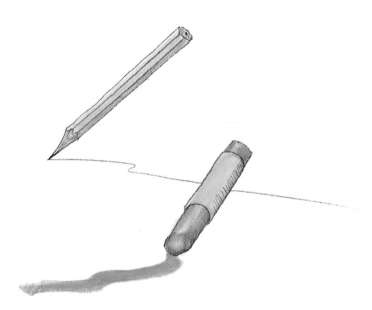

Activity: Try drawing an animal using only lines. You can draw a real or imaginary animal. What types of lines did you use? For fun try drawing an animal out of only straight lines and another out of only curved lines.

Here is a picture made only from lines. Can you name the animal? This drawing, called *The Swan*, is by the French artist Henri Matisse [on-REE ma-TEECE]. What type of lines does Matisse use for the neck of the swan? Curved lines can seem graceful. Look for some of the other curved lines in the drawing.

Henri Matisse, *The Swan*, 1932.

Here is a painting by the American artist Georgia O'Keeffe. In this painting, called *Shell No. 1*, do you see one type of line that stands out

more than the others? Do you see the spiral line? A spiral line is a line that keeps curving inside itself. Have you ever slid down a spiral sliding board? Put your finger at the center of the shell and follow the spiral.

Georgia O'Keeffe loved things of nature like flowers, bones, and shells. She painted them very carefully, and she often made them much bigger than they really were so that people could not miss them! For example, the little shell O'Keeffe painted was only an inch or two from side to side, but she painted it the size of a beach ball.

Get in Shape!

When lines join together, they make shapes. Anytime you cut something out or draw on paper, you are creating shapes. Here is the shape of a person, cut out of construction paper. The shape of a real person can change as the person moves. But other shapes remain pretty much the same. Can you name these shapes?

Here are three other shapes: a rectangle, an oval, and a diamond?

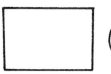

Different shapes can sometimes make you feel and think different things. Look again at the circle and the square. Which one makes you think of something moving? Circles roll: think of wheels, marbles, balls. Squares and rectangles seem to rest in one place: think of a big rectangular object, like a refrigerator. Triangles have points, and the points can make you think of something moving in a certain direction, like a rocket rising into the sky.

Activity: Make a shapes collage. You'll need construction paper of different colors, a piece of white paper, scissors, and glue. Using the colored construction paper, cut out the following shapes: square, rectangle, triangle, diamond, circle, semicircle, and oval. You can cut more than one of each shape, in different colors and sizes. Paste your shapes onto the white piece of paper. Now, can you point to each shape and say its name? If you like, you can label one of each shape by writing its shape name on it with a crayon or a marker.

Let's try something: we're going to look at a picture and try to focus our eyes just on the shapes in it. Try not to notice all the colors and patterns, but instead look at the way the painter uses basic shapes in his painting.

Look at the painting called *Stone City, Iowa,* by the American artist Grant Wood. Have you ever been up so high that when you looked down everything seemed to look like little shapes? Can you tell that we are looking down in this picture? Look at the houses: they look like rectangles with triangular roofs. What shape does Wood use for the treetops?

Activity: If you have a piece of tracing paper, place it over the picture of Grant Wood's painting here and trace over the basic shapes: squares, rectangles, circles, triangles. When you finish, look at your tracing. Where do you see most of the circular shapes? Where does the artist place most of the rectangles?

Let's look at shapes in another painting, called *Parade* (on the next page). It's by the African American artist Jacob Lawrence. Look at the people in the bottom left corner of the painting. What shapes does Lawrence use to paint their bodies? Can you see how their heads are circles, and from their shoulders down they form boxes like rectangles? Can you find other rectangles in the painting? Look near the top, at the windows, the door, and the pattern on the wall. Now look at the band members marching in the parade. Can you see shapes in the way the artist has painted their bodies?

Of course, you see more than just shapes in *Parade*. What else do you notice in the painting? If you could march in this parade, which costume would you like to wear? What do you think you would hear around you?

Activity: If you have a piece of tracing paper, place it over the picture. Look at the man almost in the middle, dressed all in black. Draw a line from the top of his hat, down the left side of his body to his foot, then across to the other foot, then back up to his hat. What shape have you drawn? Did you make a triangle? Do you see how many of the people marching in the parade can be outlined in a triangle? You could almost say that Jacob Lawrence has painted a parade of marching triangles!

Look Closely!

You've looked at colors, lines, and shapes in different paintings. Let's look at all of them in this painting. It's called *Piñata,* by the Mexican artist Diego Rivera [dee-AY-go ree-VAIR-ah]. (Do you know what a *piñata* is? If you don't, you can find out on page 150 in this book.) What colors do you see in this painting? Can you find different lines and shapes, and point to them and name them?

Texture: Oh, What a Feeling!

Imagine that you're holding a kitten. How do you think it would feel? Did you think of a word like "soft" or "furry"?

Now imagine that you're holding a frog that has just jumped out of a swamp. How do you think it would feel? Did you think of a word like "slimy" or "bumpy"?

When you talk about the way something feels, you're talking about its *texture*. When you describe the texture of an object, you might use a word like "rough," "scratchy," "prickly," "bumpy," or "crinkly."

Activity: Gather some everyday items with different textures, for example: leaves, marbles, nuts and bolts, cereal, a sponge, a blanket, cotton balls, wood, aluminum foil, shells. Feel each object and then try to think of a word to describe its texture.

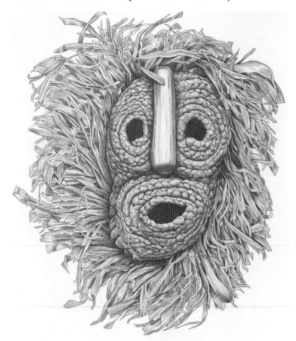

Look at this Native American mask. This mask was made for a member of the Iroquois Husk Face Society. The Iroquois Indians wore these masks in special ceremonies in which they asked the harvest spirits they believed in to help the crops grow. Can you tell what the mask is made of? Corn husks! Do you see how the artist has braided strands of corn husks to create the pattern of a face? The artist left other husks loose so they look like flowing hair. What words can you think of to describe its texture?

Sometimes artists use texture to make their art look very real. Look at this sculpture, made over a hundred years ago by a French artist named Edgar Degas [day-GAH]. The body of the dancer is cast out of a hard substance, but Degas has added other materials. The dancer has a shiny satin ribbon in her hair, and she wears a tutu of a soft material called muslin. When people in France first saw this sculpture, they were shocked. They were used to seeing statues made out of hard substances like stone. But they were surprised to see a

The Little Dancer of Fourteen Years.

statue dressed in materials that a real person might wear!

Some painters use different ways of painting to help you imagine the texture of the objects in the picture. They can paint a dress that looks smooth or a mountainside that looks rough. You might not be able to touch the objects, but you can imagine how they feel. Look at this painting called *Young Hare* by the German artist Albrecht Dürer [AL-brekt DUR-er]. He used short, separate brush strokes and touches of white to imitate the fluffy texture of the rabbit's fur. It almost makes you want to reach out and pet it!

Looking Good: Portraits

Have you had your picture taken at school? Or is there a picture of you on a wall or shelf at home? Then that's your *portrait*. That's what we call a picture of a person.

Portraits can be taken with a camera, or they can be drawn or painted. Perhaps the most famous portrait in the world is the *Mona Lisa*. It was painted by the Italian artist Leonardo da Vinci [dah VIN-chee] about five hundred years ago. Look at the expression on Mona Lisa's face. For hundreds of years, people have been fascinated by her expression. Is she happy? Is she looking at you or at something else? What do you think she might be thinking?

Some portraits can tell a lot about a person and the times in which he lived. Look at the portrait called *Edward VI as a Child* by Hans Holbein [HOLE-bine], the Younger. Edward's father was a king, King

Henry VIII of England (who lived more than four hundred years ago). The writing at the bottom of the painting (in an old language called Latin) tells Edward to grow up to be like his father. In this portrait, Edward is a little over one year old. Is this how most one-year-old children look? What's the first thing you notice about this child? Some people notice his fine red-and-gold clothing or his fancy hat with an ostrich feather. Do you see the rattle he holds in his left hand? It's made of gold! Where does young Edward seem to be looking? Notice how still and straight he sits. Now, imagine how long it would take to paint a portrait like this. Do you think the real baby Edward sat still in this pose for as long as it took the painter to finish the painting?

Let's look at a portrait of another little boy. Unlike the portrait of Edward VI, this portrait shows the boy's whole body. You might think at first that he's a girl, because of his long hair, red lips, and fancy costume. Little boys in wealthy families sometimes dressed like this a couple of hundred years ago. This little boy's name is Manuel, and his portrait was painted by the Spanish artist Francisco Goya [GOI-yuh]. How does Goya draw your attention to the boy? Look at the color of his clothes: they're bright red, with a shiny sash around his waist. Look at the light that seems to be shining around his head.

But there's more to this portrait than the boy. Don Manuel is holding a string. Where does it go? Can you follow it down and see how it's tied to the leg of the boy's pet bird? But wait a minute: what's that sitting in the darkness behind the bird? Cats! How many cats can you find? You can see two pretty clearly, and if you look very carefully, you can see the eyes of a third cat glowing dimly just a little above the other cats' heads. What are the cats looking at? Cats like to pounce on birds, but does Don Manuel seem to know this?

Don Manuel Osorio Manrique de Zúñiga.

Self-Portraits: Take a Good Look at Yourself

Sometimes an artist paints a portrait of himself. This is called a *self-portrait*. A self-portrait doesn't have to look like a photograph. You can paint yourself in many different ways, and each way will say something different about the way you feel about yourself, and the way you want other people to see you. The Dutch painter Vincent van Gogh [van GOH*] painted many self-portraits. This one shows him when he was thirty-six years old.

How does van Gogh look to you? Does he seem calm or worried? Are you surprised by the color he used to paint the shadows under his eyes? The patches of green contrast with the red of his hair and beard.

Look back for a minute at the *Mona Lisa* (page 191). Do you see what is behind her? There's a landscape with mountains and a river. Now look at what van Gogh painted in the background of his picture—swirling lines of blue and green. Where else can you find curving blue lines in van Gogh's painting?

You get a very different feeling from a self-portrait painted by an American artist, Norman Rockwell. In this painting, called *Triple Self-Portrait*, Rockwell has fun with the idea of painting a picture of himself. How many times does Norman Rockwell show himself here? He paints a picture of himself looking in a mirror to paint a picture of himself! Do you see how, in the mirror, his eyes are hidden by his glasses, but shown clearly in the painting he is working on? In this picture, Rockwell has copies of other famous self-portraits tacked to the upper right of his canvas. Can you find a self-portrait of van Gogh among Rockwell's collection?

*You may also hear his name pronounced van-KHOKH, especially outside of the United States.

Triple Self-Portrait by Norman Rockwell.

Activity: Try making your own portrait. You can work in pairs with a partner, or use a mirror to do a self-portrait. You can use crayons, markers, paints, or colored chalk. Use a piece of paper at least 8 by 10 inches. How much of the person will you show: the whole body or only the head and shoulders? What will be in the background? Will you include any objects—such as toys, pets, or books—that tell about the person? Remember, your portrait or self-portrait doesn't have to look like a photograph.

Hold Still!

You've learned about one kind of painting, called a portrait. Now let's look at another kind, called a *still life*. It's called a still life because the objects in the painting don't move. Are people ever included in a still life? No, because after a while they would move!

To paint a still life, an artist first has to decide what objects to paint. Still lifes often include flowers, fruit, books, china, silverware, furniture, or other small objects. Once the artist knows what to paint, he or she has to decide how to arrange the objects. What shapes and colors will go next to one another? Where will the light fall? Will the still life include objects with several different textures?

Irises

Apples and Oranges

Let's look at two still lifes. The first is called *Irises*. If you look at the way it's painted with energetic brush strokes, you may be reminded of an artist you met not long ago when you saw his self-portrait. It's Vincent van Gogh. Van Gogh liked to paint still lifes of flowers, such as irises and sunflowers. Do you find mostly curved or straight lines in this painting?

The other still life, called *Apples and Oranges*, is by a French artist, Paul Cézanne [say-ZAHN]. What shapes do you see in this painting? Do you see how Cézanne outlined the apples and oranges in dark tones, which makes it easy to see their circular shapes?

Activity: Let's do a still life. What do you have to do first? You need to decide what objects you want to include and how you will arrange them. You can paint a still life of many things: fruits, flowers, cans and boxes of food, the toys in your room. What materials will you use to make your still life? You can try paints, markers, crayons, colored pencils, or colored chalk.

Murals:
Paintings on Walls

Most of the paintings you've been looking at in this book were painted on canvas. They are the kind of painting that you can put in a frame and hang on a wall. But here's an idea: how about painting *the wall itself?*

That's what some artists like to do: they like to paint *murals*. A mural is a large painting done on a wall. On the next page you can see a mural painted on a hospital wall in Mexico City. It was painted in 1953 by the Mexican artist Diego Rivera. (Did you look at his painting called *Piñata* on page 189?) This mural is called *The History of Medicine in Mexico*. Of course, you're looking at only a small photograph of the mural: the real painting is huge! It tells the history of Mexican medicine. The right side shows the kind of medicine practiced by the ancient Aztec civilization in Mexico (if you don't know about the Aztecs, you can learn more about them in this book on pages 139–42). The left side of the mural shows how medicine is practiced in modern times. In the center, Rivera painted the Aztec goddess who was believed to make things clean by touching them. Why do you think Rivera chose to put this figure in a mural about medicine?

Activity: Would you like to make your own mural? Well, your parents or teachers may not like you painting on the walls! So here's what you can do instead. Get two brown-paper grocery bags. Cut each down one side, then cut out the bottom. Flatten them out and tape them together to create a long sheet of paper. Colored markers show up well on this kind of paper. Plan before you start. Think what you want your mural to

be about: the story of your family, your school, your favorite things to do, your favorite books? Now think about how you will arrange all the images. Will you, like Rivera, make a big central figure, with smaller scenes on either side? Or will your mural unfold like a story from left to right? Your mural is a big picture, so take your time. It might take a few days. You might work on it with friends. When you're finished, get an adult to help you hang it on the wall where people can see it.

IV.

Music

INTRODUCTION

We encourage you to give your child a wide range of musical experiences—singing songs, listening to all kinds of music, dancing around at home, attending local musical performances.

One of the best activities, and one of the easiest, is *singing with your child.* We suggest some favorite songs in this section (see pages 219–29). If you don't feel confident about your own singing voice, remember that in your own home, you're the star! It's fine to play tapes and compact discs for your child (we suggest some below), but the more you sing with your child, the more comfortable you'll feel and the more you'll both enjoy music together.

The previous book in this series, *What Your Kindergartner Needs to Know,* introduced activities in which children played with the basic elements of music, such as rhythm, pitch, and tempo. We encourage you to continue these activities with your first grader.

In this book, we introduce many kinds of music, including jazz, classical music, and opera, as well as different kinds of dance. We suggest ways to become familiar with great composers. We introduce some basic terms and concepts, such as melody, harmony, and rhythm, and the notion that music is written down in a language of its own. Further knowledge of musical notation will be developed in later books in this series.

Some families will choose to provide lessons that will lift children to a level of musical competence beyond what we describe in the following pages. Different children will develop musical appreciation and skills at different rates and to different degrees. It's important for everyone to enjoy music, and we hope this book will increase that enjoyment through experience and understanding.

Suggested Recordings of Favorite Songs for Children

Disney's Children's Favorites, Vols. 1–4 (Disney Songtapes)
Family Folk Festival: A Multi-Cultural Sing-Along by various artists (Music for Little People). To order call 800-727-2233
Shake It to the One That You Love the Best: Play Songs and Lullabies from Black Musical Traditions, produced by Cheryl Warren Mattox (Warren-Mattox Productions, 1989)
Wee Sing: Sing-Alongs (Price Stern Sloan, 1990)

Instruments and Their Families

What is a family? Who is in your family? Does everyone in your family look the same?

Musical instruments have families, too. And, just as in your family, some instruments in the same family look alike but are not exactly the same.

There are different families of instruments. Let's meet the *percussion* family, the *string* family, the *wind* family, and the *brass* family.

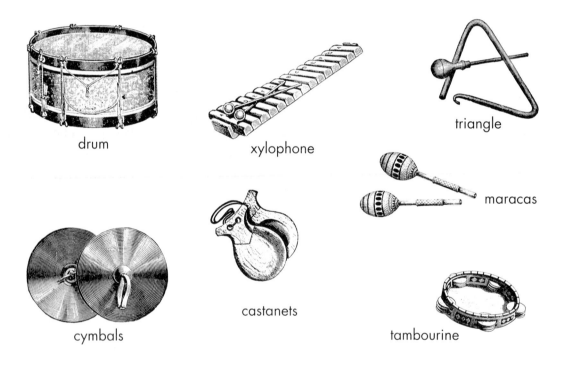

drum

xylophone

triangle

maracas

cymbals

castanets

tambourine

The percussion family. Percussion instruments are fun to play: you shake them or hit them with your hand, a stick, or a mallet. Can you name a percussion instrument? Did you think of a drum? A xylophone? A tambourine? One percussion instrument is easy to recognize: it's called a triangle. When you hit it, it makes a *ding-a-ling-a-ling* sound. Another member of the percussion family looks like lids from two big pots. These are cymbals, and when you hit them together, they can make a sound like a loud *crash!*

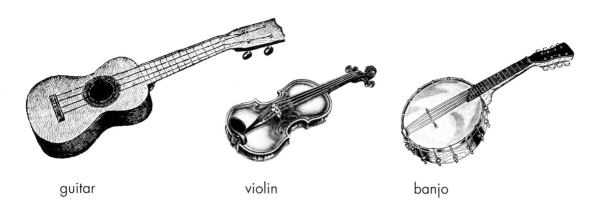

guitar   violin   banjo

The string family. Do you know any instruments with strings? How about a guitar? A banjo? A violin? These instruments don't look the same, but they all have strings. You play stringed instruments either by strumming or plucking them with your fingers or by playing them with a bow.

recorder   bassoon   clarinet

The wind family. How do you think you play instruments in the wind family? Think about the name—*wind*. You play wind instruments by blowing air into them. Sometimes the wind family is called the *woodwind* family. Some wind instruments are made of wood, and some aren't. In the pictures here, the recorder is made of wood, but the flute is made of metal. A flute can sound like a bird singing.

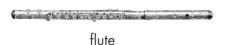

flute

oboe

Many woodwind instruments have a small piece of wood near where you put your mouth. That small piece of wood is called a reed, and it helps the instruments to make their sounds when you blow into them. Some woodwind instruments with reeds are the clarinet, the oboe, and the bassoon. (The recorder and the flute do not have reeds.)

Peruvian boys playing two different kinds of flutes.

French horn

tuba

trumpet

The brass family. Most instruments in the brass family are made of a hard, shiny metal called brass. If you have ever watched a marching band in a parade, you've seen and heard some brass instruments—and you've probably felt like marching as they went by. You play brass instruments as you play wind instruments: by blowing into them. A trumpet, a trombone, a French horn, and the big tuba are members of the brass family.

You can have fun making homemade instruments. These two books show you how:

Let's Make Music: An Interactive Musical Trip Around the World by Jessica Baron Turner and Ronny Susan Schiff (Hal Leonard, 1995)
My First Music Book by Helen Drews (Dorling Kindersley, 1993)

The Orchestra

Members of all the families of instruments—percussion, strings, winds, and brass—come together in an *orchestra*. It takes many musicians playing many instruments to make up an orchestra.

With so many musicians playing so many different instruments, you might think that an orchestra could sound like a mixed-up mess. But the musicians all play together, and the orchestra makes beautiful music! Partly that's because they have a conductor. The conductor usually does not play an instrument. The conductor is a man or woman who stands in front of the orchestra and helps the musicians stay together and play when they are supposed to. The conductor is like the coach of a ball team: he or she makes sure that all the members of the orchestra play their best and do their job at the right time. To show respect, people sometimes address the conductor as "Maestro" [MICE-troh], which means "Master."

A conductor leads an orchestra.

Here are some ways to get to know the instruments in the orchestra:

- A fun way to meet the orchestra is to listen to *Peter and the Wolf* by the Russian composer Sergei Prokofiev [SAIR-gay pruh-KOF-yef]. Many fine recordings of this work are available on cassette and compact disc, and even some on video. *Peter and the Wolf* introduces the orchestra by telling a story in which different instruments play the parts of different characters. An oboe plays a duck. A clarinet plays a cat. Stringed instruments play the hero, Peter. And brass instruments play the wolf. Many recordings feature a narrator who tells the story of Peter's adventures along with the music.

- Read *Meet the Orchestra* by Ann Hayes (Gulliver Books/Harcourt Brace, 1991). This book provides a playful introduction to the orchestra by depicting an orchestra of animals as they prepare for a concert.
- Attend a junior high or high school band concert, or watch an orchestra on television. Notice how the families of instruments sit together on the stage. Watch the conductor and see what kinds of things he or she does during the concert.

Great Composers

Some people are so good at what they do that almost everybody knows who they are. Can you think of a great basketball player that almost everybody knows? Or someone who sings popular songs on the radio? Or someone who has written famous books?

In music, there are some people who write such great music that almost everyone knows who they are. A person who writes music is called a *composer*. Some great composers wrote their music long before you, your parents, or even your grandparents were ever born. But because their music is so wonderful, people still listen to it and play it and enjoy it.

Let's meet one of these great composers. His name is Wolfgang Amadeus Mozart [MOTES-art]. That's a long name, so most people call him Mozart. He lived a long time ago in a country in Europe called Austria. Mozart lived to be only thirty-five years old, but he wrote over six hundred works to sing and to play on instruments.

Mozart.

Mozart started writing music when he was just a little boy. He was an amazing child, a real genius. He had a sister who was a very good musician herself. He called her by a nickname, "Nannerl."

Let's hear a story about Mozart when he was a child. Some words in this story may be new to you. Here is what they mean:

> *clavier* [kla-VEER]: an instrument that, like a piano today, has a keyboard
> *minuet* [min-yoo-ET]: a kind of dance
> *allegro* [uh-LEG-row]: an Italian term used to describe music that is fast and lively

"Mozart the Wonder Boy"

Nannerl was having a music lesson. Her father, Leopold, was teaching her. Little Wolfgang Mozart was watching and listening to every note she played. When her lesson was over he asked, "Please may I have a lesson, Papa?"

"You are too little, Wolfie!" said Father Mozart.

When Father Mozart and Nannerl left the room, little Wolfgang went up to the clavier and pressed the keys. He smiled. The music sounded beautiful. Father Mozart heard him and came to see. Wolfgang was playing correctly without anyone helping him. Father Mozart decided to give his little boy music lessons.

Soon Wolfgang was playing as well as his big sister, Nannerl. He learned so quickly, his father was very pleased. But when Wolfgang started to write his own music, to compose, Father Mozart was delighted. No one could believe that a little boy of five could write such beautiful music.

Now Father Mozart decided to take his two bright children on a concert tour to Munich [MYOO-nik], Germany. It was a long trip. Inside the coach it was very bumpy. But still they had to work. Father Mozart made them practice on make-believe keyboards.

As soon as they arrived in Munich, people began to talk about the talented little Mozart children. Dressed in their best clothes, they played for Prince Joseph. The concert was a huge success. Everyone clapped and gave them presents of jewels and lace. Father Mozart was very proud of them.

One large lady was so excited that she ran over to the little boy, picked him up in her arms and gave him a loud sloppy kiss! "Yeuch!" said Wolfgang, as he wriggled away and wiped his face!

Back home in Salzburg, Austria, Wolfgang was so pleased to see his mother and his funny little dog, Bimperl. He had missed them very much. Wolfgang hugged Bimperl and then wrote a little minuet to celebrate his return. It was January 1762—just days before his sixth birthday.

A few days later, Father Mozart gave Wolfgang a present. It was a little violin. That night, when Papa's friends arrived carrying their instruments, Wolfgang ran to get his own little fiddle. But Papa shook his head.

"No, Wolfgang. You cannot possibly play with us until you have had some lessons and lots of practice." Wolfgang burst into tears.

One of Mr. Mozart's friends, Mr. Schachtner, felt sorry for Wolfgang.

"Come on, Leopold," he said. "Let the child stand near me. I don't mind."

"Oh, very well," said Father Mozart, "but remember to play softly, Wolfgang, so no one will hear you."

Wolfgang smiled through his tears and, standing next to Mr. Schachtner, he began to follow the music. Gradually Mr. Schachtner played softly—still more softly—and then he stopped playing altogether. Little Wolfgang continued playing. Father Mozart could not believe his eyes or ears. How could his little boy play such difficult music without any lessons?

Their next trip was to Vienna, Austria, and this time Mother came too. One day, an important invitation arrived. Wolfgang and Nannerl were to play at the royal palace for the Emperor and Empress. There was such excitement! Clothes were washed and ironed. Shoes were polished till they shone like mirrors. Then they all climbed into the coach and started off for the palace.

The Emperor, the Empress and the royal children were waiting in the Throne Room. "What are you going to play, little one?" asked the Emperor, smiling.

"I shall play my Allegro in B flat major," Wolfgang replied.

"Very good," said the Emperor, "but first of all I wish to place this over the keys." He held up a large black cloth.

Mozart sighed. It made no difference to him. He could play the clavier without looking at the keys. The Emperor put the black cloth over the keyboard. Wolfgang placed his hands on the cloth and played his Allegro perfectly.

"Well done!" cried the Emperor and Empress.

Father Leopold took Nannerl and Wolfgang to many different countries. One trip lasted three years and five months! Wherever they went, they gave concerts. Everyone admired them and gave them presents. They called Wolfgang, "Mozart the Wonder Boy"!

Wolfgang grew up to become one of the greatest composers of all time. Even today, people all over the world love to perform and to listen to his wonderful music.

Get to Know Great Composers
and Their Music

- There are *many* recordings of Mozart's music. A good work to start with is called *A Little Night Music*. A convenient collection of favorite works is a compact disc called *Mozart: Greatest Hits* (Sony Classical MLK 64053).

- The *Classical Kids* series (BMG Music; produced by Susan Hammond) is a fun way to get to know some composers and their music. This award-winning series, on cassette tape and compact disc, includes *Mozart's Magic Fantasy, Tchaikovsky Discovers America*, and *Vivaldi's Ring of Mystery*. Each title mixes fact and fiction, and weaves familiar musical selections into the telling of a lively and engaging story.

- If you would like to read about other composers, check your library for Ann Rachlin's *Famous Children* series (published by Barron's, 1992–94). Besides the story about Mozart (part of which you read above), there are books on many other composers. Other titles include *Bach, Beethoven, Brahms, Chopin, Handel, Haydn, Schubert, Schumann*, and *Tchaikovsky*.

- Music by Mozart and other composers—such as Bach, Beethoven, and Tchaikovsky—is often called *classical music*. One special kind of classical music is called a *symphony*. A symphony is written to be played by an orchestra. Symphonies are usually long pieces of music, sometimes half an hour or more. Mozart wrote forty-one symphonies. A composer named Ludwig van Beethoven wrote nine great symphonies. The beginning of Beethoven's Fifth Symphony is one of the most famous moments in all of classical music. Try to hear it sometime, but be prepared—when the music starts, it may make you jump!

Music Can Tell a Story

What are some of your favorite stories? Sometimes music and stories go together. Some songs tell stories. If you've ever sung "Oh! Susanna" you've sung a story. Let's try it:

I come from Alabama with a banjo on my knee;
I'm goin' to Lou'siana, my true love for to see.
It rained all night the day I left, the weather it was dry;
The sun so hot I froze to death, Susanna don't you cry.

Oh! Susanna, don't you cry for me;
I come from Alabama with my banjo on my knee.

I had a dream the other night, when everything
* was still;*
I thought I saw Susanna dear, a-coming down the hill.
The buckwheat cake was in her mouth, the tear was in
* her eye;*
Said I, I'm coming from the south, Susanna don't you cry.

Oh! Susanna, don't you cry for me;
I come from Alabama with my banjo on my knee.

Check your library for these picture books based on songs that tell stories:

Abiyoyo, written by Pete Seeger and illustrated by Michael Hays (Macmillan, 1986)
The Fox Went Out on a Chilly Night: An Old Song, illustrated by Peter Spier (Doubleday/Dell Yearling, 1961)
What a Wonderful World, written by Bob Thiele and George D. Weiss, and illustrated by Ashley Bryan (Sundance, 1995)

The story in "Oh! Susanna" gets a little silly, but that's what makes it fun. Do you know some other story songs, like "Billy Boy"? (You can find the words to this song on page 221 in this book.)

Sometimes music *without* words can also seem to tell a story. The sounds can almost make you see pictures in your mind. Some music can make you imagine good guys and bad guys, birds singing, a big storm, ships at sea, and even brooms marching.

What's that—brooms marching? Yes, that's part of the story told in a famous piece of music for orchestra by a French composer named Paul Dukas [do-KAH]. The music is called *The Sorcerer's Apprentice*.

Do you know what a sorcerer is? He's like a wizard or magician. An apprentice is somebody who is both a helper and a learner. *The Sorcerer's Apprentice* is an old story that has been told in many ways. The story that Paul Dukas tells in his music is about a young man who helps a sorcerer while he is learning to become a sorcerer himself. One day the sorcerer leaves the house, and leaves the apprentice alone. The apprentice is tired of working, but he still has to carry water in a bucket from the river. "Oh," he thinks, "I would rather do magic than all this work!"

Then the apprentice decides to do something he shouldn't. He takes the sorcerer's magic wand and casts a spell: he makes an old broom come alive! The broom picks up a bucket and fills it with water—it does the apprentice's work for him!

When you hear the music for *The Sorcerer's Apprentice*, you can imagine what's happening. Quiet, mysterious-sounding music makes you think of the sorcerer and his magic. Later, when the apprentice casts his spell on the broom, the music turns into a kind of funny little march, which helps you imagine how a broom might walk!

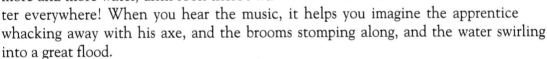

But then something goes wrong with the apprentice's spell. He can't make the broom stop! It keeps filling the bucket with water and bringing it back and pouring more and more water on the floor. The apprentice says all the magic words he can think of, but the broom won't stop. So the apprentice grabs an axe and, *whack*, chops the broom in half. That does it. But no, it doesn't! Each piece gets up, grabs a bucket, and gets more and more water, until soon there's water everywhere! When you hear the music, it helps you imagine the apprentice whacking away with his axe, and the brooms stomping along, and the water swirling into a great flood.

Many recordings of *The Sorcerer's Apprentice* are available, including one in the collection called *Classics for Kids* (RCA Victor/BMG Classics, 1993), a compact disc that presents many catchy classical selections. You can hear *and* see the musical story of *The Sorcerer's Apprentice* in the Walt Disney animated movie *Fantasia*, with a classic animated sequence in which Mickey Mouse plays the apprentice. The movie is available on video. If you get a chance to watch the video, try this: leave the picture on but turn off the sound. Do you see how important the music is to the story?

Dramas with Music: Opera

Imagine that you wake up one day and find that everybody is singing instead of talking. You're in bed and you hear your mother sing (to the tune of "On Top of Old Smoky"):

It's time to get up now,
Get ready for school.
Put on your red sweater
'Cause outside it's cool.

When you get to school, your teacher sings (to the tune of "Yankee Doodle"):

All right, children, settle down,
It's time to practice writing.
Please make sure your pencil's sharp,
And Billy stop that biting!

When you get home from school, *you* sing (come on, sing now, to the tune of "Twinkle, Twinkle Little Star"):

I worked hard at school all day,
Now I'm ready for some play.

Wow! Wouldn't that be weird, but fun, too? It would be like living in an *opera.*

Two singers in the leading roles of the opera *Hansel and Gretel.*

What is an opera? An opera is like a play in which the words are sung. Have you ever seen a play, or been in one? In a play people put on costumes, then go onstage to act out a story. Now imagine if the actors didn't speak their lines but sang them instead. And imagine that while they were singing, an orchestra was playing music for them to sing along with.

You've just imagined an opera. Operas tell stories, sometimes funny, sometimes sad. Some operas tell stories you probably know. Two famous operas are called *Cinderella* and *Hansel and Gretel.*

Many operas were written by composers who lived in European countries, such as Italy, Germany, and France. That's why many operas are sung in languages other than English. The opera

Cinderella is sung in Italian. The opera *Hansel and Gretel* is sung in German. But because the singing and music are so beautiful, many people love to listen to operas even if they don't understand all the words.

To hear some opera, try these recordings:

Mozart's Magic Fantasy, produced by Susan Hammond (BMG Music). Part of the award-winning *Classical Kids* series, on cassette tape and compact disc, this is the story of a little girl who is magically transported into the world of Mozart's opera *The Magic Flute.*

My Favorite Opera for Children, presented by Luciano Pavarotti (London 443 817-2 LM). This compact disc includes excerpts from Mozart's *Magic Flute,* Humperdinck's *Hansel and Gretel,* and Bizet's *Carmen.*

Music Can Make You Move

What happens when you hear a fast, happy song you like? Do you clap your hands? Do you tap your toes?

Sometimes music just makes you want to move. Dancing is moving to music. People around the world love to dance—do you? You can dance just by moving in whatever way the music makes you feel. Or you can do one of many special kinds of dance, such as tap dancing or square dancing or ballet.

Tap dancers have flat pieces of metal, called taps, on the bottoms of their shoes. They quickly move their feet and legs, and the metal taps make tap-tap-tapping noises as they dance.

Square dancing is popular in our country. Men and women stand in a square and listen to a "caller," a person who calls out

Brothers Maurice and Gregory Hines tap-dancing.

what to do next. As the fiddler plays, the caller might say, "Swing your partner, 'round you go. Turn to your right and do-si-do."

One kind of dance, called ballet, can tell a story. In a ballet there is music, often played by an orchestra, but no one sings or talks. Instead, in many ballets the dancers tell a story through the way they move. Some ballets tell stories you may know, like the story of "Sleeping Beauty."

Ballet dancers have to practice for years to learn all they need to know. They have to work very hard and have very strong legs. They have to work at balancing themselves and controlling their bodies. Sometimes they dance only on the tips of their toes. Sometimes they spin around and around. Sometimes they make high leaps into the air.

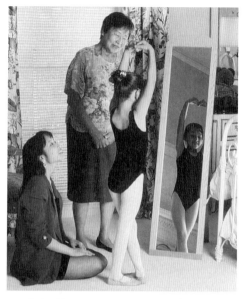

A ballerina prepares to dance.

A beloved ballet, performed every year around Christmastime, is *The Nutcracker* by the Russian composer Peter Illyich Tchaikovsky [chy-KAHV-skee]. *The Nutcracker* tells a story about a toy nutcracker that magically comes to life and, with a little help from a girl named Clara, battles and defeats a Mouse King. Check your library for books that tell the story of the ballet, such as *The Nutcracker Ballet* by Vladimir Vagin (Scholastic, 1995). Wonderful performances of *The Nutcracker* are available on video, including the American Ballet Theatre's production with Mikhail Baryshnikov (Jodav Productions, 1977).

Clara dances with the Nutcracker.

Jazz

A special kind of music was born in America, and now it's liked by people around the world. This music, called *jazz*, was invented by African Americans. Many people say that jazz is America's most important gift to music.

There's one big difference between jazz and most other music. If you sing, "Row, row, row your boat," you don't change the words or the tune. But every time a jazz mu-

An early New Orleans jazz group.

sician plays a song, it comes out a little different. Different jazz musicians can play the same songs in different ways. A jazz musician may start with a familiar tune, but then he or she changes the tune while playing it, so that it sounds a little different every time.

When you make something up as you go along, you are *improvising*. When jazz musicians play, they improvise. Can you imagine how you could improvise on a familiar song? You might start out singing something you know, like this:

Row, row, row your boat
Gently down the stream,
Merrily, merrily, merrily, merrily,
Life is but a dream.

Now sing it again, but have fun by changing the words and the tune. As you improvise, your words might come out something like this (you'll have to imagine your own tune!):

Row, row, row-ba-doh-ba-doh,
Row my little piddle-paddle boat.
Row so merrily, be-bop-a-bearily,
Down the ice cream peanut-butter dreamy stream!

Check your library for these two "jazzy" books:

Ben's Trumpet, written and illustrated by Rachel Isadora (Greenwillow, 1979)
Charlie Parker Played Be Bop, written and illustrated by Chris Raschka (Orchard Books, 1992)

One of the first great jazz musicians was Louis Armstrong. Some people called him by a nickname, "Satchmo," and others called him "Pops." When Louis was a boy, he lived in New Orleans, a city in Louisiana famous for its jazz music. He became very good at playing jazz even when he was young. He learned to play the cornet (an instrument like the trumpet) so well that the other musicians in his band would stop playing, or play very quietly, and let him play a solo ("solo" means "alone"). He played and sang with many different jazz musicians and bands during his life, and he was loved by people all over the world. You can always recognize his warm and gravelly voice.

Louis Armstrong.

The city of New Orleans, where Louis Armstrong grew up, is where one important kind of jazz got started. A song that jazz musicians in New Orleans liked to improvise on is called "When the Saints Come Marching In." Let's sing part of it:

Oh, when the saints come marching in,
When the saints come marching in,
I want to be in that number,
When the saints come marching in.

Melody and Harmony

Can you hum? What is your favorite song? Try humming it now. You've just hummed the *melody*. Sometimes people call the melody of a song the tune. Have you ever played "Name That Tune"? To play the game, you take turns humming a song. Your partner tries to guess the name of the song.

> Try playing "Name That Tune" with some of your favorite songs and with some of the songs in this book (see pages 219–29).

You only hum a little of the song at first. If your partner can't guess it, then you hum some more. When he guesses it, then it's his turn to hum and your turn to guess.

Have you ever sung in a group or heard a choir sing? If you have, maybe you've heard how a lot of different voices can go together in a way that makes a lovely sound. In music, some sounds go together well. But some don't. It's kind of like clothing: some clothes go together and some don't. If you put on a red-striped shirt with purple-and-green-checked pants, your clothes don't match. When you put on clothes that match, they go together. Music is like that. When the sounds match, or go together, they make *harmony*. Instruments can make harmony, and voices can make harmony.

Listen to some of your favorite songs to see what instruments are playing at the same time. Listen to a choir sing. If there are men and women singing together, try to hear how the men's low voices and the women's high voices go together.

I've Got Rhythm!

Now that you know what melody and harmony are, let's find out about another important part of music—*rhythm*.

Rhythm is what makes music move. All music has rhythm. In fact, some kinds of music are mainly rhythm. Some Native American music is mainly rhythm. African drummers play music that is mainly rhythm.

A big part of rhythm is called the beat. Some musicians beat a drum or a piece of wood to keep the beat. What does it mean to "keep the beat" in music? Think about this: have you ever noticed how some music makes you want to clap your hands or tap your feet? When that happens, you don't clap or tap at just any old time. Instead, when you listen to the music, it tells you when to clap, in a regular, steady way,

Darryl Rose of the Chihamba dance troupe plays an African drum.

right in time with the music. That's because you keep hearing the strongest sound in the music, the beat, coming over and over again at the very moment that you expect it to come. If you clap your hands or tap your feet every time you know the strong sound is going to come, then you are "keeping the beat." "Keeping the beat" is also called "keeping time" to the music.

Here is part of a song you may know, "Yankee Doodle." Let's try keeping time to it by clapping our hands on the strong beat every time we know it's going to come. (In the song, the strong beat falls on the underlined parts of the words.)

Yankee Doodle went to town,
A-riding on a po—ny,
Stuck a feather in his cap
And called it macaro—ni.

Reading and Writing Music

PARENTS: *Here we introduce your child to some musical notes to convey the idea that music can be written down. Later books in this series will explain more about musical notation.*

Have you ever seen music written down on paper? It looks like this:

Twin-kle, twin-kle, lit-tle   star,   How I   won-der what you   are!

That's the way you write down the music for "Twinkle, Twinkle, Little Star." Reading music is like reading words—it takes time and practice!

When you write words, you use letters. But when you write music, you use notes and other special marks. What the notes look like, where they are, and how many of them are together tell the musician what to do on his or her instrument. Here you can see some musical notes and their names.

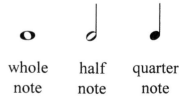

whole note   half note   quarter note

When you sing or play a whole note, it lasts twice as long as a half note. When you sing or play a half note, it lasts twice as long as a quarter note.

Music is written down so that anyone who reads music can play it. Two people might live very far away from each other and be very different, but they can play the same music the same way if they both can read music. Writing music down on paper helps people to share the music they like.

A Few Favorite Songs

PARENTS: *Here are a few familiar songs to sing with your child. You can find words to more songs earlier in this Music section, and words to "Yankee Doodle" on page 170. We encourage you to sing many other songs with your child as well. Children enjoy listening to and singing along with recordings, too, such as the ones suggested on page 201.*

America the Beautiful

O beautiful for spacious skies,

For amber waves of grain,

For purple mountain majesties

Above the fruited plain!

America! America!

God shed his grace on thee

And crown thy good with brotherhood

From sea to shining sea!

Blow the Man Down

Come all ye young fellows that follow the sea,
To me way, hey, blow the man down!
Now pray, pay attention and listen to me,
Give me some time to blow the man down!

As I was a-walking down Paradise Street,
To me way, hey, blow the man down!
A pretty young damsel I chanced for to meet,
Give me some time to blow the man down!

She hailed me with her flipper, I took her in tow,
To me way, hey, blow the man down!
Yard-arm to yard-arm away we did go,
Give me some time to blow the man down!

La Cucaracha
(The Cockroach)

La cucaracha, la cucaracha,
Running up and down the house,
La cucaracha, la cucaracha,
Quiet as a little mouse.

He gets in trouble, a lot of trouble,
Snooping here and everywhere,
La cucaracha, la cucaracha,
Always keeps the cupboard bare.

Billy Boy

Oh, where have you been,
   Billy Boy, Billy Boy,
Oh, where have you been
   charming Billy?
I have been to seek a wife,
She's the joy of my life,
She's a young thing and cannot leave her mother.

Did she ask you to come in,
   Billy Boy, Billy Boy,
Did she ask you to come in,
   charming Billy?
Yes, she asked me to come in,
There's a dimple in her chin,
She's a young thing and cannot leave her mother.

Can she make a cherry pie,
   Billy Boy, Billy Boy?
Can she make a cherry pie,
   charming Billy?
She can make a cherry pie
Quick as a cat can wink her eye,
She's a young thing and cannot leave her mother.

Down by the Riverside

Gonna lay down my sword and shield,

Down by the riverside,

Down by the riverside,

Down by the riverside,

Gonna lay down my sword and shield,

Down by the riverside,

Ain't gonna study war no more.

Ain't gonna study war no more, ain't gonna study war no more,

    Ain't gonna study war no more.

Ain't gonna study war no more, ain't gonna study war no more,

    Ain't gonna study war no more.

Gonna lay down my burden,

Down by the riverside,

Down by the riverside,

Down by the riverside,

Gonna lay down my burden,

Down by the riverside,

Ain't gonna study war no more.

Ain't gonna study war no more, ain't gonna study war no more,

    Ain't gonna study war no more.

Ain't gonna study war no more, ain't gonna study war no more,

    Ain't gonna study war no more.

For He's a Jolly Good Fellow

For he's a jolly good fellow,

For he's a jolly good fellow,

For he's a jolly good fellow,

Which nobody can deny.

Which nobody can deny,

Which nobody can deny.

For he's a jolly good fellow,

For he's a jolly good fellow,

For he's a jolly good fellow,

Which nobody can deny.

Down in the Valley

Down in the valley, the valley so low,

Hang your head over, hear the wind blow.

Hear the wind blow, dear, hear the wind blow,

Hang your head over, hear the wind blow.

Roses love sunshine, violets love dew,

Angels in heaven know I love you.

Know I love you, dear, know I love you.

Angels in heaven know I love you.

Writing this letter, containing three lines,

Answer my question, "Will you be mine?"

Will you be mine, dear, will you be mine?

Answer my question, "Will you be mine?"

Dry Bones

Ezekiel cried, "Them dry bones!"
Ezekiel cried, "Them dry bones!"
Ezekiel cried, "Them dry bones!"
Now hear the word of the Lord.

The foot bone connected to the leg bone,
The leg bone connected to the knee bone,
The knee bone connected to the thigh bone,
The thigh bone connected to the hip bone,
The hip bone connected to the back bone,
The back bone connected to the neck bone,
The neck bone connected to the jaw bone,
The jaw bone connected to the head bone,
Now hear the word of the Lord.

Them bones, them bones gonna walk around,
Them bones, them bones gonna walk around,
Them bones, them bones gonna walk around,
  Now hear the word of the Lord.

Them bones, them bones, them dry bones,
Them bones, them bones, them dry bones,
Them bones, them bones, them dry bones,
Now hear the word of the Lord.

Frère Jacques/ Brother John

[French]

Frère Jacques, Frère Jacques,

Dormez-vous, dormez-vous?

Sonnez les matines, sonnez les matines,

Din, din, don. Din, din, don.

[English]

Are you sleeping, are you sleeping

Brother John, Brother John?

Morning bells are ringing, morning bells are ringing,

Ding, dang, dong. Ding, dang, dong.

Michael, Row the Boat Ashore

Michael, row the boat ashore, Hallelujah,

Michael, row the boat ashore, Hallelujah.

Sister, help to trim the sail, Hallelujah,

Sister, help to trim the sail, Hallelujah.

Jordan's River is chilly and cold, Hallelujah,

Chills the body but not the soul, Hallelujah.

The river is deep and the river is wide, Hallelujah,

Milk and honey on the other side, Hallelujah.

Michael, row the boat ashore, Hallelujah.

Michael, row the boat ashore, Hallelujah.

On Top of Old Smoky

On top of Old Smoky,
All covered with snow,
I lost my true lover
For courting too slow.

Well, courting's a pleasure
And parting is grief,
But a false-hearted lover
Is worse than a thief.

On top of Old Smoky,
All covered with snow,
I lost my true lover
For courting too slow.

She'll Be Comin' Round the Mountain

She'll be comin' round the mountain when she comes,
She'll be comin' round the mountain when she comes,
She'll be comin' round the mountain,
She'll be comin' round the mountain,
She'll be comin' round the mountain when she comes.

She'll be drivin' six white horses when she comes, [*etc.*]

Oh, we'll all go out to meet her when she comes, [*etc.*]

She'll be wearing pink pajamas when she comes, [*etc.*]

She'll be comin' round the mountain when she comes, [*etc.*]

Skip to My Lou

[*chorus*]
Skip, skip, skip to my Lou,
Skip, skip, skip to my Lou,
Skip, skip, skip to my Lou,
Skip to my Lou, my darling!

Lost my partner, what'll I do?
Lost my partner, what'll I do?
Lost my partner, what'll I do?
Skip to my Lou, my darling!

[*repeat chorus*]

I'll find another one, prettier, too,
I'll find another one, prettier, too,
I'll find another one, prettier, too,
Skip to my Lou, my darling!

[*repeat chorus*]

Flies in the sugar bowl, shoo, fly, shoo,
Flies in the sugar bowl, shoo, fly, shoo,
Flies in the sugar bowl, shoo, fly, shoo,
Skip to my Lou, my darling!

Skip, skip, skip to my Lou,
Skip, skip, skip to my Lou,
Skip, skip, skip to my Lou,
Skip to my Lou, my darling!

There's a Hole in the Bucket

There's a hole in the bucket, dear Liza, dear Liza.
There's a hole in the bucket, dear Liza, a hole.
Well, mend it, dear Henry, dear Henry, dear Henry.
Well, mend it, dear Henry, dear Henry, mend it.

With what shall I mend it? dear Liza, dear Liza,
With what shall I mend it? dear Liza, with what?
With a straw, dear Henry, dear Henry, dear Henry.
With a straw, dear Henry, dear Henry, with a straw.

But the straw is too long, dear Liza, dear Liza.
The straw is too long, dear Liza, too long.
Then cut it, dear Henry, dear Henry, dear Henry.
Then cut it, dear Henry, dear Henry, cut it.

With what shall I cut it? dear Liza, dear Liza,
With what shall I cut it? dear Liza, with what?
With an ax, dear Henry, dear Henry, dear Henry.
With an ax, dear Henry, dear Henry, with an ax.

But the ax is too dull, dear Liza, dear Liza.
The ax is too dull, dear Liza, too dull.
Then sharpen it, dear Henry, dear Henry,
   dear Henry.
Then sharpen it, dear Henry, dear Henry, sharpen it.

With what shall I sharpen it? dear Liza, dear Liza,
With what shall I sharpen it? dear Liza, with what?
With a stone, dear Henry, dear Henry, dear Henry.
With a stone, dear Henry, dear Henry, with a stone.

But the stone is too dry, dear Liza, dear Liza.
The stone is too dry, dear Liza, too dry.
Then wet it, dear Henry, dear Henry, dear Henry.
Then wet it, dear Henry, dear Henry, wet it.

With what shall I wet it? dear Liza, dear Liza,
With what shall I wet it? dear Liza, with what?
With water, dear Henry, dear Henry, dear Henry.
With water, dear Henry, dear Henry, with water.

In what shall I carry it? dear Liza, dear Liza,
In what shall I carry it? dear Liza, in what?
In a bucket, dear Henry, dear Henry, dear Henry.
In a bucket, dear Henry, dear Henry, in a bucket.

But there's a hole in the bucket, dear Liza, dear Liza.
There's a hole in the bucket, dear Liza, a hole.
Well, mend it, dear Henry, dear Henry, dear Henry.
Well, mend it, dear Henry, dear Henry, mend it!

Take Me Out to the Ball Game

Take me out to the ball game,
Take me out to the crowd.
Buy me some peanuts and Cracker Jack,
I don't care if I never come back.
And it's root, root, root for the home team,
If they don't win it's a shame.
For it's one, two, three strikes, "You're out!"
At the old ball game.

V.

Mathematics

INTRODUCTION

In this section we sometimes address your child and sometimes address you as parents, particularly in the directions for activities you can do with your children.

We encourage you to give the topics and activities in this secvtion some special emphasis. In international evaluations of math performance by students in various countries, students in the United States have consistently performed near the bottom. One reason is that students in other countries begin building a secure foundation in mathematics in the earliest years of their schooling, and that they receive more consistent practice and more challenging work than students in the U.S.

In school, any successful program for teaching math to young children follows these three cardinal rules: (1) practice, (2) practice, and (3) practice. Not mindless repetition, of course, but thoughtful and varied practice, in which children are given opportunities to approach problems from a variety of angles, and in which, as they proceed to learn new facts and operations, they consistently review and reinforce their earlier learning.

In school, first graders should practice math daily, in order to ensure that they can effortlessly and automatically perform the basic operations upon which all problem solving and other sophisticated math applications depend. Some well-meaning people fear that practice in mathematics—for example, memorizing the addition and subtraction facts up to 12, or doing timed worksheets with 25 problems—leads to joyless, soul-killing drudgery. Nothing could be farther from the truth. The destroyer of joy in learning mathematics is not practice but anxiety—the anxiety that comes from feeling that one is mathematically stupid or lacks any "special talent" for math.

We adults must be careful not to convey to our children any feelings that we "don't like math" or are "not good at math" or any other symptoms of what has been called "math anxiety." By engaging our children in the kinds of activities suggested in this section, we can let them know that math is important and interesting to us. Keep in mind, however, that *the activities suggested here are supplemental ways for parents to reinforce their children's learning at home. They are not sufficient for teaching math in school,* where children need more regular and structured opportunities for practice and review.

Suggested Resources

Books

Family Math by Jean Kerr Stenmark, Virginia Thompson, and Ruth Cossey (Regents of the University of California, 1986); to order call (510) 642-1910.

Software

Early Math (Sierra); *Math Rabbit* (The Learning Company); *Math Workshop* (Broderbund).

Patterns and Classifications

PARENTS: *Learning to see likenesses, differences, and patterns is an essential part of mathematical thinking. A first grader should be able to sort objects according to some specific attributes, such as color, shape, and function; to define a set of items by what the items have in common; to tell which item does not belong in a set; and to recognize patterns and predict how a pattern will continue. To review these skills, see* What Your Kindergartner Needs to Know. *Your first grader should also learn to recognize likeness and difference in printed symbols. For example, ask your child to look at the following groups of squares and to point to the one in each group that is different. Also, check your library for* Anno's Math Games *(Putnam, 1987).*

Numbers and Number Sense

PARENTS: *By now your first grader has probably had many experiences with numbers and counting. She knows her age and her address and can probably recite her telephone number. She can probably count to 30 or more, and she understands that each number stands for a specific quantity of items. (To review these concepts, see the section on Numbers and Number Sense in* What Your Kindergartner Needs to Know.) *Now your child is ready to learn that there are different ways of counting. By the end of first grade she should know how to count to 100 by ones, twos, fives, and tens, both forward and backward. She should also learn to write the words for the numbers from one to twelve.*

First graders should be learning to compare numbers to see which is greater and which is less, and to have a sense of how big 100 is. They can also begin to understand that a digit in the tens place of a number means something different from a digit in the ones place. In school, your child should also be introduced to number lines, tallies, and simple bar graphs and pictorial graphs.

Some Things to Prepare in Advance:
It helps to have real things for children to count. If you can gather and prepare these items in advance, you'll have a useful supply of materials to use for activities in this section and the Computation section.

- *Keep a ready supply of countable things, such as dried beans, buttons, paper clips, or small pasta shapes like elbow macaroni.*
- *It's very handy to have a set of number cards numbered from 0 to 100 for all sorts of games and counting activities. You can buy number cards at teacher supply stores and many toy stores, or you can make them out of index cards.*

Numbers from 1 to 10

Count out loud from 1 to 10. Afterward, practice writing the words for the numbers from one to ten.

1	one	★
2	two	★★
3	three	★★★
4	four	★★★★
5	five	★★★★★
6	six	★★★★★★
7	seven	★★★★★★★
8	eight	★★★★★★★★
9	nine	★★★★★★★★★
10	ten	★★★★★★★★★★

ZERO

Zero is a special number. It tells how many you have when you don't have any. How many elephants do you have in your pocket?

0

One More and One Less

In counting, the number that comes after another number is always 1 more. For example, 6 is 1 more than 5. If you had 5 star stickers and you got 1 more, you would have 6 star stickers.

☆☆☆☆☆ + ☆ = ☆☆☆☆☆☆

In counting, the number that comes before another number is always 1 less. For example, 3 is 1 less than 4. If you had 4 pencils and you gave 1 away, you would have 3 pencils left.

To figure out what 1 less is, you can count backward. Learn to count backward from 10 to 0, like this:

10, 9, 8, 7, 6, 5, 4, 3, 2, 1, 0

Numbers for Things in Order

Here are ten fish. One fish is out of line. Which one? The seventh fish.

When you say "seventh," you are using a special kind of number called an *ordinal number*. Ordinal numbers name the number of something in an order. Practice saying and writing the first ten ordinal numbers in order. Except for first, second, and third, ordinal numbers end in "th."

Which one of the fish is facing the wrong way?

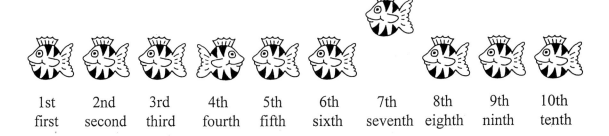

1st	2nd	3rd	4th	5th	6th	7th	8th	9th	10th
first	second	third	fourth	fifth	sixth	seventh	eighth	ninth	tenth

Place Value

10 is a number with two digits. A digit is any of the single numbers from 0 to 9. 10 has 2 digits, a 1 and a 0.

In the number 10, we say that the first digit is in the tens place, and the second digit is in the ones place. The 1 in the tens place means 1 group of ten.

A group of ten is called a ten. The 0 in the ones place means 0 ones.

Tens	Ones
1	0

The number after 10 is 11.
11 means 1 ten and 1 one.

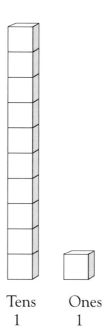

Tens   Ones
 1   1

The next number is 12, which is 1 ten and 2 ones.

The numbers continue: 13, 14, 15, 16, 17, 18, 19.

19 means 1 ten and 9 ones.
After 19 the next number is 20.
20 means 2 tens and 0 ones.

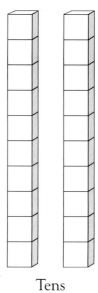

Tens   Ones
 2   0

Here are the words for the numbers from 11 to 20: eleven, twelve, thirteen, fourteen, fifteen, sixteen, seventeen, eighteen, nineteen, twenty.

Place Value from 21 to 100

After 20, the numbers continue:
21, 22, 23, 24, 25, 26, 27, 28, 29, 30.
25 means 2 tens and 5 ones.

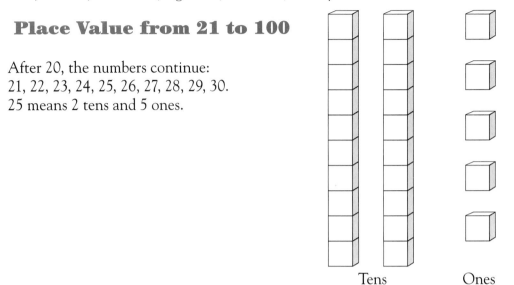

Tens   Ones

Let's count by tens: 10, 20, 30, 40, 50, 60, 70, 80, 90. The words for these numbers are ten, twenty, thirty, forty, fifty, sixty, seventy, eighty, ninety.

30 means 3 tens and 0 ones.
40 means 4 tens and 0 ones.
67 means 6 tens and 7 ones.

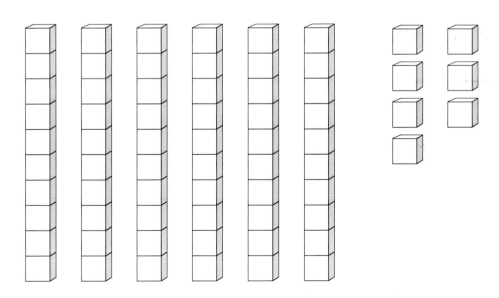

Tens   Ones

The numbers continue to 99, which is 9 tens and 9 ones. Do you know what comes after 99? The number after 99 is 100, which is written in words as one hundred.

Counting to 100

Practice counting out loud from 1 to 100, so that you can do it easily.

Practice counting to 100 by tens: 10, 20, 30, 40, 50, 60, 70, 80, 90, 100. Practice counting to 100 by fives: 5, 10, 15, 20, 25, 30, 35, 40, and so on.

You should also practice counting by tens starting on different numbers, like this: 14, 24, 34, 44, 54, 64, 74, 84, 94. Notice that when you count by tens, the ones place stays the same but the tens place gets 1 number larger each time.

Also practice counting backward from one ten to another. For example, try counting backward from 30 to 20, like this: 30, 29, 28, 27, 26, 25, 24, 23, 22, 21, 20.

You should also be able to say the name of any number between 0 and 100. For example, when you see 78, you say "seventy-eight."

You should be able to read any number between 0 and 100 when it is spelled out. For example, eighty-three is 83.

Twelve Is a Dozen

When you have 12 of something, you have a *dozen*. At the grocery store, eggs often come in cartons of a dozen.

If you need half a dozen eggs to bake a cake, how many eggs do you need? (A half dozen is 6.)

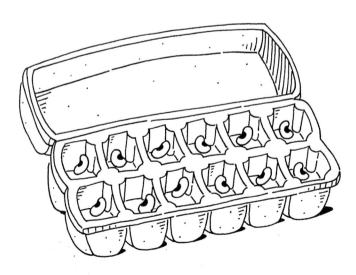

Greater Than and Less Than

Which number is greater, 5 or 4? 5 is greater than 4 because 5 is 1 more than 4. For example, 5 baseball mitts are more than 4 baseball mitts.

We say 5 is greater than 4, and we write that like this:

$$5 > 4$$

The sign > means "is greater than." When you count, 5 comes after 4. Numbers that are greater come after in counting.

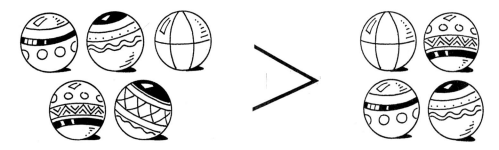

The number 3 is less than the number 4. For example, 3 nickels are less than 4 nickels.

We say 3 is less than 4, and we write that like this:

$$3 < 4$$

The sign < means "is less than." When you count, 3 comes before 4. Numbers that are less come before in counting.

Learn to compare numbers using the signs >, <, and =. Remember that =, the equals sign, means "is the same as." Notice that the small end of the signs < and > always points to the smaller number. What sign would you put between each pair of numbers here?

$$10 \underline{\phantom{<}} 3 \qquad 6 \underline{\phantom{<}} 8 \qquad 9 \underline{\phantom{<}} 9$$

Activity: BEFORE AND AFTER

PARENTS: Show your child a book with numbered pages. Try to use a book with at least 96 pages. If your child is not familiar with reading numbers over 100, you may want to try to find a book that has only about 100 pages. Leaf through the book with your child and talk about how the pages are numbered in order.

Have your child open the book to any right-handed page. Ask her to predict the page number that comes right after that page. Then have her turn the page to check her prediction. Close the book then open it again at random. Have her look at the number on a left-handed page, then ask her the number of the page just before. Have her turn back and check. Later you can ask your child to predict the page that comes before page 42, after page 13, and before page 60. Then try a more complicated task that asks her to count backward, such as predicting, in order, the pages that go from page 63 to page 56. Each time, have her say the numbers first and then check the book.

Activity: NUMBER FLASH CARD ACTIVITIES

PARENTS: You will need a deck of flash cards with the numbers from 0 to 100. You can make these from index cards, or buy them at many toy stores and teacher supply stores. Here are some activities you can do quickly and occasionally repeat for practice:

- Hold up a card and have your child say the number on the card.
- Hold up two cards and ask which number is greater.
- Hold up two cards and ask your child to count forward or backward from one of the numbers to the other.
- Pick a card without showing it. Have your child guess the number by solving a number clue such as, "This number is one more than 63," or "This number is one less than 35," or "This number is between 59 and 61."
- After you use your 0 to 100 number cards, they'll probably be out of order. Before putting them away, ask your child to rearrange them in the correct order. This will provide an extra chance to practice counting from 0 to 100 in order.

Using Graphs

The children in Ms. Williams's class took a vote on their favorite color. Different children chose red, blue, green, pink, and purple. The teacher counted their votes and put them on a special kind of chart called a *graph*. Here it is:

red										
blue										
green										
pink										
purple										

Look at the graph and see if you can answer these questions:

- Which color was chosen as the favorite by the most children?
- Which color was chosen as the favorite by the fewest children?
- Which two colors were chosen as favorites by the same number of children?
- How many children chose each color?

The children in Ms. Johnson's class voted on their favorite flavor of ice cream. Seven children voted for chocolate. Five children voted for vanilla. Three children voted for strawberry. Show how the children in Ms. Johnson's class voted by filling in a graph like the one below. Use a different color for each flavor of ice cream, such as brown for chocolate, yellow for vanilla, and pink for strawberry.

chocolate									
vanilla									
strawberry									

Fractions

A fraction is a part of something. $^1/_2$ is a fraction. If something is divided into two equal parts, each part is $^1/_2$. $^1/_2$ is written in words as one half.

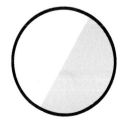

$^1/_3$ is also a fraction. If something is divided into 3 equal parts, each part is $^1/_3$. $^1/_3$ is written in words as one third.

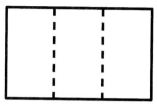

Each part is 1/3 of the rectangle.

If something is divided into 4 equal parts, each part is $^1/_4$. $^1/_4$ is written in words as one fourth. Sometimes people say "one quarter" instead of "one fourth"—they mean the same thing.

Each part is 1/4 of the apple.

When you divide something into parts, the parts are equal only if they are the same size. For example, the parts of this rectangle are equal. But the parts of this square are not equal.

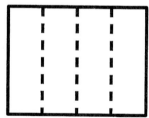

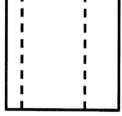

The rectangle has 4 parts.
The parts are equal. Each part is 1/4.

The square has 3 parts.
The parts are not equal.

Learn to recognize the fractions $^1/_2$, $^1/_3$, and $^1/_4$.

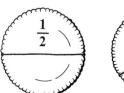

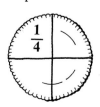

Computation

PARENTS: *From kindergarten, your child should understand that in a group of up to 10 objects there are ways to change the number of objects by adding to them and taking away from them, and that these changes can be shown in writing: for example, 2 + 2 = 4, or 4 − 3 = 1. In first grade, your child should learn more about how addition and subtraction work, and with repeated and varied practice, he or she should know addition and subtraction facts to 12, as well as learn how to apply these memorized facts when solving problems that ask your child to add or subtract two-digit numbers (without having to carry or borrow). Your child should also gain a firmer grasp of the connection between number sentences and the physical objects they represent.*

From Manipulatives to "Mental Math": *As children begin to learn to add and subtract, they may sometimes use countable objects, such as buttons, beans, or paper clips. Such objects, often called "manipulatives" in schools, can help children make the connection between numbers, which are symbols, and the actual items that are being added or subtracted. The goal in first grade, however, is for children to become more competent at working computations in their heads, without using countable objects. While children who are just learning their math facts should not be discouraged from using objects or counting on their fingers, they should, with repeated practice, make the transition to more "mental math."*

You can help your child by playing the number games we suggest below, by using addition and subtraction flash cards (available at many toy stores and teacher supply stores), and, if you have access to a computer capable of running the software, by having your child play the computation games in such programs as Math Rabbit or Math Workshop.

Learn a Fact a Day: *You can use the charts on pages 246–247 to help your child learn one addition or subtraction fact a day. Pick one fact and beginning in the morning, repeat it aloud together. For example, "Nine minus seven is two." Say it over many times. Add a little fun by saying it in different voices (high, low, squeaky, growly), or even sing it! Repeat it often throughout the day. Later, use the charts for review and practice.*

Addition Facts to 12

Sum of 0
0 + 0 = 0

Sum of 1
1 + 0 = 1
0 + 1 = 1

Sum of 2
2 + 0 = 2
1 + 1 = 2
0 + 2 = 2

Sum of 3
3 + 0 = 3
2 + 1 = 3
1 + 2 = 3
0 + 3 = 3

Sum of 4
4 + 0 = 4
3 + 1 = 4
2 + 2 = 4
1 + 3 = 4
0 + 4 = 4

Sum of 5
5 + 0 = 5
4 + 1 = 5
3 + 2 = 5
2 + 3 = 5
1 + 4 = 5
0 + 5 = 5

Sum of 6
6 + 0 = 6
5 + 1 = 6
4 + 2 = 6
3 + 3 = 6
2 + 4 = 6
1 + 5 = 6
0 + 6 = 6

Sum of 7
7 + 0 = 7
6 + 1 = 7
5 + 2 = 7
4 + 3 = 7
3 + 4 = 7
2 + 5 = 7
1 + 6 = 7
0 + 7 = 7

Sum of 8
8 + 0 = 8
7 + 1 = 8
6 + 2 = 8
5 + 3 = 8
4 + 4 = 8
3 + 5 = 8
2 + 6 = 8
1 + 7 = 8
0 + 8 = 8

Sum of 9
9 + 0 = 9
8 + 1 = 9
7 + 2 = 9
6 + 3 = 9
5 + 4 = 9
4 + 5 = 9
3 + 6 = 9
2 + 7 = 9
1 + 8 = 9
0 + 9 = 9

Sum of 10
9 + 1 = 10
8 + 2 = 10
7 + 3 = 10
6 + 4 = 10
5 + 5 = 10
4 + 6 = 10
3 + 7 = 10
2 + 8 = 10
1 + 9 = 10

Sum of 11
10 + 1 = 11
9 + 2 = 11
8 + 3 = 11
7 + 4 = 11
6 + 5 = 11
5 + 6 = 11
4 + 7 = 11
3 + 8 = 11
2 + 9 = 11
1 + 10 = 11

Sum of 12
11 + 1 = 12
10 + 2 = 12
9 + 3 = 12
8 + 4 = 12
7 + 5 = 12
6 + 6 = 12
5 + 7 = 12
4 + 8 = 12
3 + 9 = 12
2 + 10 = 12
1 + 11 = 12

Subtraction Facts from 0 to 12

From 0
$0 - 0 = 0$

From 1
$1 - 0 = 1$
$1 - 1 = 0$

From 2
$2 - 0 = 2$
$2 - 1 = 1$
$2 - 2 = 0$

From 3
$3 - 0 = 3$
$3 - 1 = 2$
$3 - 2 = 1$
$3 - 3 = 0$

From 4
$4 - 0 = 4$
$4 - 1 = 3$
$4 - 2 = 2$
$4 - 3 = 1$
$4 - 4 = 0$

From 5
$5 - 0 = 5$
$5 - 1 = 4$
$5 - 2 = 3$
$5 - 3 = 2$
$5 - 4 = 1$
$5 - 5 = 0$

From 6
$6 - 0 = 6$
$6 - 1 = 5$
$6 - 2 = 4$
$6 - 3 = 3$
$6 - 4 = 2$
$6 - 5 = 1$
$6 - 6 = 0$

From 7
$7 - 0 = 7$
$7 - 1 = 6$
$7 - 2 = 5$
$7 - 3 = 4$
$7 - 4 = 3$
$7 - 5 = 2$
$7 - 6 = 1$
$7 - 7 = 0$

From 8
$8 - 0 = 8$
$8 - 1 = 7$
$8 - 2 = 6$
$8 - 3 = 5$
$8 - 4 = 4$
$8 - 5 = 3$
$8 - 6 = 2$
$8 - 7 = 1$
$8 - 8 = 0$

From 9
$9 - 0 = 9$
$9 - 1 = 8$
$9 - 2 = 7$
$9 - 3 = 6$
$9 - 4 = 5$
$9 - 5 = 4$
$9 - 6 = 3$
$9 - 7 = 2$
$9 - 8 = 1$
$9 - 9 = 0$

From 10
$10 - 1 = 9$
$10 - 2 = 8$
$10 - 3 = 7$
$10 - 4 = 6$
$10 - 5 = 5$
$10 - 6 = 4$
$10 - 7 = 3$
$10 - 8 = 2$
$10 - 9 = 1$

From 11
$11 - 1 = 10$
$11 - 2 = 9$
$11 - 3 = 8$
$11 - 4 = 7$
$11 - 5 = 6$
$11 - 6 = 5$
$11 - 7 = 4$
$11 - 8 = 3$
$11 - 9 = 2$
$11 - 10 = 1$

From 12
$12 - 1 = 11$
$12 - 2 = 10$
$12 - 3 = 9$
$12 - 4 = 8$
$12 - 5 = 7$
$12 - 6 = 6$
$12 - 7 = 5$
$12 - 8 = 4$
$12 - 9 = 3$
$12 - 10 = 2$
$12 - 11 = 1$

Practice Your Addition

One way to practice addition is with things you can count. For example, if you have 3 keys, and you get 5 more keys, how many will you have?

You start with 3 keys:

You get 5 more keys:

Now count how many keys you have in all. So, 3 + 5 = 8.

Another way to practice addition is to count forward. What does 5 + 2 equal? You want the number that is 2 more than 5. So count forward 2 numbers from 5, like this: 5 → 6 → 7. So, 5 + 2 = 7.

When you know how to add by counting forward, keep practicing your addition facts until you know them by heart, without counting. Practice writing and saying the addition facts a lot. It's important that you learn how to give the sums of addition facts quickly, without making mistakes.

Addition Facts with the Same Sum

Learn to give all the addition facts that have the same sum. For example, if you were asked for all the addition facts with a sum of 6, you would write:

6 + 0 = 6
5 + 1 = 6
4 + 2 = 6
3 + 3 = 6
2 + 4 = 6
1 + 5 = 6
0 + 6 = 6

Try this: can you write all the addition facts with a sum of 5?

Things to Know About Addition

- When you add numbers together, the answer you get is called the *sum*. The sum of 3 + 2 is 5. The sum of 3 + 4 is 7. What is the sum of 5 + 3?
- When you add zero to a number, you get the same number. That's because zero means "nothing," so if you add 0, you're adding nothing. For example, 5 + 0 adds up to 5. What is the sum of 8 + 0? How much is 27 + 0?
- It does not matter what order you add numbers in, the sum is still the same. 3 + 4 = 7 and 4 + 3 = 7. So, if you know that 2 + 6 = 8, you also know what 6 + 2 equals.
- You can write addition problems across or up and down. They both mean the same thing. For example:

$$5 + 3 = 8 \text{ is the same as } \begin{array}{r} 5 \\ +3 \\ \hline 8 \end{array}$$

Activity: DICEY ADDITION

PARENTS: For this activity you will need number cards from 2 to 12, pencil and paper, and two six-sided dice.

Give your child a pencil and a sheet of paper. Ask her to place the number cards face up in order. Now have her roll the dice, then add the two numbers that are rolled. She should say the numbers she has rolled aloud and then write them as an equation on her paper. For example, if she rolls a 6 and a 2, she writes (and reads aloud)

$$6 + 2 = 8.$$

If she needs to, your child can count the dots on the dice to add the numbers. When she finds the correct sum, she turns the number card representing that sum face down. When all the number cards from 2 to 12 have been turned face down, the game is over. (You can also adapt this game to include two or more players.)

Adding Three Numbers

To add three numbers, begin by adding the first two numbers. For example:

$$
\begin{array}{r} 4 \\ 2 \\ +1 \end{array}
\qquad
\text{First add}
\begin{array}{r} 4 \\ +2 \\ \hline 6 \end{array}
\qquad
\text{So}
\begin{array}{r} 4 \\ 2 \\ +1 \end{array}
\begin{array}{r} \\ \longrightarrow 6 \\ +1 \\ \hline 7 \end{array}
$$

Can you solve this problem? Remember, begin by adding the first two numbers.

$$
\begin{array}{r} 5 \\ 2 \\ +3 \\ \hline \end{array}
$$

Subtraction: Taking Away Leaves the Difference

Subtraction means taking a number away. Pretend you have five toy robots. You take away 2 toy robots and give them to a friend. How many are left?

There were 5, but you took away 2. 5 take away 2 is 3. Or you can say, "Five minus

two equals three." And you can write that in two ways:

$$5 - 2 = 3 \qquad \text{is the same as} \qquad \begin{array}{r} 5 \\ -2 \\ \hline 3 \end{array}$$

The number you have left after you subtract is called the *difference*. So, the difference of $5 - 2$ is 3. What is the difference of $7 - 4$? The difference is 3.

You can practice subtraction by counting backward. What does $9 - 4$ equal? You want the number that is 4 less than 9, so you can start at 9 and count backward 4 numbers, like this: $9 \rightarrow 8 \rightarrow 7 \rightarrow 6 \rightarrow 5$. So, $9 - 4 = 5$.

Practice your subtraction facts until you know them without having to count backward. Practice writing and saying the subtraction facts up to 12 many times. (See the chart on page 247.) With practice, you will learn them so well that you don't have to stop and figure them out.

You know what happens when you add zero to a number. What is $8 + 0$? Yes, it's 8. What do you think happens when you subtract zero from a number? When you subtract zero, you take away nothing, so you get the same number.

$$5 - 0 = 5 \qquad 12 - 0 = 12 \qquad 43 - 0 = 43$$

Comparing Differences and Sums

You know these signs:

> > greater than
> < less than
> = equals

You can use these signs to compare differences and sums. Here are some examples:

$$10 - 2 > 6 \qquad 6 - 4 < 5 - 1 \qquad 8 - 4 = 7 - 3$$

What sign belongs in the squares here?

$$5 + 3 \ \square \ 6 + 2 \qquad 9 - 7 \ \square \ 2 + 6 \qquad 10 - 3 \ \square \ 6 - 1$$

Fact Families

A family is a group of related people. In math, a *fact family* is a group of related math facts.

A fact family brings together addition facts with their opposite subtraction facts. For example, here is a fact family:

$$5 + 2 = 7 \qquad 7 - 2 = 5$$
$$2 + 5 = 7 \qquad 7 - 5 = 2$$

Here is another fact family:

$$6 + 2 = 8 \qquad 8 - 2 = 6$$
$$2 + 6 = 8 \qquad 8 - 6 = 2$$

If you are given $4 + 2 = 6$, can you figure out all facts in the fact family? Here they are:

$$4 + 2 = 6 \qquad 6 - 2 = 4$$
$$2 + 4 = 6 \qquad 6 - 4 = 2$$

Practice finding the facts in a fact family. For example, try to figure out the fact family for $3 + 2$. Try to figure out the fact family for $4 + 3$.

Activity: FIND THE MYSTERY NUMBER
PARENTS:
You will need:
index cards
marker or crayon
number cards from 0 to 12
countable objects such as buttons, dried beans, or macaroni

Write a plus sign, a minus sign, an equal sign, and a question mark on individual index cards. If you do not have ready-made number cards, make cards for the numbers 0 to 12. Tell your child that you're going to ask him to solve some number problems.

Tell your child this number story. As you tell the story, use the cards to show what's happening. Say, "I have 5 buttons. I'll use this card with the number 5 to show how many buttons I have. Then I bought some more buttons. I'll use the plus sign to show that some buttons were added. This question mark shows that we don't know how many buttons were added. Now I have 9 buttons. I can show the equals sign and the sum of 9."

Ask your child to figure out the mystery number. This process is hard for many children, so be encouraging about his guesses, and help him as necessary to use the countable objects. Your child might need to set up 5 countable objects and then to add one object at a time as he counts onward from 5 to find the mystery number.

When your child gets the correct answer, have him replace the question mark with the appropriate number card, then ask him to read the equation using the correct mathematical language, for example: "Five plus four equals nine."

Repeat the process with a subtraction story, such as: "I had 7 buttons in a box. Then I took away some of those buttons to sew on a jacket. Now I have 2 buttons left in the box. How many buttons did I take away?" Repeat the process using the cards to show the following:

$$7 - ? = 2$$

Have your child find the missing number, using countable objects as necessary, and again have him read the equation using the correct mathematical language. Continue with other addition and subtraction stories that you make up.

As your child becomes more confident with addition and subtraction, encourage him to try figuring out the missing number without using the countable objects.

Activity: ADDITION AND SUBTRACTION STORIES

PARENTS: Make up little stories that ask your child to add and subtract with numbers of 12 or less. Have on hand some countable objects (beans, buttons, macaroni, etc.) for your child to use as necessary, but encourage her to try to do these problems on paper or in her head.

For your addition and subtraction stories, you can use real-life or imaginary situations. For example:

- "Pretend you have a box of ten crayons. Two of the crayons roll under the bed and you can't find them. How many crayons are left in the box?"
- "Once a spaceship from another planet landed on Earth. Out of the ship came 3 space people. Then 5 more space people came out. How many space people came out of the ship in all?" After she has solved that problem, you can continue the same story if you wish. For example: "That's right, there were 8 space people in all. But four of them got homesick and decided to go back to their own planet. How many stayed on Earth?"

Activity: A HUNDRED TABLE

PARENTS: Show your child the 1 to 100 number table on page 255. Show your child how the table is laid out by counting with him from 1 to 21, having him point at the numbers as he counts. Then ask questions like these:

- "What's the largest number in the table?" (100)
- "What's the same about the number in the first box in each row?" (They all end in 1.)
- "What's the same about the number in the last box in each row?" (They all end in 0.)

The hundred table highlights number patterns that will help reinforce your child's understanding of place value and adding and subtracting with tens. This is a first step toward being able to compute with two-digit numbers. Here are some questions you can ask:

- "Look at the third row, with the numbers from 21 to 30. Look at the last number in the row: what's in the tens place?" (3 is in the tens place in the number 30.) "How is that different from all the other numbers in the row?" (All the other numbers have a 2 in the tens place.) "So, how many tens are in 30?" (3 tens are in 30.) "How many tens are in 25?" (2 tens are in 25.)
- "Find the number 53. Count to find 10 more than 53. What number do you get? Look at where 53 and 63 are on the table. What do you see?"
- "Let's look at the table again, but this time let's not count. What do you think 28 + 10 is? Now count to see if you were right."
- "What do you think will happen when you add 17 + 20? How can you figure it out using the number table?" (Look two rows down from 17 to find 37.)

1	2	3	4	5	6	7	8	9	10
11	12	13	14	15	16	17	18	19	20
21	22	23	24	25	26	27	28	29	30
31	32	33	34	35	36	37	38	39	40
41	42	43	44	45	46	47	48	49	50
51	52	53	54	55	56	57	58	59	60
61	62	63	64	65	66	67	68	69	70
71	72	73	74	75	76	77	78	79	80
81	82	83	84	85	86	87	88	89	90
91	92	93	94	95	96	97	98	99	100

Later you can use the same kind of questions with several cases of subtracting 10 from a number.

Two-Digit Addition

You can use the addition facts you have learned so far to add numbers that have two digits. Let's look at this problem:

$$\begin{array}{r} 43 \\ + 25 \\ \hline \end{array}$$

First you add the 3 and the 5 in the ones place:

$$\begin{array}{r} 43 \\ + 25 \\ \hline 8 \end{array}$$

Then add the 4 and 2 in the tens place:

$$\begin{array}{r} 43 \\ + 25 \\ \hline 68 \end{array}$$

So, the sum is 68. Altogether you have 6 tens and 8 ones.

Sometimes one of the numbers you are adding has two digits, but the other has only one digit. For example, look at this problem:

$$\begin{array}{r} 22 \\ + \ 6 \\ \hline \end{array}$$

To solve that problem, you begin in the same way. First you add the numbers in the ones place. Then, since there are no tens to add to the 2 in the tens place, you just bring the 2 down into your answer.

add the ones   *bring down the 2 in the tens place*

$$\begin{array}{r} 22 \\ + 6 \\ \hline 8 \end{array} \qquad \begin{array}{r} 22 \\ + 6 \\ \hline 28 \end{array}$$

So, the sum is 28, which is 2 tens and 8 ones. Do not forget to bring down the 2 tens into your answer!

Two-Digit Subtraction

You can use the subtraction facts you have learned to do subtraction with two-digit numbers.

Find the difference:

$$\begin{array}{r} 7\ 6 \\ -3\ 4 \end{array}$$

First you subtract the numbers in the ones place:

$$\begin{array}{r} \text{tens}\ \text{ones} \\ 7\ 6 \\ -3\ 4 \\ \hline 2 \end{array}$$

Then subtract the numbers in the tens place:

$$\begin{array}{r} \text{tens}\ \text{ones} \\ 7\ 6 \\ -3\ 4 \\ \hline 4\ 2 \end{array}$$

So, the difference is 42, which is 4 tens and 2 ones.

Let's look at another problem:

	subtract the ones	*bring down the 5 in the tens place*
$\begin{array}{r} 57 \\ -6 \\ \hline \end{array}$	$\begin{array}{r} 57 \\ -6 \\ \hline 1 \end{array}$	$\begin{array}{r} 57 \\ -6 \\ \hline 51 \end{array}$

In a problem like that, don't forget to bring down the number in the tens place. Practice doing many two-digit addition and subtraction problems, like these:

$$\begin{array}{ccccc} 34 & 25 & 52 & 68 & 75 & 49 \\ +13 & -12 & +\ 7 & -\ 5 & +12 & -27 \end{array}$$

Money

PARENTS: *Your first grader should already be familiar with the names of the coins and understand that each one has a particular value; if not, see the Money activities in* What Your Kindergartner Needs to Know. *Once your child is comfortable with different coin values, as well as with some basic addition (see above, Computation), you can do the following activity, which shows that different combinations of coins can equal the same amount of money.*

Activity: COIN COMBINATIONS

PARENTS: You will need:
pencils and several sheets of plain paper
pennies, nickels, dimes, and quarters

Before you start counting coins, make sure your child can name each one and tell you how many cents it is worth. A fun way to review the names of the coins is to make coin rubbings by placing a coin under a sheet of paper and rubbing a pencil lightly over the coin until an impression shows up.

To get started, ask your child to show a combination of coins worth 11¢. Then ask her to show another coin combination worth the same amount. Offer help as needed. For example, your child might decide to show a dime and a penny, and eleven pennies. Then ask, "Can you think of any other ways to show 11¢? How about using two nickels? If you use just one nickel, what else do you need to make 11¢?"

Now repeat the above steps with a combination of coins of another amount up to 25¢.

To focus on the idea that different combinations of coins can be worth the same amount of money, ask questions like the following (have some real coins on hand for your child to use if she needs them to answer the questions):

- "What coin is worth the same as two nickels?"
- "If I give you two dimes and one nickel, what coin would you give me that is worth the same?"

- "If I have a dime and a nickel, and you have a dime and five pennies, does one of us have more money?"

When your child is comfortable with combinations up to 25¢, try combinations of coins from 26¢ to 35¢. Start with 26¢, and provide enough coins for your child to make as many possible combinations as you and she can think of.

Geometry

Flat and Solid Shapes

Math that has to do with shapes is called *geometry*. You probably know the names for many flat shapes. A shape with three sides is called a triangle. Here are two triangles. Count the sides on each.

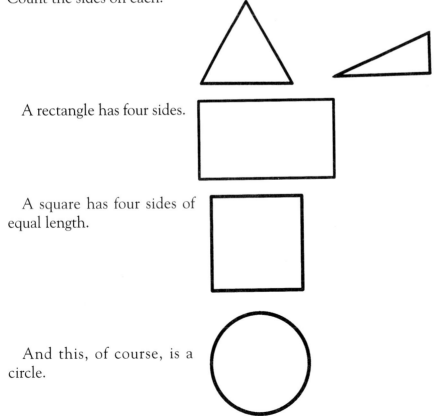

A rectangle has four sides.

A square has four sides of equal length.

And this, of course, is a circle.

When two shapes are the same size and shape, we say they are *congruent*. Two of these triangles are congruent.

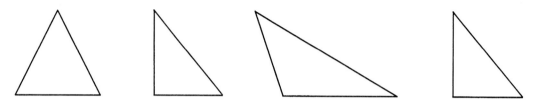

Here are six shapes. Two of them are congruent. Congruent means they are the same size and shape. But they may not be in the same position. Can you find the congruent shapes here?

Learn the names of these solid shapes, and look around your home or school for examples, such as a juice can (cylinder) or ball (sphere).

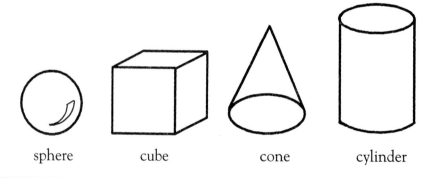

sphere   cube   cone   cylinder

PARENTS: Children often enjoy playing with a tangram, a 7-shape puzzle thought to have been created in China long ago. Check your library or bookstore for books like *Tangram* by Joost Elffers (Penguin, 1977) and *Fun with Tangrams Kit* or *Tangrams ABC Kit* by Susan Johnston (Dover Publications, 31 East 2nd Street, Mineola, NY 11501).

Activity: SIMON SAYS

PARENTS: In first grade, your child should continue to refine her sense of spatial orientation, and become more secure using terms of location such as *left, right, top, middle,* and *bottom,* as well as terms of relative position such as *on, under, over,* and *between.* At home, you can adapt the old favorite game of Simon Says so that it helps your child practice direction words. To practice direction words, use commands that incorporate words like *over, under, left, right, behind, between,* and *around* as part of the game. For example, "Simon says put your left hand under your chin. Simon says walk around the kitchen table. Simon says hold your right knee between your hands."

Measurement

PARENTS: *By the end of first grade, children should become more familiar with a few standard measuring tools, as well as units such as inches and centimeters; cups, quarts, and gallons; pounds; and degrees Fahrenheit. To understand measurement, first graders need many opportunities to measure things.*

First graders also need plenty of practice in measuring time. They need to work with terms and concepts such as before and after, and yesterday, today, and tomorrow. They should know the days of the week and the months of the year (see the Language Arts section of this book for the poem, "Thirty Days Hath September"). By the end of first grade, your child should be able to read a clock face and tell time to the half hour. You can help her by regularly showing her a calendar and clock as you plan various tasks. Don't rely exclusively on digital clocks or watches; use a clock or watch with hands.

> See "Measurement: How Long, How Much, How Hot" in the Science section of this book (pages 294–299) for activities involving length, volume, and temperature.

Calendar Time

There are seven days in a week. Can you name them? (Sunday, Monday, Tuesday, Wednesday, Thursday, Friday, Saturday.) Of those seven days, five are called the weekdays and two days make up the weekend. Can you tell me which two days are the weekend days? (Saturday and Sunday.)

There are twelve months in a year. Can you name them, starting with the first month? They are (1) January, (2) February, (3) March, (4) April, (5) May, (6) June, (7) July, (8) August, (9) September, (10) October, (11) November, and (12) December. Make sure you know the names of the months of the year, in order.

You remember ordinal numbers, the numbers that help you put things in order? For the last two months of the year, you can learn two new ordinal numbers, eleventh and twelfth. (Notice the funny spelling of "twelfth.") November is the eleventh month, and December is the twelfth month.

PARENTS: To strengthen your child's sense of calendar time, display the calendar for the current month and occasionally ask questions like the following:

- "What day is today?" (Ask for the day of the week as well as the month, day, and year.)
- "What day of the week was yesterday?"
- "What day of the week will tomorrow be?"
- "Can you show me where yesterday was on the calendar? Can you tell me what the date will be next Sunday?"

Activity: TELLING TIME

PARENTS: *What follows is not so much a one-time activity as an explanation you can read aloud to your child, then refer back to on many occasions. Most children need repeated practice and reinforcement before they master the skill of telling time. In school, your child should get plenty of practice in learning to tell time. If you want to supplement this, check your library or bookstore for books like* My First Book of Time *by Claire Llewellyn (Dorling Kindersley, 1992). Many teacher supply stores and some toy stores sell "hands-on" kits for learning to tell time.*

Get Ready: As you read aloud the following section to your child, it will be helpful to have a paper clockface to work with. You can make one from a paper plate, a sheet of colored paper, and a brad. To make clock hands, cut two narrow strips of paper from the sheet: one strip should be longer than the other. Then have your child help you turn the paper plate into a clockface by numbering around the rim from 1 to 12. Finally, use the brad to attach the ends of both strips to the center of the clockface. Your child can use this homemade clockface to show different times.

Go: Ask your child to show the times on a homemade clockface as you read aloud the following:

Look at the clock. What time does this clock say it is?

When the long hand is on the 12 and the short hand is on the 8, then the time is 8 o'clock. We can write that in two ways:

8:00 *means the same as* **8 o'clock**

The long hand on a clock is also called the *minute hand*. The short hand is also called the *hour hand*. On this clock, the minute hand is on the 12 and the hour hand is on the 4. Can you tell me what time it is?

Look at this clock. Tell me where the minute hand is, and where the hour hand is. Then can you tell me what time it is?

Yes, that clock shows 10 o'clock. Can you show me 10 o'clock on your paper clock?

Your clock could be showing 10:00 in the morning or 10:00 at night. If you want to tell someone to meet you at 10:00, how can you make sure he knows that you mean 10:00 in the morning and not 10:00 at night? One way is to say, "Meet me at 10 A.M." A time before noon is called A.M. A.M. is in the morning. Time after noon is called P.M. P.M. is in the afternoon or at night. [*Note:* You may want to ask your child if he can recognize noon on a clock, and show him if he doesn't know how.]

Do you eat breakfast closer to 8 A.M. or 8 P.M.? Do you go to bed closer to 8 A.M. or 8 P.M.? Can you think of some things you normally do at about 10 A.M.? What are you normally doing at 10 P.M.?

Now let's look at this clock. What number is the minute hand on? And look at the hour hand—do you see how it's between 7 and 8? This clock is showing half past seven. Another way of saying half past seven is seven-thirty, which we can write like this:

7:30

When we say seven-thirty, we mean that it's 30 minutes after seven o'clock. Seven-thirty is the same as saying "half past seven" because 30 minutes is half of an hour. A whole hour is 60 minutes. Sixty minutes is how long it takes for the minute hand to go around the clock once, starting at the 12 and coming back to the 12. While the minute hand makes one whole trip around the clock, the hour hand moves from one number to the next.

Can you tell what time it is on this clock?

Some clocks do not have hands. On a digital clock, the time appears in numbers. These two clocks are showing the same time in different ways. Can you tell me what time they are showing?

These two clocks are showing the same time in different ways. Can you tell me what time they are showing?

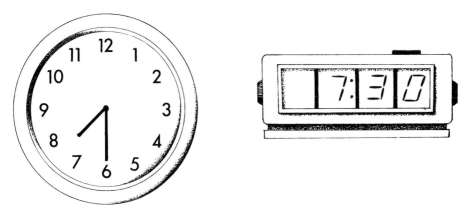

VI.

Science

INTRODUCTION

Children gain knowledge about the world around them in part from observation and experience. To understand animals and their habitats, or human body systems, or electricity, a child needs firsthand experience with many opportunities to observe and experiment. In the words of *Benchmarks for Science Literacy* (a 1993 report from the American Association for the Advancement of Science): "From their very first day in school, students should be actively engaged in learning to view the world scientifically. That means encouraging them to ask questions about nature and to seek answers, collect things, count and measure things, make qualitative observations, organize collections and observations, discuss findings, etc."

While experience counts for much, book learning is also important, for it helps bring coherence and order to a child's scientific knowledge. Only when topics are presented systematically and clearly can children make steady and secure progress in their scientific learning. The child's development of scientific knowledge and understanding is in some ways a very disorderly and complex process, different for each child. But a systematic approach to the exploration of science, one that combines experience with book learning, can help provide essential building blocks for deeper understanding at a later time. It can also provide the kind of knowledge that one is not likely to gain from observation: consider, for example, how people long believed that the earth stood still while the sun orbited around it, a misconception that "direct experience" presented as fact.

In this section, we introduce first graders to a variety of topics consistent with the early study of science in countries that have had outstanding results in teaching science at the elementary level. The text is meant to be read aloud to your child, and it offers questions for you and your child to discuss, as well as activities for you to do together.

Suggested Resources

Living Things and Their Habitats
Desert; *Forest*; *Mountain*; and *Ocean*, four books by Ron Hirschi (Bantam, 1992, 1991, 1992, and 1991)
A Walk in the Desert by Caroline Arnold (Simon and Schuster Education Group/Silver Press, 1990)
Who Eats What? Food Chains and Food Webs by Patricia Lauber (HarperCollins, 1995)

Dinosaurs
Dinosaur Time by Peggy Parish (HarperCollins, 1974)

My Visit to the Dinosaurs (1985) and *Digging Up Dinosaurs* (1988) by Aliki (Harper-
Collins)

Oceans and Undersea Life
Amazing Fish by Mary Ling (Knopf, 1991)
The Magic School Bus on the Ocean Floor by Joanna Cole (Scholastic, 1992)

The Human Body
Germs Make Me Sick! by Melvin Berger (HarperCollins, 1985)
What's Inside? My Body (Dorling Kindersley, 1991)
Your Insides by Joanna Cole (Putnam and Grosset, 1992)

Matter
Air Is All Around You by Franklyn M. Branley (HarperCollins, 1986)
It Could Still Be Water by Allan Fowler (Childrens Press, 1992)
What Happened? by Rozanne Lanczak Williams (Creative Teaching Press, 1994)

Introduction to Electricity
All About Electricity by Melvin Berger (Scholastic, 1995)
Experiment with Magnets and Electricity by Margaret Whalley (Lerner, 1994)

Astronomy
The Moon Seems to Change by Franklyn M. Branley (HarperCollins, 1987)
My Picture Book of the Planets by Nancy E. Krulik (Scholastic, 1991)
The Sun Is Always Shining Somewhere by Allan Fowler (Childrens Press, 1991)

Inside the Earth
Earth by Dennis B. Fradin (Childrens Press, 1989)
The Magic School Bus Inside the Earth by Joanna Cole (Scholastic, 1987)
Rocks and Minerals by Illa Podenforf (Childrens Press, 1982)
Volcanoes by Franklyn M. Branley (HarperCollins, 1985)

Living Things and Their Habitats

Do you recognize this big furry fellow? He's a polar bear. He lives near the North Pole. What's the weather like there? Brrr! Yes, it's cold, *cold*, **cold.** Look at what's all around the polar bear: ice, and lots of it.

The polar bear lives where it's cold and icy all the time, but he doesn't seem to mind at all. Look at him again. See his thick, furry coat? With all that thick fur, he stays pretty cozy, even at the North Pole.

Now, imagine that the polar bear decides to go on a vacation. (Of course, you and I know that bears don't take vacations, but let's pretend.) He goes on a trip to Hawaii. How do you think he would like it? What would our big furry friend think of the sunny, sandy beaches of Hawaii?

Well, if you've ever been to the beach, *you* might like it, but you can take off your clothes and wear nothing but a bathing suit. The polar bear can't take off his fur!

Poor polar bear! He wouldn't enjoy a trip to warm, sunny Hawaii. It's a lovely place, but not for him. It's not his *habitat*.

What's a habitat? For an animal, a habitat is the place where the animal lives, eats, sleeps, makes its home, has babies, and gets along (mostly) with other animals. But it's not just *any* kind of place. An animal's habitat is a special place suited to the animal because the animal is suited to it.

The big furry polar bear isn't suited to the warm beach, but he gets along fine at the icy North Pole. A fish that swims in the ocean couldn't possibly survive in the mountains, could it? Would a worm that crawls through the moist, rich soil of the forest be happy living in the hot, sandy desert?

Different animals live in different habitats. The way an animal lives has a lot to do with its habitat. Let's explore a few habitats and get to know some animals living in them.

The Forest Habitat

Imagine you're taking a walk through a beautiful forest. Oak and maple trees stand tall around you. Their highest branches reach upward and form a leafy canopy, which makes it cool and shady for you as you walk along below.

What's that tap-tap-tapping sound? It's a bird called a woodpecker. Woodpeckers peck into the trunks of old trees, looking for insects to eat. The woodpecker lives in this forest habitat.

A squirrel scampers up a tree. The squirrel also lives in this forest habitat. Squirrels build nests in the tree branches and gather acorns from the oak trees in the fall.

Pew! What could that awful smell be? It's a skunk! You must have scared it. A skunk sends out a stinky spray to defend itself against larger animals that threaten to eat it (not that you would ever eat a skunk!). Skunks burrow into holes in the ground or into rotten tree trunks. They eat berries and insects and eggs they steal from the nests of birds that also live in the forest habitat.

Ooh, what's that sticky stuff on your face? You've walked into the threads of a spider

What You're Called and What You Eat

Here's a fact you know is true every time your tummy growls: animals need to eat. Some animals eat plants. Some animals eat other animals. And some animals eat both. Scientists use special names for animals, depending on whether they eat plants, meat, or both. Let's learn these special names: they're big words, so get ready!

Do you eat both plants and meat? Then you're an *omnivore* [AHM-nuh-vore]. An omnivore is an animal that eats both plants and animals. Bears are omnivores. They eat berries, and they eat small animals like fish. They also use their sharp claws to rip open logs and eat the insects they find there.

Animals that eat only plants are called *herbivores* [HUR-buh-vores]. Some human beings choose to eat only plants and no meat. Many animals, including mice, cows, and horses, eat only plants. Even huge elephants eat only leaves, fruits, nuts, and grasses.

Some animals would rather eat meat most of all. Can you think of any? Dogs and cats, lions and tigers, sharks and snakes eat meat. They are called *carnivores* [CAR-nuh-vores]. A carnivore eats animal flesh, or meat.

web, strung across your path. Spiders weave their webs where insects fly, hoping to trap some bugs for dinner. Yummy!

Down on the forest floor, the leaves fall and pile up. Snails and other animals eat the leaves. Along comes a raccoon, which eats the snails (and many other things—raccoons aren't very picky eaters!).

Woodpecker, squirrel, skunk, spider, snail, raccoon—all these animals and many, many more live in the forest habitat. For their homes and food, they depend upon the plants and other animals that live in the forest with them.

The Underground Habitat

Imagine that you brought a shovel with you on your walk through the forest. Take it out and dig down under the twigs, leaves, and mushrooms on the forest floor. What can you see?

A slimy brown earthworm slithers deeper underground. A little white grub curls up in the soil. Soon it will grow into an insect and creep among the forest ferns and mosses.

The worm and the grub live together in the forest's underground habitat. Even some furry animals, like moles, live underground with them. Moles have long, slender paws just right for digging. They burrow underground, and they look for things to eat: things like roots, ants, and—sorry, little worm—worms. Actually, moles don't really "look" for

things to eat, since they can't see very well. Instead, moles find their way around underground with a keen sense of smell.

So, moles have paws for digging, and even though they have weak eyes, they have a strong sense of smell. Do you see how the mole is suited to its underground habitat?

What is this mole eating?

The Desert Habitat

Let's look at the desert, which is a very different habitat from the forest. Can you think of some differences between the forest and the desert?

The forest is often cool. The desert is often hot.

The forest is moist. The desert is dry.

The forest is dark and shady. The desert is bright and sunny.

Sometimes it snows and rains in the forest, but it rarely does in the desert.

Compared to the forest, the desert is a very different habitat for plants and animals. So, do you think you'll find the same kind of animals and plants in the desert that you found in the forest?

This lizard lives in a desert in Arizona.

Lizards live in the hot desert. Their bodies do well in the heat. They like to lie on warm rocks and bask in the blazing sunshine. Lizards match the desert habitat.

Cactus plants grow in the desert. They can grow for a long time without any rain at all. They like heat and a lot of sunshine. Cactus plants do well in the desert habitat.

But not many animals or plants live in the desert. In fact, the desert is almost deserted—which is how it got its name.

A big cactus.

Water Habitats

Can you name some animals that live in water?

Fish live in water, such as ponds, lakes, and streams. They eat smaller fish, plants, and insects.

Think of the ways that a fish is suited to its water habitat. Fish don't have feet, because they don't walk. They live in a water habitat, and so they swim. You can't breathe underwater, but fish can because they have gills. But a fish out of water is in trouble! A fish can't survive outside its water habitat.

The Great Blue Heron's long neck helps it reach fish under water.

Have you ever heard the saying "like a fish out of water"? Since fish can't breathe out of water, people use this saying to mean that someone is very uncomfortable in a new or unusual situation.

For example, a shy child who is asked to sing a song in front of the whole school might think, "I don't want to sing in front of all those people. I've never been onstage before. I'd feel like a fish out of water."

Many other animals do best in a water habitat, too. Some live all their lives underwater, like oysters and starfish. Some live part of their lives underwater and part on land, like frogs and salamanders. Some live on the land near the water, like herons and hermit crabs. All of these animals depend upon the water, the plants, and the other animals nearby.

Not all water habitats are the same. Ponds, lakes, and rivers are different from oceans. Do you know why? If you've ever played in the waves at the ocean, you know how that water tastes: very salty. Oceans contain salt water. But most ponds, lakes, and rivers contain fresh water. What's the difference?

Here's an experiment to answer that question. Fill a glass with drinking water. Take a sip. It tastes refreshing. That's the kind of water found in most lakes and rivers.

Now stir in two teaspoons full of salt. Take a sip—a *very small* sip. Yuck! You wouldn't call that refreshing, would you? That glass now contains salt water, like the water in the ocean.

You may not like the taste of salt water, but many plants and animals depend upon it to live. Clams, oysters, and jellyfish live in the salty ocean, along with plants such as seaweed. Whales, dolphins, sharks—*all* the animals that live in an ocean habitat—need salt water. If you put them into water without

Shark!

salt, they wouldn't survive. And if you put a freshwater fish in salt water, it wouldn't survive. Each water animal and plant needs to be in the kind of water habitat to which it's suited.

The Food Chain

As you've learned about different habitats, you've heard a lot about animals and what they eat. Has it made you hungry? You've got to eat to live. Not just you, but every living thing needs food to survive. Plants make their own food out of sunshine, air, water, and nutrients from the soil in which they grow. But animals can't do that. Animals eat other living things, including plants and other animals. Big animals may eat little ones. And when the big animal dies, it may be eaten by little animals. All this eating is called the *food chain*. Let's see how it works.

Imagine a green plant growing by the side of a river. A caterpillar comes along and chews on the leaves. Later the caterpillar grows into a flying insect. The insect flies across the river, when suddenly, *swoosh*, a fish leaps out of the water and swallows it.

A food chain.

The fish splashes back into the water, feeling full and happy—but not for long. A big bear reaches into the river and grabs the fish in his paw. The bear has caught a tasty supper.

Later that year the bear dies, and through the winter its body rots away. The rotting body turns to nutrients that soak into the soil by the side of the river. When spring comes, the nutrients help green plants grow. One of those green plants grows by the side of the river. A caterpillar comes along and chews on the leaves and . . .

Do you see? It's a cycle, starting over, and going round and round again. It's a cycle of one creature feeding upon another, a cycle of life and death and life again.

People call this cycle the food chain because it seems to link together the plants and animals in nature. Animals eat plants, and these animals are sometimes eaten by other animals. Plants and animals die and rot, which returns nutrients to the soil, which helps more plants grow. It's all a part of the food chain that keeps nature alive, and it all starts with plants growing from sunshine, air, water, and nutrients.

Animals and Plants Need Their Habitats, So Be Careful

You've seen that there are many different kinds of habitats, and many different kinds of animals and plants in each one. Different plants are suited to different habitats: an oak tree does fine in the forest but could not grow in the desert. Most animals are so well suited to living in one kind of habitat that it would be difficult for them to live in another. They might not be able to find the right kind of food, or the right kind of water, or the materials they need to make a home or nest.

Sometimes people can mess up a habitat. People cut down forests to get trees for lumber or to make space for new houses and office buildings. People bring water to the desert so that they can make more farms. People fill in ponds with dirt so that they can build houses. What happens to the animals and plants when their habitat is destroyed? Sometimes they die.

In one habitat, the world's rainforests, many animals and plants are in danger. That's because people are cutting down too many trees in the rainforests. Rainforests are tall, dense green forests that grow in the hottest parts of the world. They are called rainforests because there is always moisture in the air, and it drips off the leaves as if it were

always raining. Not many people live in the rainforests, but thousands of different plants and animals do. We need to be careful not to hurt this precious habitat or we will lose even more of the animals and plants that live there.

When a habitat is destroyed, plants and animals die. When something happens that causes *all* of a certain kind of plant or animal to die off, then we say that kind of plant or animal is *extinct*, which means it no longer exists anywhere in the world: it has died off, never to be seen again.

The jaguar is in danger of becoming extinct.

You may know about some very famous extinct animals: the dinosaurs. They became extinct—no one knows exactly why—millions of years ago. But extinction is not just something that happened millions or thousands or even hundreds of years ago. Today many different kinds of animals and plants are *endangered*, which means that there are not many of them left in the world and they are in danger of becoming extinct. They are sometimes endangered because of things that people do to hurt their habitats: things like cutting down trees or polluting the land and water.

> Rachel Carson understood the importance of protecting the natural world. You can find out more about her on page 319.

If people make problems, they can also solve them. Many people today understand that it is not a good thing to destroy the habitats of plants and animals. These people are working to make sure that we find ways to protect the different habitats and the living things that depend on them.

The orangutan is endangered.

Extinct but Still Popular: Dinosaurs

They haven't been around for millions of years, but many people are crazy about them. How about you? Do you like dinosaurs?

Some dinosaurs, like the huge Brachiosaurus [BRAK-ee-uh-SAWR-us], were taller than a house. Like many dinosaurs, the Brachiosaurus was a herbivore (which means it ate only what?). Other dinosaurs were carnivores: they ate animal flesh, including other dinosaurs. One fierce carnivore was the Tyrannosaurus rex.

Dinosaurs have been extinct for so long that no one has ever seen one. So how do we know they ever lived at all? Because dinosaur bones have been found in the ground all around the world. From these remains, scientists can figure out a lot about what dinosaurs looked like and how they lived.

To learn more about dinosaurs, check your library for the *many* good books that will tell you more about these fascinating creatures.

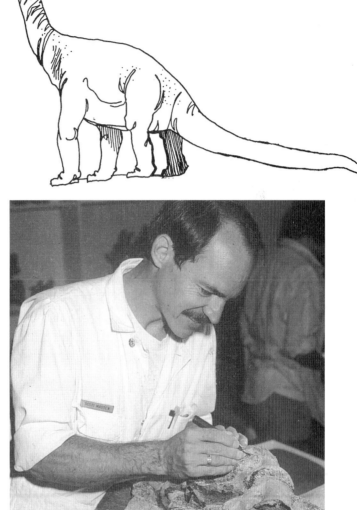

Brachiosaurus.

Tyrannosaurus rex.

This scientist is cleaning the backbone of a dinosaur.

Oceans and Undersea Life

The Oceans and the Tides

Take a look at a globe or a map of the world and notice how much of its area is covered in water. How much? A lot! Water covers three fourths of the earth.

Where will you find most of this water? In the oceans. Look at a globe or map (like the one on page 135) and see if you can find these big oceans: the Pacific Ocean, the Atlantic Ocean, the Indian Ocean, and the Arctic Ocean.

The place where the ocean meets the land is called the *shore*. If you've ever walked along the shore of an ocean, you may have noticed that sometimes the water comes way up on the shore, and sometimes it stays farther out.

Every day, twice a day, in a regular pattern, the level of the ocean rises and falls as it meets the shore. These changes are called the ocean's *tides*.

If you were to spend a day on the beach (wouldn't that be nice?), you could see how

Low tide. High tide.

the tide changes from high to low and back again. At high tide, the edge of the ocean comes way up, covering the beach, so that all you see is a little stretch of sand. At low tide, the water level drops and the edge of the ocean moves farther away, leaving a broad sandy beach. At high tide, that beach was covered with water.

Ocean Currents

The water in the ocean moves all the time. The wind moves it and forms the ocean surface into waves. The tides move it, up toward shore and back down again.

In some parts of the ocean, water moves in great streams, almost like rivers flowing through the ocean. We call these moving streams *ocean currents*. When ship captains sail the ocean, they pay close attention to currents because a current can carry a ship along with it, just as a river carries a stick or a paper boat downstream.

When ship captains sail across the Atlantic Ocean, they pay special attention to a current called the Gulf Stream. The Gulf Stream runs from the Gulf of Mexico, up the coast of Florida, and then north up the coast of the United States as far as North Carolina before it crosses the Atlantic Ocean. Use your finger on the map to trace the path of the Gulf Stream.

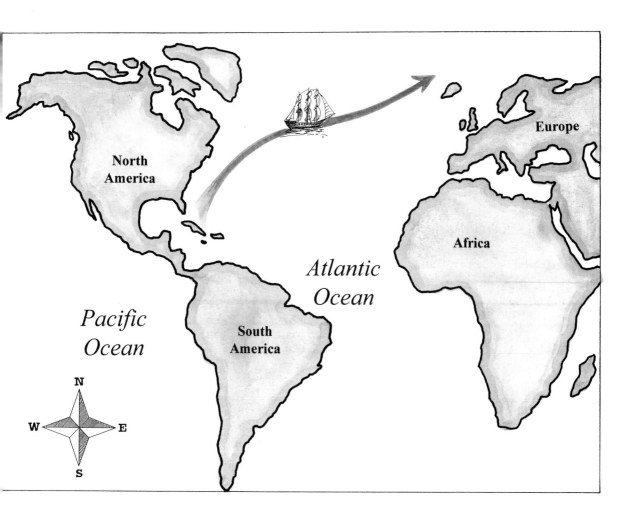

The water in the Gulf Stream is warmer than the ocean it flows through. If a ship sailing out of Florida wants to go straight east, the Gulf Stream will push it to the north. So, if you were steering the ship, you would have to know about the strong currents of the Gulf Stream if you planned to get where you wanted to go!

Under the Ocean

The ocean floor has hills and valleys just like the dry parts of the earth.

Let's take a look beneath the surface of the ocean. Put on your scuba-diving gear. Is your mask on tight? Are the air tanks full? Okay, let's jump in!

Look at the ground under the water. The sandy beach continues to slope down. We call the bottom of the ocean the ocean floor. Where the ocean is shallow, the ocean floor is close to the water's surface. Sometimes the ocean floor juts up out of the water, and that makes an island. Where the ocean is deep, the ocean floor drops way down. Long, deep valleys run across it. The deepest valleys are called ocean trenches. You can think of the ocean floor as a landscape of

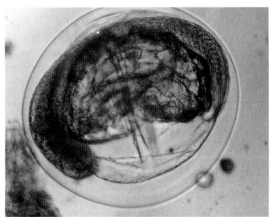

This is one of many kinds of plankton that live in the ocean. This picture was taken with a special camera to make the plankton big enough to see.

mountains, valleys, and trenches, stretching out for thousands of miles underwater.

So many different animals live in the ocean. Can you name some? Did you think of fish, sharks, dolphins, octopuses, and others? Did you know that if you scoop up a handful of ocean water, you're holding a bunch of living creatures? These creatures are so tiny that you can't see them. It would seem as if you were holding just a handful of water, but really the water is full of little living things! There's a special name for all these teeny-tiny animals, along with many teeny-tiny plants, that drift in the ocean's waters: they're called *plankton*.

The ocean is home not only to teeny-tiny plankton but also to some of the world's largest creatures. Can you name any of these big ocean creatures? Did you think of whales? The blue whale, the biggest whale of all, can grow to 98 feet long and weigh 165 tons (1 ton is 2,000 pounds). It's hard to imagine how big that is! If about thirty children your size were to lie down

How big is a blue whale? Compare it to an elephant.

in a line, head to toe, they might add up to the length of a blue whale. But to add up to the weight of a blue whale, it would take about six thousand children your size!

There's a food chain for animals and plants in the ocean, just as there is for animals and plants on land. One ocean food chain is amazing: some whales eat only plankton. Think about it: some of the biggest ocean animals eat only some of the littlest plants and animals! How would you like to have the same thing every day for breakfast, lunch, dinner, and snacks, and never see what you're swallowing?!

Humans and the Ocean World

People all over the world depend upon the ocean. Ships travel on the ocean, moving things from one continent to another. Fishermen catch food in the ocean for us to eat. Tuna fish comes from the ocean. So do shrimp. And many people around the world enjoy eating some kinds of seaweed.

The ocean helps the world's people. It has many different habitats for many different plants and animals. It helps the planet earth stay healthy. That's why people have to be careful not to do things to hurt the ocean.

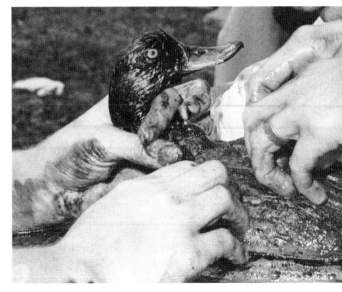

This duck is getting cleaned up after an oil spill.

People can hurt the ocean by putting the wrong things in it, like garbage and litter. Sometimes people put things in by accident. When an oil tanker spills oil into the ocean, the surface of the water turns black and dingy. An oil spill kills many fish and birds. It also kills plankton, which may be too small to see but is important to the ocean habitat. When an accident like an oil spill happens, people may come quickly to the rescue, but such a big mess is very hard to clean up.

People can also hurt the ocean by taking too much from it. For example, fishermen can "overfish" if they catch the same kind of fish for a long time in one small region of the ocean. Sometimes, if fishermen catch too many of one kind of fish, not enough fish are left behind to have babies, and then that kind of fish can become extinct. When one kind of fish disappears, it can disturb the lives of other animals and plants living in that part of the ocean. Today many states and countries have laws telling how many fish people are allowed to catch and during what time of the year people can catch them. These laws are one way to keep overfishing from damaging the ocean habitat forever.

The Human Body

PARENTS: *In this book, we introduce the major body systems. Later books in this series present the body systems in greater detail.*

Have you ever thought about what happens inside your body when you breathe? When you eat? When you stand up? When you jump? When you run? Your body can do so many things! Different parts of your body work together to let you breathe, eat, stand up, jump, run, and lots more. Let's find out about what's going on inside. Let's learn about some of the systems of your body.

The Skeletal System

Hold up a jacket by the collar. It just falls limp. Now, put the jacket over a coat hanger. The hard coat hanger gives the soft jacket a shape.

Inside your body there's something that gives you a shape. No, not a bunch of coat hangers, but a bunch of bones—more than two hundred of them! These bones make up your *skeleton*. Your skeleton is the hard part inside your body. It looks something like the drawings you might see around Halloween time.

Squeeze one of your fingers: do you feel the hard bone inside? Now, tap your head with your knuckles— not too hard! The sound you hear is the sound of the bone inside your finger knocking against your skull, which is the bone inside your head.

Bones are hard, but they can break, such as when a person takes a bad fall. Doctors can help fix most broken bones. They use a special machine called an X-ray machine. An X-ray machine takes a picture through your skin and let's the doctor see the broken bone. Often the doctor will wrap the injured part of the body in a hard cast, which will protect the broken bone and keep it straight until it grows back together again.

You can find the words to a funny song about the skeleton, "Dry Bones," on page 224 of this book.

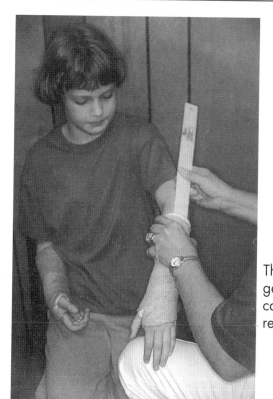

There are more than two hundred bones inside you.

This is an X-ray of a broken leg bone.

This girl is getting her cast removed.

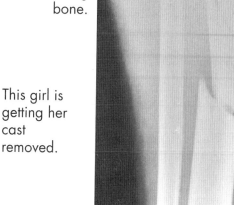

The Muscular System

Squeeze one of your arms and you can feel the solid bone inside. You feel something firm around it, too: that's a *muscle*.

Muscles wrap around bones and stretch from one bone to another. Hold one hand around your arm, between your wrist and your elbow. Make a tight fist with the arm that you're holding. Do you feel something tighten up inside? That's your muscle.

Muscles make you move. You use your muscles to walk, run, jump, draw, stretch, and lift. You even use your muscles to talk, yawn, laugh, wink, and sing.

Your muscles help you move.

The Circulatory System

Now put your hand on your chest. Do you feel something beating inside? If you don't, run around fast and then try again. That beating you feel is a very important muscle: it's your heart.

Your heart is beating all the time, day and night. When your heart beats, it pumps blood. It pumps blood through tubes that go all around your body and then come back to your heart. By beat-beat-beating, your heart keeps the blood *circulating* to every part of your body ("circulating" means going round and round).

Your circulatory system moves your blood around your body.

The Digestive System

Your blood carries good things from the food you eat to all parts of your body. But how did your food get into your blood?

It got there because your body *digested* it. Whatever you eat—corn on the cob, a bagel, a peanut butter sandwich, a carrot, a glass of milk, an egg roll—your body has to digest it. Here is how that happens.

When you put a piece of food in your mouth, you chew it with your teeth, which break the food into little pieces. There's a watery fluid in your mouth, called saliva, that also helps break down the food. When you swallow, the food goes down a tube into your stomach. (When you drink something, you just swallow, and the liquid you're drinking goes down the same tube to your stomach.)

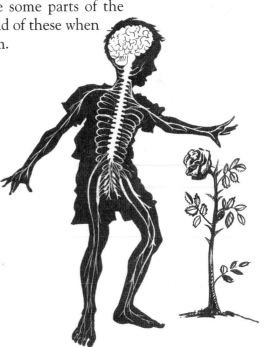

After you eat, have you ever heard your stomach make some squichy, gurgling noises? These noises show that your stomach and other body parts are continuing the work of digesting your food.

Once your food is digested, it's broken into very tiny bits. The most valuable parts go into your blood and give you the energy you need to do all the things you like to do. Your body cannot use some parts of the food you eat; you get rid of these when you go to the bathroom.

Your digestive system breaks your food down so your body can use it.

The Nervous System

Tap your head—gently!—with your knuckles one more time. There's your skull. Do you know what's inside it? A very important part of your body: your brain.

Your brain is what you use to think, remember, and learn. Your brain tells the rest of your body what to do. Your brain is in charge: it's like the captain of a ship or the pilot of an airplane.

Your brain sends messages to all parts of your body and gets messages back. These messages are carried through the *nerves*, which go from your brain all through your body. The nerves look something like the branches of a tree, but they're *much* thinner.

Your nervous system carries messages to and from your brain.

Your nerves carry messages from your five senses. Do you remember learning about your five senses (in the Kindergarten book in this series)? Can you name them?

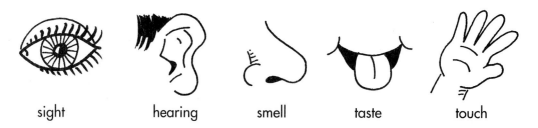

| sight | hearing | smell | taste | touch |

When you feel an itch on the tip of your nose, nerves are sending a message from your nose to your brain. Then your brain sends a message along the nerves to your fingers. The messages says, "Reach up and scratch that itchy nose!" Ahh, does that feel better? Nerves sent that "feel-better" message from your nose back to your brain.

In Sickness and in Health

Ah-choo! Whew, that was a big sneeze. Well, that's okay, it was just one and—*ah-choo! ah-choo!*

Uh-oh. You can't stop sneezing. Your nose is runny. You're starting to feel a little hot. And maybe your tummy aches.

Everybody gets sick now and then. It's no fun. You can feel just terrible.

Some germs can make your body sick. You can't see germs, but you sure can feel what the bad ones do to you! When your body gets sick, it fights the germs. Sometimes when your body is working really hard to fight the germs, you have a fever—which means that your body's temperature rises.

Many illnesses, like colds and flu, can be spread from one person to another. If a friend with a cold sneezes right in your face, his cold germs could get into your body

through your nose and mouth. Then, in a few days, you might catch that cold, too.

Try not to spread your germs: cover your face when you sneeze or cough. Use tissues when you blow your nose. Wash your hands after using the bathroom and before every meal. Your hands can pick up many germs without your even knowing it.

Sometimes when you're sick, you go to a doctor. The doctor may use a thermometer to check your temperature. She may ask you to open your mouth wide and say "Ah" so that she can look down at your throat. (What's down there? Ask an adult to let you look inside.) The doctor may listen to your heartbeat with a tool called a stethoscope.

The doctor may decide that you need medicine to help you get better. Never take any medicine without permission, and take only as much as you're supposed to. Sometimes the doctor may give you a shot. You may not like it, but be brave: the shot helps your body fight the disease.

> Edward Jenner and Louis Pasteur discovered a lot about how to keep people from getting sick. You can find out more about them on pages 314 and 316.

When you were very young, you probably got a special kind of shot called a *vaccination*. You didn't get this shot because you were sick. You got a vaccination to help keep you from getting sick with certain bad diseases. Vaccination shots might hurt a little, but they help you for a long time.

Take Care of Your Body

It's almost dinnertime at Billy's house. Have you ever heard anything like this?

MOTHER: Billy, dinner will be ready in a few minutes. Wash your hands.
BILLY: Okay, just let me finish making this last mudball.
MOTHER: Billy, come to the table, dinner's ready.
BILLY [*sitting down at table*]: Yum, I'm starved, let's eat.
MOTHER: Billy, did you wash your hands?
BILLY: Aw, Mom, come on!
MOTHER: Billy, get up and go wash your hands before you eat.
BILLY: But Mom, they're clean. I washed them yesterday!

To stay healthy and strong, you've got to do what adults keep telling you to do:

- Wash your hands after using the bathroom and before every meal.
- Eat foods that are good for you (and go easy on the "junk food").
- Get plenty of exercise.
- Take a regular bath or shower.
- Get a good night's sleep.

Did you hear that, Billy?

Matter:
Solid, Liquid, and Gas

What do these things have in common: an apple, a river, and the air we breathe?

They may seem very different, but they're alike in one way: they are all made of *matter*.

Matter is the stuff that makes up all the things in the world. Your shoes, a flower, an egg, a dog, a rock, a tire, a book, a cloud, a goldfish, a jet plane, a pencil—matter makes up every one of these things, and everything else as well. Matter even makes up your body.

Let's go back to our first three examples: an apple, a river, and the air we breathe. You can see and touch the matter in an apple. It's *solid*. Can you think of some other matter that's solid? How about a rock? A baseball? Your shoes?

You can see and touch the matter in a river, too. It's not solid, though, or hard like a rock. It's *liquid*. Can you think of some other matter that's liquid? Such as milk? Or the saliva in your mouth?

Now, what about the air we breathe? It's different: it's not a solid or a liquid. You can't see it. You can't reach out and touch it. But sometimes you can feel it, like when the wind blows. When you feel the wind blowing on your face, you are feeling the matter in the air. And think about this: when you blow up a balloon, what goes inside? Some stuff goes into the balloon and makes it bigger. That stuff is air, and air is matter. But air is a different kind of matter: it's not a solid or a liquid. Air is a *gas*.

Air Is Matter

PARENTS: *Here are two experiments you can do with your child to see that air is matter.*

You will need:
a bowl deeper than the cup
a cork
a clear plastic drinking cup or a glass
tissues or paper towels

1. Put water in the bowl but not quite to the top. Ask your child to drop in the cork and describe what happens: it floats. Have your child use her hand to push the cork to the bottom of the bowl, then let it go. What happens? It pops back up and floats again. Now take the clear plastic cup (or glass). Ask your child to lower it over the cork. What happens? The cork sinks! Ask you child, "Why do you think this hap-

pens? What is pushing the cork down?" (The air in the cup is pushing the cork down. Air is matter!)

2. Leave the water in the bowl but remove the cork. Dry the cup or glass. Now crumple a few tissues or paper towels (if you use paper towels, first tear them into strips). Stuff the crumpled paper into the bottom of the cup. The paper should stay firmly in the bottom of the cup when you turn it over. Have your child confirm that the paper in the bottom of the cup is dry. Now put the cup (open end first) into the bowl of water. Push it down until the rim of the cup touches the bottom of the bowl. Pull the cup straight out of the water, making sure to keep the open end pointing straight down. Let the water drip off the cup, then turn it over. Check the paper in the bottom of the cup. It should still be dry. Why? Ask your child, "What do you think kept the paper from getting wet?" (The air in the cup.)

Way Too Small to See: Atoms

All matter, everything in the world, is made up of teeny-tiny bits called *atoms*. Atoms are too small to see. How small? Think about this: millions of atoms could fit on the period at the end of this sentence.

The atoms in a solid are close together. That's what makes an apple feel hard. The atoms in a liquid are farther apart. That's why water takes the shape of any glass into which you pour it. The atoms in a gas are even farther apart. That's why it's hard to see and feel the air, even though it is made of matter.

Changing States of Matter

Matter doesn't always stay in the same state. Now, "state" here doesn't mean a place like Florida or California or Ohio. This is a different kind of state: the *states of matter*, which you've just learned the names of: solid, liquid, and gas. Matter can change from one state to another. A solid can become a liquid. A liquid can become a gas. Let's see how matter can change states.

Water can be a solid, a liquid, or a gas. Can you point to and name each of them in this picture?

We can do this by looking at a cup of water. If you put some water in a cup, what state of matter is the water in? Yes, it's a liquid.

If you put that cup of water into a freezer and leave it overnight, what will be its state of matter? The water freezes and becomes ice. The liquid has turned into a solid.

Now let the cup of frozen water sit for a few hours. What happens? The ice melts: the solid has turned back into a liquid. Now take the cup of water, pour it into a pan, and put it on the stove. Ask an adult to help you heat the pan. Don't get too close, but watch what happens. The water begins to boil. Soon it rises as steam. The liquid water has turned to gas. Careful—steam is very hot!

If you boil the water for a long time, eventually all the water will turn to steam and the pan will be empty. Where has the water gone? It has been turned into a gas—steam—and has mixed with the air in the room. Now the water is part of the matter that makes up the air in the room.

Measurement:
How Long, How Much, How Hot

Units of Measurement

What is this girl measuring?

You know that everything is made of matter. Sometimes we need to know things about matter. We need to know how much of something there is, or how much something weighs, or how big or little something is. To find out all this, we need to take some *measurements*.

Measuring things is a way to use numbers to say how big or small things are, or how heavy or light, or how hot or cold. Has anyone ever measured how tall you are? Has anyone ever measured how much you weigh?

You know how important measurements are if you've ever helped somebody bake a cake. When you bake a cake, you have to measure out each ingredient carefully. You use a pan that's a certain size, and you heat the oven to a certain temperature. Every step of the way, you use numbers and make measurements.

Here's a recipe for chocolate cake. But something is wrong with it.

1 sugar	1 milk
1 margarine	½ salt
4 eggs	4 chocolate
3 baking powder	2 flour

Mix the margarine and sugar together in a large bowl until soft. Add all other ingredients; then put mixture in a pan 13 long and 9 wide. Bake at 350 for 45.

Do you see what's wrong with the recipe? Could you mix and bake this cake? You would begin by measuring out one—one what?—of sugar. One teaspoon? One cup? One *ton?!* The cake will taste very different, depending on how much sugar you put in.

Is the pan 13 inches long and 9 inches wide, or 13 miles long and 9 miles wide? Inches and miles are both units for measuring length. Do we bake it for 45 minutes or 45 days or 45 years? Minutes, days, and years are all units for measuring time.

Now do you see what's wrong with the recipe? Somebody forgot to write in the *units of measurement*. Measuring means counting, but you have to know *what* you're counting. To make sense, every measurement needs a number and a unit.

Let's look at the cake recipe as it should be, with numbers *and* units of measurement:

1 cup sugar	1 cup milk
1 stick margarine	½ teaspoon salt
4 eggs	4 ounces chocolate
3 teaspoons baking powder	2 cups flour

Mix the margarine and sugar together in a large bowl until soft. Add all other ingredients; then put the mixture in a pan 13 inches long and 9 inches wide. Bake at 350 degrees Fahrenheit for 45 minutes.

Now that makes more sense. Sounds yummy, too!

How Long? How Tall?

How tall are you? Look back at the cake recipe: are there any units of measurement in it that will help you answer that question?

Are you ten *cups* tall? No. Are you three *teaspoons* tall? No. But what about *inches*? Yes, now we're talking!

To tell how tall you are, most likely you'll use a combination of *inches* and *feet*. Inches and feet measure length. You might also use a different unit of measurement called *centimeters*. Centimeters measure length, too.

PARENTS: *Show your child a 1-foot ruler and discuss the units of measurement: inches and feet (as well as centimeters, if the ruler shows them). Give him some different objects or distances to measure. For each one, have him say before measuring whether he thinks inches or feet would be a better unit of measurement. Then have him do the actual measuring (he may need some help from you). With each object, be sure that your child lines up the end of the ruler with the object that he's measuring. Here are some suggestions for things to measure:*

- *the length of your child's shoe (inches)*
- *the distance from one room to another (feet)*
- *the length of an envelope for a letter (inches)*
- *the height of the front door (feet)*
- *the height of your child (feet and inches)*

How Much Space Does It Fill?

Pretend that you're at the grocery store. You need to buy some milk. How much milk do you need to buy? What units of measurement could you use to answer that question?

You remember that inches, feet, and centimeters are some of the units we use to measure length. But if you want to know how much milk to buy, do you think about *how long* the milk is? Do you think, "I need fifteen inches of milk"? No: you're not thinking about how long the milk is, but *how much space it takes up*.

We can use many different units to measure how much space something takes up.

For example, when you shop for milk, you can buy a quart. Or you can buy a gallon. You could buy four quarts, but it would be easier to buy one gallon: that's because four quarts is the same as one gallon.

Four quarts make a gallon.

Every gallon jug holds the same amount of milk. Even if containers have different labels and come from different companies, they hold the same amount: one gallon. That's why units of measurement work: because we all agree on them.

Cups, Quarts, and Gallons

Another unit for measuring how much space something takes up is a *cup*. Not just any cup, like a paper cup or plastic cup, but a certain amount that we all agree is *one cup*. Because we all agree on how much one cup is, you can be pretty sure that if you're baking a cake that calls for one cup of sugar, your cake will not be too sweet or not sweet enough, because you and the person who wrote the recipe both agree on how much a cup is.

Let's find out how many cups are in a *quart*, and how many quarts are in a *gallon*. Try this outdoors, or somewhere you can splash a little water. You will need a 1-cup measuring cup, a 1-quart container (such as an empty quart container for milk or a quart jar), and a 1-gallon container (such as an empty gallon container for milk). A funnel might also come in handy.

Fill the measuring cup with water up to the line that marks "1 cup." Now carefully pour the water into the quart container (try not to spill). Do this again and again until the quart container is full. How many cups of water are in a quart? (Did you get four cups in a quart?)

Now fill the quart container with water and pour it into the gallon container. Repeat this until the gallon container is full. How many quarts are in a gallon? (Did you get four quarts in a gallon?)

Temperature: How Hot? How Cold?

PARENTS: *In this book, we introduce temperature only as measured in degrees Fahrenheit. Later books in this series will introduce your child to both degrees Fahrenheit and Celsius.*

Before you get in a bathtub, you might stick your finger in the water to see whether it's too cold, too hot, or just right. When you do this, you're checking the *temperature*. But fingers aren't really a very good way to measure temperature. Some things, like a hot oven, are too hot to touch. So, when we want to know how hot or cold something is, we use a thermometer. Thermometers help us measure the temperature in units called *degrees*.

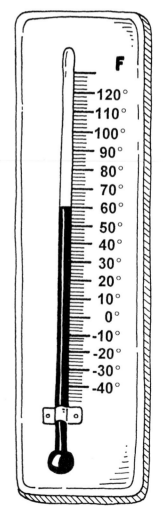

When you go to a doctor's office, the doctor or a nurse might use a special kind of thermometer to take your temperature. If you're healthy, your temperature will be 98.6 degrees, or close to that. If you're sick and have a fever, your temperature might be a little over 100 degrees.

We use a different kind of thermometer to tell us the temperature of the air around us. Look at the picture of a weather thermometer. A weather thermometer has a tube running up and down its center, usually with red or silver liquid in it. This liquid goes higher in the tube when the temperature gets warmer. And when the temperature gets cooler, the liquid goes—what do you think?—that's right, lower. To read the thermometer, you find where the liquid has stopped, then you look over to see the number nearest to the top of the liquid. Can you read the temperature on the thermometer in the picture? (It's 60 degrees.)

Can you find 70 on the thermometer? Seventy degrees is a comfortable temperature—for most people, it's not too hot and not too cold. Can you find 100? If the thermometer reaches 100 degrees, you'll be sweating! That's a very, very hot day!

Can you find 30? Now, count out loud to 2 more than 30. That takes you to 32, right? If you put a cup of water outside on a day on which the temperature is 32 degrees or lower, do you know what will happen to the water? The water will freeze: it will turn to ice. So, if the temperature outside is 32 degrees, bundle up before you go out because it's freezing outside!

Can you find 0 (zero) on the thermometer? Do you see that even more numbers appear below 0? Only on the coldest days—really supercold!—and only in some places does it ever get so cold that we have to use those numbers below 0 on the thermometer. Those are the days when we say the temperature is "below zero."

Taking the Temperature

PARENTS: In this activity it is fine for your child to read the temperature (with your help) to the nearest 10 degrees Fahrenheit. If your child is comfortable counting by twos, you can help him or her take a more exact reading. If your thermometer has both Fahrenheit and Celsius scales, you can explain the Celsius scale if you wish, or tell your child that the degrees Celsius are "different units of measurement that we'll learn about a little later."

Use a thermometer like the one in the picture on page 298. Be very careful with it because some parts may be glass and easy to break. Take the temperature indoors. What is it? Now put the thermometer in a glass of ice water. What happens to the colored liquid? About how cold is the ice water? Now put the thermometer in a bowl of warm (*not* hot) water: can you see the liquid rise? About how warm is the water? Next, take the thermometer outside and wait until the colored liquid stays in one place. Can you read what the temperature is outside?

Electricity:
An Introduction to the Shocking Facts

Look around the room and see how many things you can turn on and off. Is there a light with a light switch? Is there a radio, or a television, or maybe a computer? Is there a toy that uses batteries and moves or makes noise when you turn it on?

All of these things use *electricity*. Electricity is the power that makes them work. Electricity makes them shine, beep, show pictures, or move around.

Static Electricity

Everything in the world, even your body, carries a little bit of electricity in it. Have you ever combed your hair and noticed the hairs on your head standing up as you pull the comb away? That's electricity. Have you ever rubbed a balloon against your shirt,

then pressed it against the wall and watched it stick? That's electricity, too.

There's a special name for this electrical attraction between a comb and your hair, or between the balloon and the wall. It's called *static electricity*. Maybe you have walked across a room and touched somebody's hand and felt a little *zap!* That also happens because of static electricity. If it happens in a dark room, you might see a little flash of light. That little zap of static electricity works the same way as a lightning bolt streaking through the sky in a thunderstorm. But the lightning bolt is *a lot* more powerful!

Do you know about Ben Franklin's famous experiment with lightning? You can read about it on page 166 in this book.

On and Off

Thanks to electricity, lightbulbs shine and radios play music. When you turn on a light at home or at school, you are letting electricity flow through wires all the way to the lightbulb. Where does the electricity come from? Probably from a factory miles away, where big machines generate the electricity and send it through wires to your home and school and lots of other places.

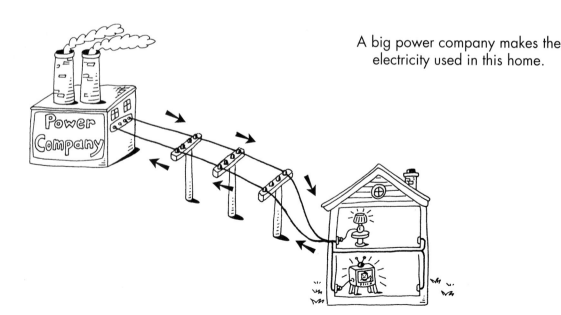

A big power company makes the electricity used in this home.

What happens when you turn on a light? Let's find out by looking at a small model. Look at the picture and find these parts: the battery, wire, the switch, the lightbulb.

Look at the picture again and find the battery. The battery is like a little electric power factory. It uses chemicals to make electricity. (*Never* try to open a battery! The chemicals inside could hurt you.)

Do you see the wire? Use your finger to follow the path of the wire. It goes from one end of the battery to a switch. Then it goes from the switch to a lightbulb. Then it goes from the lightbulb back to the other end of the battery. The wire has to be connected to both ends of the battery to make the electricity flow.

Let's follow the electricity on its path from one end of the battery to the lightbulb. Put your finger on the picture of the battery. The electricity from the battery flows through the wire, kind of like water flowing through a hose. Move your finger along the wire until you get to the switch. What happens when the electricity gets to the switch? That depends on whether the switch is turned "off" or "on." If the switch is "on," then the electricity can continue along its path to the bulb. But if the switch is "off," then the path is broken.

Here's a way to imagine what happens when the electricity reaches the switch. Pretend that you are walking along a path. You come to a river, and there you find that there's no bridge: the path is broken, so you can't keep going. But now, pretend there *is* a bridge: now there's no break in the path, and you can continue on your way.

That's like what happens with electricity: as it travels along the wire, it comes to the switch. If the switch is turned "off," it's like there's no bridge: the electricity cannot continue along the path to the lightbulb. But when the switch is turned "on," it's like there is a bridge: the electricity can keep right on going from the battery, through the wire, through the turned-on switch, through more wire, and to the bulb. When electricity flows through the lightbulb, the bulb lights up. What a bright idea!

Who invented the lightbulb, and a whole lot more? You can find out about Thomas Edison in this book (see page 317).

Conductors

Electricity flows through some materials but not through others. Materials that allow electricity to flow through them are called *conductors:* they "conduct" electricity. Copper is a very good conductor of electricity. If you look at a cord running from a lamp or radio, you'll see a plastic covering, but inside that covering is copper wire. (Do *not* try to take the plastic covering off! It is there to protect you from the electricity in the wires, which can hurt you.)

An Experiment: What Conducts?

PARENTS: *This experiment will require your time and assistance. The components of a simple tabletop electrical system like the one described below are often available at electronics and hobby shops.*

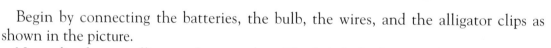

You will need:
2 batteries
a double battery holder
a bulb and bulb holder
3 wires
2 alligator clips
various items, such as a pencil, a shoelace, a metal
   spoon, a plastic utensil, a piece of paper, a safety pin,
   a crayon, a rubber band, a penny, a paper clip

Begin by connecting the batteries, the bulb, the wires, and the alligator clips as shown in the picture.

Next clip the two alligator clips together. The lightbulb should light up. When the alligator clips touch, you are making a pathway going from the batteries, through the light bulb, and back to the batteries again. Now pull the alligator clips apart. What happens? Why does the light go out?

You can use this system to test what things are good conductors of electricity. Let's test many things, such as a pencil, a shoelace, a metal spoon, a plastic utensil, a piece of paper, a safety pin, a crayon, a rubber band, a penny, and a paper clip.

To test each item, "bite" one end with one alligator clip, then attach the other alligator clip to the other end. If the object you are testing is a good conductor, what do you think will happen? The electricity will flow from the batteries, through the wires, through the object you are testing, to the bulb. If the object conducts electricity, the bulb will light up.

You can make a chart of everything you test. Make two columns: on one side, put "Conductors." On the other side put items that "Do Not Conduct." What do you find? Does plastic conduct electricity? What about paper? Do most things made of metal conduct electricity?

Safety Rules Around Electricity

A little battery puts out a little bit of electricity, so you can use it safely for your experiments. But the electricity that comes through the wires in your house or school is *much* more powerful, so you need to remember some safety rules.

Inside the walls where you live or go to school, there are big wires that carry electricity. When you plug in a light or radio or other electrical appliance, you are putting the light or radio in the pathway of the electricity. You have heard adults say, *"Don't stick your finger into the electrical outlet on the wall!"* Now do you know why? If you did, *you* would become part of the electrical pathway. Your body is a pretty good conductor of electricity. The electrical current coming through the wires to the wall outlet is so strong that it would hurt *a lot* if you stuck your finger in the outlet.

What if you held a piece of metal, like a fork or knife, and stuck it into the wall outlet? *Don't do it!* Why? Because metals conduct electricity, and you would get a terrible shock!

Another rule you may have heard is "Don't touch any electrical appliance when you are wet." Can you think why? It's because water is a good conductor of electricity. When your hands are wet or when your body is in a bathtub full of water, the electricity could flow right through you and give you an awful shock, or even kill you.

Think: Why should you never put your fingers into the socket where the lightbulb screws into a lamp? That's the place where the electricity flows into the lightbulb, isn't it? Put your finger in there and it could be you, rather than the lightbulb, that becomes part of the electrical pathway. And that would hurt!

Electricity is very useful, but it can be dangerous. Be careful, be safe, be smart. Let electricity help you, not hurt you.

Astronomy: Our Solar System

Meet two astronauts. They are some of the many scientists who have flown in powerful rockets to outer space. Sally Ride was the first woman in outer space. Neil Armstrong was the first person to walk on the moon.

Sally Ride (left),
Neil Armstrong
(right).

Far out in space, the astronauts can look back and use cameras to take pictures of the Earth. From space, this is what our planet looks like.

Our Solar System

Don't you love a sunny day? The sun makes the days bright. The sun may look like a big bright yellow ball. But did you know that the sun is a star? It's like many other stars that you see shining in the sky on a clear night. What makes the sun different from those other stars? The big difference is that the sun is closer to us than any other star.

Earth as seen from outer space.

If you could get in a rocket ship and travel far, far out in space, you would see that the sun has planets going around it. Our Earth is only one of those planets. There are eight others: some are closer than we are to the sun, some are farther away. Some are bigger than the Earth, some are smaller. Each planet goes around the sun its own special path, called an *orbit*. The sun and the planets that go around it are part of what we call the *solar system*.

Let's take an imaginary rocket ship journey. We'll start

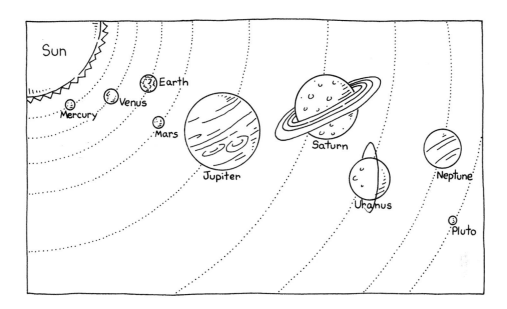

near the sun, at the center of our solar system, and move out from there. This really is an imaginary ride, because the sun is so hot you could never fly close to it. The sun is not a solid planet like the Earth. The sun is a huge ball of superhot burning gases. If a rocket really approached the sun, it would melt long before it could land.

As you fly away from the sun, what's the first planet you see? It's the planet Mercury. Mercury is a small planet, and it's the closest planet to the sun.

Next you come to Venus, the second planet from the sun. After that, you see the third planet from the sun—and it looks very familiar! It's Earth, your home planet. Earth is 93 million miles from the sun. That sounds far, but six more planets are even farther away. Better get going!

The fourth planet out from the sun is Mars. Some people nickname Mars "the red planet" because when you are lucky enough to see it in the nighttime sky, it seems to have an orangey-red color.

Next comes Jupiter, the fifth planet from the sun. Jupiter is the largest planet in our solar system.

There's something unusual about Saturn, the sixth planet from the sun. Saturn is surrounded by beautiful rings.

The next two planets, Uranus [YOOR-uh-nus] and Neptune, are very large compared to Earth. The ninth and last planet, farthest from the sun, is Pluto, the smallest planet in our solar system. Pluto is a superfrozen planet, since it's so far from the sun. How far? Three and a half billion miles away—a distance so huge it's hard to imagine!

Hey, you'd better turn that rocket around and head back to Earth at maximum speed! You don't want to be late for dinner!

The Moon

During your imaginary rocket ship journey, when you passed the Earth, you may have noticed what looked like a ball circling around it. What was that? It's something you know very well: the moon.

The moon that you see in the sky goes around the Earth. You can also say that the moon *orbits* the Earth, just as the Earth and the other eight planets orbit the sun.

Have you noticed that the moon seems to change shape? Sometimes it's a full moon, with a big round face. Sometimes it's a half-moon, shaped like a big slice of watermelon. Sometimes it's only a thin crescent. Some nights we don't see the moon at all (and when this happens, we call it a "new moon"). We call these different shapes the *phases* of the moon.

Phases of the moon.

The moon only *seems* to change shape. Really, it's always a big round ball. Sometimes we see all the ball, and sometimes we only see part of it. We see the part that is lit by the sun. Did you know that the moon itself does not shine? When the moon seems to shine, it's really reflecting light from the sun.

Sometimes when the moon is bright and big in the sky, it might almost seem as if a face is looking down at you. People even jokingly refer to "the man in the moon." But there are no people on the moon—no animals or plants either, and no trees, grass, or clouds. There is no water or air. Astronauts who visited the moon had to wear space suits to give them air to breathe. The moon may look lovely, but it's not a friendly place to visit.

So far, astronauts have visited the moon, but no astronaut has landed on another planet. Not yet, at least. Who knows what may happen when you grow up? Maybe then astronauts will make a trip to Mars. Maybe you will be one of them!

Constellations:
Connect-the-Dot Stars

On a clear night, go outside and look up at the stars. For thousands of years, people have enjoyed looking up at the stars. Long ago, people used their imaginations and found pictures among the stars, like big connect-the-dots drawings in the sky. They imagined they saw pictures of bears and horses, or a man shooting an arrow. People still look for those connect-the-dot pictures today. They are called the *constellations*.

The Big Dipper.

Here's a constellation you can look for: the Big Dipper. It got that name because it looks like a pan with a long handle, the kind you would use to dip water out of a bucket. On a clear night, ask an adult to help point your gaze toward north. In that direction, look for a square of four stars that seem to connect to form a pan. Then look for three more bright stars that seem to connect to one corner of the pan and form a curving pan handle. There are a lot of other stars in the sky near these, but if you just concentrate on the brightest ones, you can see the Big Dipper.

Our Big, Round,
Moving Earth

Photographs taken from outer space show that the earth is a big ball. Then why doesn't it seem round to us? It's because the earth is so large that you don't notice that the ground you're standing on has a curve to it. If the earth were the size of a basketball, one entire city would be no bigger than a speck of dust. That's why it's hard to get a sense of the vast curving surface of our earth.

If you could watch a boat sail away from you out into the ocean, where there's nothing but water as far as the eye can see, you could catch a glimpse of the earth's curving surface. As the boat gets farther away, it approaches the place where the sky seems to meet the sea: we call this the *horizon*. Slowly, the boat seems to sink below the horizon. You see less and less of the boat until finally all you see is the tip of the mast, and then nothing. The boat hasn't sunk or fallen off the earth! It has gone around to part of this big ball of a planet that you can no longer see.

As it sails away, a boat seems to sink below the horizon.

Try this: stand up and be as still as you can. It doesn't feel as if the ground beneath your feet is moving, does it? But in fact the earth is spinning around all the time. It spins like a top. And that's not all. As the earth spins around like a top, it is also circling through space in an orbit around the sun. Whoa, we're really moving here!

Hundreds of years ago, people used to believe that the sun went around the earth. It's easy to see why people thought so, because the sun does *seem* to travel slowly across the sky, from morning to night. But a man named Nicolaus Copernicus showed people that they had it backward. The sun doesn't move, said Copernicus; it only looks that way because really the *earth* is moving, spinning around like a top. To understand Copernicus's idea, try this: look straight ahead of you and spin around very fast. When you do this, things seem to move around you in a circle, but really you are the one doing the moving.

The earth spins like a top.

You may hear people talk about the sun rising in the morning and setting in the evening—which makes it sound as if the sun were moving through our sky. But the sun is *not* moving. It's the *earth* that does the moving. The earth spins around one complete turn every day. One complete rotation takes twenty-four hours. The spinning of the earth makes day and night. You can do an experiment to understand how.

An Experiment:
What Makes Day and Night?

To do this experiment you will need:

a globe

clay

a strong light (such as a desk lamp)

Pretend that the globe is the earth. Take a little piece of clay and stick it onto the globe. That's you!

Pretend the light is the sun. Shine the light at the middle of the globe. Now make the globe spin slowly. When the sun (the light) shines on you (the clay), it's daytime. But as the earth continues to spin around, soon the light isn't on you anymore: that's nighttime.

What about the people who live on the other side of the earth? Put another piece of clay on the opposite side of the earth from where you are. Now shine the light on the globe and slowly spin it again. What happens? When it's bright daytime for you, it's night for people on the opposite side of the earth. But when the sun shines on them, you're fast asleep!

Around and around goes the earth, spinning like a top—and that's what makes day and night.

Down to Earth

Let's take a closer look at the third planet from the sun, our home, the earth.

You already know some things about the earth. You know that its surface is covered with land and water. What are the biggest chunks of land called? Yes, the *continents*. And the biggest bodies of water? Yes, the *oceans*.

Imagine drawing a line around the middle of the earth, as though you were putting a big belt around it. We call that imaginary line the *equator*. Many world maps and globes have this imaginary line drawn on them; see if you can find it. The sun always shines strongly at the equator, so the land and oceans near the equator stay warm all year round. Do you remember learning about the warm rainforests? They are all near the earth's equator.

The top and the bottom of the earth are called *poles*. What's on top? The North Pole. And down on the bottom is the South Pole. The sun never shines as strongly at the poles as it does at the equator. In fact, the water at the poles stays frozen all year round.

If you look at a globe, you might think that people living near the South Pole must feel as if they were standing upside down. But in fact, standing up near the South Pole feels just like standing up in your own neighborhood—feet down, head up, only colder!

Inside the Earth

Have you ever started digging a hole and wondered how far you could go? What would it be like to dig way down deep down into the earth?

Scientists have used special equipment to drill deep down into the earth. They have found out that the earth has many layers. If you could slice right through the earth, you would see the different layers, all the way to the center, something like this:

The outermost layer is called the *crust*. That's the surface of the earth, the part we live on. Mountains and valleys, rivers and deserts, oceans and continents make up the earth's crust. The crust is a thin outer coating compared to the other layers inside.

Beneath the crust lies a thick layer of hot, melted rock called the *mantle*. The deeper the mantle, the hotter it gets. At the center of the earth burns a *core* of hot melted rock. No one has ever traveled through the earth's mantle to the core. No one would want to! It gets as hot as 7,000 degrees down there!

Sometimes holes open in the earth's crust. When these holes open, hot gas and liquid can escape from deep down in the earth.

At some places, boiling hot steam explodes out of a hole in the ground, spewing high up into the air. Do you know what we call this? A *geyser*. In the state of Wyoming, at least two hundred geysers

"Old Faithful."

shoot up out of the ground. The most famous one shoots 11,000 gallons of water—boiling hot, so it's steam—150 feet up, far above the treetops around it. For a long time, this geyser has seemed to shoot up regularly, nearly once an hour, so people call it "Old Faithful."

At other places, red-hot melted rock bursts out of the ground. What do we call this event? A *volcano*. Volcanoes give us an idea of what it's like beneath the earth's crust. We know that the melted rock comes from deep down inside the earth's mantle layer. Then it can spurt out through the top of a mountain. The melted rock, called *lava*, can travel in fiery streams down the mountainside, burning everything in its path.

Sometimes a volcano can erupt, then remain quiet for many years, and then erupt again. In 1980, Mount St. Helens erupted in the state of Washington. People knew that the mountain was a volcano, but it hadn't erupted for more than one hundred years.

Mount St. Helens erupting in 1980.

The Earth Makes Different Kinds of Rocks

The next time you have a chance, pick up a handful of rocks and look at them. You'll notice how *different* rocks can be. Some seem all one color, while others are streaked with different colors. Some are dark, while some are light; some are so light that you can almost see through them, like looking through a foggy glass. Some are so smooth that it almost makes you want to rub them, while others are rough and jagged.

So many different rocks—granite, quartz, coal, shale, limestone, and many more. Scientists put each of these different rocks into one of three groups, depending on how the rock was formed. Here are the names that scientists use for the three types of rocks. Like the names of dinosaurs, they're big words, and fun to say aloud. Ready?

igneous [IG-nee-us]
sedimentary [said-ih-MEN-tuh-ree]
metamorphic [met-ah-MORE-fik]

Let's see what those fancy names mean.

Granite.

Sandstone.

Igneous means "made by fire." Granite is one of the most common igneous rocks. It is made underground, where it's very hot. Some igneous rocks come from volcanoes. Volcanoes have been erupting on earth for millions of years. Whenever lava flowed out, it cooled and hardened into rock. Pumice is an igneous rock that's full of little holes. Pumice is so light that it floats in water!

Sedimentary means "made by settling down." Sometimes, often under the sea or in a riverbed, lots of little rocks settle down on top of one another. Over thousands and thousands of years, they press down until they form one big rock. Sandstone is a sedimentary rock. You can see and feel the grains of sand that settled down together to form sandstone.

Metamorphic means "made through change." Deep inside the earth, powerful forces and superhot heat are squeezing and cooking the material down there. All this squeezing and cooking can change rocks. For example, look what can happen to limestone, which is a kind of sedimentary rock. Deep in the earth, limestone can get heated and squeezed and changed into a rock called marble. Marble is a metamorphic rock: it was made through change. Some artists like to make statues out of marble. Marble is often used for the walls and stairs of big buildings. People like to build with it because of its beautiful streaks of color, formed over long periods of time by forces under the earth.

Marble.

The Earth's Important Minerals

Just as it takes different ingredients to bake a cake, lots of different ingredients go into making rocks. Each of these ingredients is a *mineral*. Most rocks are made up of more than one kind of mineral.

We can find lots of different minerals in the earth. Gold is a mineral. When you think of gold, maybe you think of jewelry or pirate's treasure. For thousands of years, people have used gold to make the things they consider most valuable, such as coins, rings, and crowns. All the gold in the world comes from the earth.

Uncut diamonds.

Diamonds are minerals. Have you ever seen a diamond in a ring or necklace? Just like gold, all the diamonds in the world come from the earth. In the earth they don't look like they do in a ring or necklace: it takes a lot of work to make them so pretty and shiny. People use diamonds for more than jewelry. Diamonds are harder than any other rock or mineral, so people use diamonds to help cut other rocks!

Quartz.

Quartz is a mineral. Quartz is much more common than gold and diamonds. In many places, you can find quartz lying on the ground. Quartz comes in many forms, such as white quartz, rose quartz, amethyst, and tiger's eye. Some sandpaper is made with little bits of quartz glued to a paper backing.

People have learned how to find minerals in the earth, and how to dig them out, or *mine* them. We mine the mineral called halite, then use it to make salt for our food. We mine the mineral iron ore, then use it to make steel, which goes into cars, refrigerators, and bicycles. We mine the mineral copper, then use it to make cooking pots, electrical wiring, and pennies.

Stories About Scientists

Edward Jenner

Today children around the world receive vaccinations. Do you remember being vaccinated? The shot may have hurt a little, but it helped a lot to keep you safe from serious diseases.

Vaccinations work in a way that might surprise you. Most keep you from getting a disease by actually putting *a little bit* of the disease germs in you. Your body fights these germs, and from then on your body is ready to keep you from catching the disease.

More than two hundred years ago, before anyone knew about vaccination, many people died of a disease called smallpox. They would get terrible sores on their bodies, and those who managed to survive could end up blind, weak, and covered with scars for the rest of their lives. But those that survived knew they would never catch the disease again—just the way you know that after you have had chicken pox, you will never catch it again.

Doctors in those days started thinking that maybe, just maybe, they could figure out a way to make people catch a mild case of smallpox. Then they might get a little sick, but they would never catch smallpox again. So doctors tried taking a little fluid from a sick person's smallpox sore and putting it into a cut on a well person's arm.

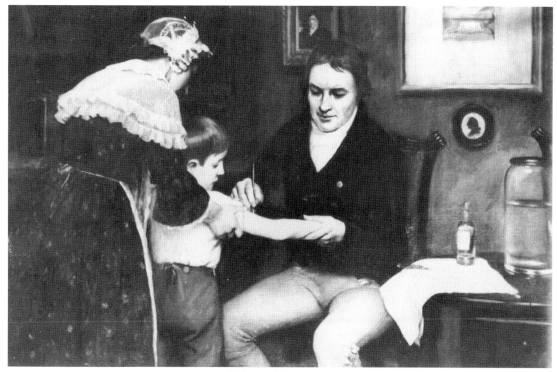

Edward Jenner.

Sometimes this worked. The person would get a little sick but soon feel better, and then he would never catch smallpox again. But sometimes the people got very sick, and even died. In those cases, it seemed as if the doctor was spreading the smallpox disease.

The problem concerned Edward Jenner, an English doctor. Once, when he met a woman who worked on a dairy farm, she showed him her hands; they were covered with the marks of old sores. But she told Jenner, "It can't be the smallpox. I've already had the cowpox. Everybody knows you never get smallpox after you've had cowpox."

Jenner had seen cattle with the disease called cowpox. The cows got sores on their body, just as humans with smallpox did. Jenner had seen people with cowpox, too. They got a little sick, and they got a few sores, but then they got better. Jenner began asking questions and studying. He started to think that it might be true: by catching cowpox, a person could keep from catching smallpox.

Finally Jenner was ready to try an experiment. On May 14, 1796, he took fluid from a cowpox sore and put it into a cut on the arm of an eight-year-old boy named James Phipps. James caught cowpox. He came down with a fever, headaches, and sores, but he soon got better. Now came the important and risky next step: on July 1, Jenner infected the boy with fluid from a smallpox sore. For days and weeks, Jenner watched and waited. James Phipps stayed healthy. The cowpox kept him from catching smallpox.

Jenner told other doctors about his discovery, but at first they didn't believe him. But Jenner believed in his idea, and he kept giving people cowpox. He believed so much, he even gave his own baby son the cowpox germs. Finally he wrote a book explaining his discovery. He called it "vaccination," from the Latin word *vacca* for "cow."

As Jenner vaccinated more people successfully, his work became well known. The King and Queen of England asked to be vaccinated. Thomas Jefferson, our third President, received a vaccination and encouraged other Americans to do the same.

Other scientists learned from Edward Jenner's ideas, and they worked to make vaccinations even safer and more reliable. Today vaccinations protect us against many serious diseases, such as polio, tuberculosis, and measles. Jenner's bold experiments, and the work of the scientists who learned from his ideas, have helped to save many, many lives.

Louis Pasteur

Louis Pasteur.

Take a look at the label on almost any carton of milk and you're likely to see the word PASTEURIZED [PASS-chuh-rized]. What does that mean? Let's find out by meeting Louis Pasteur [pass-TUR].

Louis Pasteur was born in 1822 in a little town in France. As he grew up, he loved to paint. He loved to look at the world around him.

When he went to the university in Paris, he turned his attention to looking through a microscope. A microscope makes things look a lot bigger; it lets you see things you can't see just with your eyes. Looking through a microscope, Pasteur observed a living world in a drop of water. He saw and drew pictures of the tiny living creatures—he called them "microbes" or "germs"—that squirmed in a drop of water.

One day a winemaker came into the laboratory, hoping that someone could help him solve a problem. "Sometimes my wine tastes delicious, but sometimes it turns sour," he said to Pasteur. "Can you help me find out why?"

Pasteur put some drops of the wine under the microscope. He noticed that the sour wine had some unusual germs. If he could kill these germs, maybe he could keep the wine from turning sour. He experimented with different ways to kill the germs. He tried freezing, then electric shock. But in the end, heating the wine seemed to work best. The winemaker tried it, and every bottle of wine tasted good.

Pasteur's idea worked for other people, too. When dairies heated milk, it didn't sour so quickly. When breweries heated beer, it tasted better. People called the process "pasteurization"—heating a liquid to kill harmful germs. Aren't you glad that the milk you drink has been pasteurized?

Louis Pasteur's good ideas didn't stop there. He also worked on vaccinations, building upon the discoveries of Edward Jenner. He developed a vaccine to treat rabies, a serious disease carried by some dogs, wolves, and other wild animals. Rabies made the animals vicious, and if they bit a person, the person would get terribly sick and die. Pasteur was still experimenting with his rabies vaccine when one day a sick little boy named Joseph Meister was brought to Pasteur. Joseph's parents said, "We know we are taking a risk, letting you experiment on him, but he will die of rabies soon unless you try your medicine." Joseph Meister was the first person to receive a rabies vaccine—and it worked. In just weeks he was feeling well.

Louis Pasteur's countrymen recognized how important his discoveries were to the health of the world. They honored him by building a great laboratory, called the Pasteur Institute, where they could continue the work Pasteur had begun. Later, a man came to work at the Institute, taking care of one of the buildings: a man named Joseph Meister, who recognized that he owed his life to the great scientist, Louis Pasteur.

Thomas Edison

Do you like being able to turn on a light when it's dark? Do you like movies? Do you enjoy listening to music through a stereo? If you like any of these things, you have a reason to say, "Thanks, Thomas Edison!"

Born in Ohio in 1847, Thomas Alva Edison had a restless mind. As a child, he was always asking questions that confused many adults. He wanted to know how things worked—and if someone couldn't tell him, well, he would just figure it out for himself. He experimented with chemicals, batteries, and wires. Sometimes his experiments got out of hand: he got in trouble when he set things on fire or sent broken glass flying into the air!

As he grew up, Thomas Edison was fascinated by the new science of electricity. He began inventing new machines, such as a machine that used electricity to send news to offices in New York City. People began to believe in Edison and his inventions. Finally he had enough money to build a science laboratory in Menlo Park, New Jersey, where he and his helpers could work day and night on new inventions.

One day Edison invited his friends into his lab to see a new invention. It looked like

Thomas Edison and his phonograph.

a big metal drum with a handle. He turned the handle, and as he did so he said, "Mary had a little lamb." He adjusted the machine, then turned the handle again. The machine made a noise, then it played back the words "Mary had a little lamb"! Thomas Edison had invented the first phonograph. Today we have tape recorders and compact disc players, but they all began with the ideas of Thomas Edison. People began calling him "the Wizard of Menlo Park."

Next, Edison put his mind to the problem of electric light. For hundreds of years, the only things that people had to light their way in the dark were oil lamps, candles, or fire. Using fire for light was not very safe or clean. So people began to try to find a way to use electricity to make light. But so far, no one had found a safe, easy, and inexpensive way to do it.

Thomas Edison asked a glassblower to make him a round bulb with a long neck. Inside the bulb he placed a thin wire. He connected the wire to a source of electricity. The wire glowed—but then it burned out, very fast. He tried making the other wires out of many different materials. For months everything he tried would not work: all the wires just burned out. People began to wonder if maybe the Wizard of Menlo Park had lost his magic touch.

But Thomas Edison didn't give up. He kept on trying until he finally got it right. He sent electricity through a wire in a bulb, and the electricity lit up the wire—and it didn't burn out! He had invented the lightbulb.

He built a small electric power factory at Menlo Park and put his new lightbulbs in lamps all around his laboratories. Soon people from all over the world came to see this wonderful new marvel: electric light—a clean, steady light without flame, without smoke!

Thomas Edison's mind jumped to another project. He thought, "If I can record sound, perhaps I can record pictures, too." He invented a machine that moved a strip of film pictures past a light and projected the pictures onto a wall. This was the first movie! It wasn't very exciting—it showed a man sneezing—but people were so amazed to see moving pictures that they gladly watched that man sneeze over and over.

The phonograph, the lightbulb, and the motion picture are considered Thomas Alva Edison's most important inventions. But they are only a few of the more than a *thousand* things he invented! What a genius! But as Edison himself said, "Genius is one percent inspiration and ninety-nine percent perspiration." In other words, it helps to be smart, but it helps a lot more to work hard.

Rachel Carson

Rachel Carson was born in 1907 and grew up on a farm in Pennsylvania. She played in the woods, she wrote stories, and she drew pictures of the things in nature she loved. She made those pictures into books and proudly showed them to her parents.

Rachel Carson's parents admired their daughter's abilities. When she grew up, they encouraged her to attend a women's college. In college she studied biology—the science of plants and animals. Later, her biology teacher invited her to study all summer in Massachusetts, right on the ocean shore.

That sounded wonderful to Rachel Carson. She had always been fascinated by ocean life, even though she had never lived near the water before. In a time when few women even attended college, Carson continued her education and worked hard to learn even more about ocean biology.

She had a special combination of talents. She knew a lot about the science of plants, animals, and the ocean. And she was a very good writer. When she went to Washington, D.C., to look for a job, she heard that the government needed someone to write booklets and radio programs—someone who knew a lot about fish and the ocean, and could explain things in a way that made sense to everyone. Rachel Carson took the job, and she did very well at it.

At night she wrote books of her own. She wanted to help other people love the ocean as she did. She wrote two books about the sea and sea life. The second book, called *The Sea Around Us*, was very successful and even won awards. Hundreds of people wrote letters to her, thanking her for showing them the beauty of the sea.

As Carson continued to study and write about nature, she learned things that disturbed her. The natural world was beautiful, but people did not always take good care of it. Sometimes people even hurt the world they lived in.

One day Rachel Carson received a letter from a friend. The friend said she was finding dead songbirds outside her back door. She thought they were dying because people nearby had been spraying an insect poison called DDT. The DDT was supposed to kill

Rachel Carson.

the mosquitoes bothering the neighborhood.

Rachel Carson thought about what was happening. If the poison spray got into mosquitoes, and the birds ate the mosquitoes, then the birds must be eating poison, which would make them die. Carson also knew that farmers used DDT to keep insects off pigs and cows. But when the animals licked themselves, some of the poison must be going into their systems. That must mean that when humans ate pork and beef, they were eating a little insect poison, too.

To be sure her ideas were right, Carson read and studied for several years. Then she wrote a book called *Silent Spring*. The title was meant to warn people that unless they were more careful about the way they used poisons and treated nature, then springtime might be silent: the natural world might die, and then there would be no birds to sing in the springtime.

When *Silent Spring* came out in 1962—not very long ago—it made a lot of people angry. It angered the chemical companies that produced DDT. It angered government officials, because they had been saying that DDT was safe. It angered farmers who wanted to use DDT.

Rachel Carson's book changed things. The United States government passed laws that limited the use of DDT and other poisons. And many people began to think about the natural world in a new way. They began to avoid using chemicals that could harm natural habitats.

Rachel Carson never stopped observing, thinking, reading, and writing. Her ideas and her writing have made a big difference in our world. Rachel Carson helped people understand, as she wrote, that "man is a part of nature."

Illustration and Photo Credits

Animals Animals/Earth Scenes
  © Doug Allan/Oxford Scientific Films: 142(c)
  © Miriam Austerman: 280
  © Carson Baldwin, Jr.: 276(b), 285(b)
  © W. Gregory Brown: 277
  © Frank Burek: 276(a)
  © E. R. Degginer: 284(b), 313(b)
  © M. P. L. Fogden: 139(a)
  © Mickey Gibson: 115
  © Breck P. Kent: 143(a, b), 281(c), 312(a, b), 313(a), 314
  © Gérard Lacz: 279
  © Terry G. Murphy: 169
  © Len Rue, Jr.: 271(a)
  © Leonard Lee Rue III: 273
  © Ann Sanfedele: 275(a)
  © Barrie E. Watts: 274
American Antiquarian Society: 158
American Museum of Natural History, Courtesy Department Library Services, Neg. No. 326597 and
  Neg. No. 334110: 141(a, b)
Art Resource, NY/Alinari: 116(a), 117, 123(a)
Art Resource, NY/Giraudon
    Vincent van Gogh, *Self-Portrait*. Musee d'Orsay, Paris, France: 194
    James Abbott McNeill Whistler, *The Artist's Mother*. 1871. Musée d'Orsay, Paris, France: 183
Art Resource, NY/Erich Lessing
    Paul Cézanne. *Still Life with Apples and Oranges*. Musée d'Orsay, Paris, France: 196(b)
    Leonardo da Vinci. *Mona Lisa*. 1503–1506. Louvre, Paris, France: 191(b)
    Albrecht Dürer, *Hare*. 1502. Watercolor. Graphische Sammlung Albertina, Vienna, Austria: 191(a)
    Claude Monet, *Tulip Field in Holland*. 1886. Musée d'Orsay, Paris, France: 181(b)
Art Resource, NY/Foto Marburg: 120(b)
Art Resource, NY/Scala: 180(b)
Art Resource, NY/SEF: 116(b)
Art Resource, NY/Vanni: 181(a)
Ashlawn Summer Festival, © Peter Emerson: 212
The Bettmann Archive: 111, 120(a), 131, 134(b), 146, 153(a), 163, 165, 168(a), 275(a), 311(a), 315,
316, 318
Corbis/Bettmann: 118(b), 205, 213, 216
UPI/Bettmann: 304(a, b, c), 320
Catherine Bricker: 217
CCI: 8,9
Edgar Degas, *Dressed Ballet Dancer (Petite Danseuse de Quatorze Ans)* 1880–1881. Plaster cast; height,
  1.003 m (39 1/2″). Collection of Mr. and Mrs. Paul Mellon, © 1996 Board of Trustees, National
  Gallery of Art, Washington: 190(b)
Leslie Evans: 74, 75
Jonathan Fuqua: 190(a), 292, 307
Wanda Gag, from *Tales from Grimm*, © 1936 Wanda Gag. Used by permission of the Wanda Gag estate:
  46, 47, 48

Francisco de Goya y Lucientes (1746–1828), *Don Manuel Osorio Manrique de Zúñiga* (1784–1792). Oil on canvas. Copyright © 1994 The Metropolitan Museum of Art, The Jules Bache Collection, 1949 (49. 7.41): 193

The Granger Collection, New York: 119, 121(b), 123(b), 138(b), 142(a), 147, 151, 152, 153(b), 155, 157(a, b), 161, 166, 174, 180(a)

Julie Grant: 61(a, b), 62(a), 63

Steve Henry: 136, 184(a), 186(b), 211, 224, 226, 236, 237, 238, 239, 240, 243, 245, 248, 249, 250, 251(b), 254, 255, 263(a), 271(b), 289(b), 290(a, b), 291, 293, 294, 297 (a, b, c), 298, 300(a, b), 305, 310(b)

Hans Holbein, the Younger, *Edward VI as a Child*. Probably 1538. Oil on panel, .568 × .440 m (22 3/8″ × 17 3/8″); framed, .838 × .698 m (33″ × 27 1/2″). Andrew W. Mellon Collection, © 1996 Board of Trustees, National Gallery of Art, Washington: 192

Hannah Holdren: 186(a)

Sara Holdren: 137(a), 138(a), 139(b), 142(b)

The Image Bank

   © David W. Hamilton: 214(a)

   © Paul Loven: 204(a)

   © Hans Neleman: 207

Phillip Jones: 4

Bob Kirchman: 114, 124, 133, 135, 140, 148, 159, 173, 283, 285(a), 301(a, b), 302

Jacob Lawrence, *Parade*. Hirshorn Museum and Sculpture Garden, Smithsonian Institution, Gift of Joseph H. Hirshorn, 1966, © Lee Stalsworth: 188

Edward Lear: 24, 25

Library of Congress: 172

The Louvre, *Code d'Hammurabi*, © R.M.N.: 125

Henri Matisse, *The Swan*. Page 123 from Poésies by Stéphane Mallarmé. Lausanne, Albert Skira & Cie, Editeurs, 1932. Etching printed in black; plate: 11 15/16″ × 8 3/4″ (30.3 × 22.3 cm). The Museum of Modern Art, New York. The Louis E. Stern Collection. Photograph © 1996 The Museum of Modern Art, New York: 185(a)

Gail McIntosh: ii, iii, 1, 18(a), 22, 26, 30, 38, 40, 41, 42, 44, 45, 68, 73, 101, 103, 107, 127(a), 132, 162, 167, 177, 182, 184(b), 199, 231, 257(b), 261, 267, 272, 278, 282, 284(a), 286, 287(a), 288(a, b), 289(a, c), 296, 306, 308(a), 309

The Metropolitan Museum of Art, photography by Egyptian Expedition. The Metropolitan Museum of Art: 121(a)

Georgia O'Keeffe, *Shell No. 1*. 1928. Oil on canvas, .178 × .178 m (7″ × 7″); framed, .203 × .203 × .033 m (8″ × 8″ × 15/16″). Alfred Steiglitz Collection, Bequest of Georgia O'Keeffe, © 1996 Board of Trustees, National Gallery of Art, Washington: 185(a)

Beatrix Potter, *The Tale of Peter Rabbit*. Copyright © Frederick Warne & Co., 1902, 1987. Reproduced by permission of Frederick Warne & Co.: 95(b, c), 96, 97

Richmond Ballet, from production of *The Nutcracker*. Copyright © 1995, Suzanne Grandis: 214(b)

Diego Rivera, *The History of Medicine in Mexico: The People's Demand for Better Health*. 1953. Mural, (c. 7.4 × 10.8 m). Hospital de la Raza, Mexico City, Mexico, © Bob Schalkwijk: 189

Diego Rivera, *Piñata*. 1953. Tempera on canvas. Hospital Infantil de Mexico "Frederico Gómez," Mexico City, Mexico, © 1996 Bob Schalkwijk: 198

Norman Rockwell, *Triple Self-Portrait*. Photo courtesy of The Norman Rockwell Museum at Stockbridge; printed by permission of the Norman Rockwell Family Trust. Copyright © 1960, the Norman Rockwell Family Trust: 195

Bob Schalkwijk: 149, 150

E. H. Shepard, from *The House at Pooh Corner*. Used by permission of Dutton Children's Books, a division of Penguin Books USA Inc.: 55, 56, 58, 60

Nic Siler © 1996: 134(a), 287(b)

Courtesy of Tulane University Library, William Ransom Hogan Jazz Archive: 215

United States Capitol Art Collection, *Landing of Columbus At The Island Of Guanahani*. Architect of the Capitol: 145

U.S. Geological Survey: 311(b)

University of Pennsylvania, The University Museum: 122

University of Virginia Library, Special Collections Department/Alderman Library: 168(a)

University of Virginia Medical Center: 287(c)

Vincent van Gogh, *Irises*. Oil on canvas. Copyright © 1985 The Metropolitan Museum of Art, Gift of Adele R. Levy, 1958 (58.187): 196(a)

Grant Wood, *Stone City, Iowa*. Josyln Art Museum, Omaha, Nebraska: 187

While every care has been taken to trace and acknowledge copyright, the editors tender their apologies for any accidental infringement where copyright has proved untraceable. They would be pleased to insert the appropriate acknowledgment in any subsequent edition of this publication.

Text Credits and Sources

POEMS

"Hope," from *Collected Poems* by Langston Hughes. Copyright © 1994 by the Estate of Langston Hughes. Reprinted by permission of Alfred A. Knopf, Inc.

"I Know All the Sounds that the Animals Make," from *Something Big Has Been Here* by Jack Prelutsky. Copyright © 1990 by Jack Prelutsky. Used by permission from Greenwillow Books, a division of William Morrow and Company, Inc.

"The Pasture," by Robert Frost, from *Complete Poems of Robert Frost* (Holt, Rinehart, and Winston © 1949).

"Rope Rhyme," by Eloise Greenfield, from *Honey, I Love and Other Poems* by Eloise Greenfield. Text copyright © 1978 by Eloise Greenfield. Selection reprinted by permission of HarperCollins Publishers.

"Sing a Song of People," from *The Life I Live* by Lois Lenski. Used by permission from the Lois Lenski Covey Foundation.

STORIES

"All Stories Are Anansi's," adapted from *The Hat-Shaking Dance and Other Tales* from the Gold Coast by Harold Courlander (Harcourt, Brace & World, Inc., 1962). Used by permission of the author, Harold Courlander.

"The Boy at the Dike," adapted from "The Leak in the Dike," in *Everyday Classics Third Reader* by Franklin Baker and Ashley Thorndike (Macmillan, 1920); and *Child Life in Many Lands: A Third Reader* by Etta and Mary Frances Blaisdell (Macmillan, 1908). Concluding stanza of poetry adapted from the narrative poem by Phoebe Cary (1824–1871), "The Leak in the Dike."

"Brer Rabbit Gets Brer Fox's Dinner," by Julius Lester, from *More Tales of Uncle Remus* by Julius Lester. Copyright © 1988 by Julius Lester. Used by permission of Dial Books for Young Readers, a division of Penguin Books USA Inc.

"The Frog Prince," by Wanda Gag, from *Tales from Grimm* by Jacob and Wilhelm Grimm. Copyright © 1936 by Wanda Gag. Used by permission of the Wanda Gag Estate.

"Hansel and Gretel," adapted from *Household Stories from the Collection of the Brothers Grimm*, translated by Lucy Crane (1886).

"In Which Tigger Comes to the Forest and Has Brkfst," by A. A. Milne, illustrations by E. H. Shepard, from *The House at Pooh Corner* by A. A. Milne, illustrations by E. H. Shepard. Copyright 1928 by E. P. Dutton, renewed © 1956 by A. A. Milne. Used by permission of Dutton Children's Books, a division of Penguin Books USA Inc.

"Issun Boshi: One-Inch Boy," retelling by Lindley Shutz and John Holdren from multiple sources.

"It Could Always Be Worse," adapted from *A Treasury of Jewish Folklore* by Nathan Ausubel. Copyright © 1948, 1976 by Crown Publishers, Inc. Used by permission of Crown Publishers, Inc.

"Jack and the Beanstalk," adapted and condensed from *English Fairy Tales* by Joseph Jacobs (Putnam's, 1892).

"The Knee-High Man," from *The Knee-High Man and Other Tales* by Julius Lester. Copyright © 1972 by Julius Lester. Used by permission of Dial Books for Young Readers, a division of Penguin Books USA Inc.

"Medio Pollito," a retelling by E. D. Hirsch, Jr. from multiple sources.

"Mozart the Wonder Boy," from *Mozart* by Ann Rachlin. Copyright © 1992 by Aladdin Books Ltd. Text copyright © Ann Rachlin/Fun with Music, reprinted by arrangement with Barron's Educational Series, Inc., Hauppauge, New York.

"The Pied Piper of Hamelin," a new retelling freely incorporating and adapting lines from the famous poem by Robert Browning, and also from versions in *The Merrill Fourth Reader* by Franklin Dyer and Mary Brady (Merrill, 1916); *The Progressive Road to Reading: Book Two* by Georgine Burchill et al. (Silver, Burdett and Co., n.d.); and *Child Life in Tale and Fable: A Second Reader* by Etta and Mary Frances Blaisdell (Macmillan, 1909).

"Pinocchio," retelling based on episodes from C. Collodi, *The Adventures of Pinocchio*.

"The Princess and the Pea," an original retelling based on the story by Hans Christian Andersen, versions in *Story Hour Readers Revised: Book Two* by Ida Coe and Alice Dillon (American Book Company, 1923), and *Everyday Classics Third Reader* by Franklin Baker and Ashley Thorndike (Macmillan, 1917).

"Puss-in-Boots," adapted from "The Master Cat or Puss in Boots" in *The Blue Fairy Book*, edited by Andrew Lang (Longmans, Green, and Co., 1889), and "Puss in Boots" in *Fables and Folk Stories*, retold by Horace E. Scudder (Houghton, Mifflin, 1890).

"Rapunzel," adapted from *Household Stories from the Collection of the Brothers Grimm*, translated by Lucy Crane (1886).

"Rumpelstiltskin," adapted from *Household Stories from the Collection of the Brothers Grimm*, translated by Lucy Crane (1886).

"Sleeping Beauty," adapted from *Household Stories from the Collection of the Brothers Grimm*, translated by Lucy Crane (1886), and *Third Year Language Reader* by Franklin Baker et al. (Macmillan, 1919).

The Tale of Peter Rabbit, by Beatrix Potter. Copyright © Frederick Warne & Co. Used with permission from Frederick Warne & Co.

"Tom Thumb," adapted from *Household Stories from the Collection of the Brothers Grimm*, translated by Lucy Crane (1886), and *Fables and Folk Stories* by Horace Scudder (Houghton, Mifflin, 1890).

"Why the Owl Has Big Eyes," retelling by Lindley Shutz, based on multiple sources.

While every care has been taken to trace and acknowledge copyright, the editors tender their apologies for any accidental infringement where copyright has proved untraceable. They would be pleased to insert the appropriate acknowledgment in any subsequent edition of this publication.

Index

ABOUT THE EDITOR

E. D. Hirsch, Jr., is a professor at the University of Virginia and the author of *The Schools We Need* and the bestselling *Cultural Literacy* and *The Dictionary of Cultural Literacy*. He and his wife, Polly, live in Charlottesville, Virginia, where they raised their three children.

"The best year of teaching I ever had. This year has
been so much fun: fun to learn, fun to teach."

Joanne Anderson, Teacher,

Three Oaks Elementary School

Fort Myers, Florida

Collect the entire Core Knowledge series

ISBN	TITLE	PRICE
0-385-48117-9	What Your Kindergartner Needs to Know	$24.95/$34.95Can
0-385-48119-5	What Your First Grader Needs to Know (Revised Edition)	$24.95/$34.95Can
0-385-41116-2	What Your Second Grader Needs to Know	$22.50/$28.00Can
0-385-41117-0	What Your Third Grader Needs to Know	$22.50/$28.00Can
0-385-41118-9	What Your Fourth Grader Needs to Know	$22.50/$28.00Can
0-385-41119-7	What Your Fifth Grader Needs to Know	$22.50/$28.00Can
0-385-41120-0	What Your Sixth Grader Needs to Know	$22.50/$28.00Can
Also available:		
0-385-31640-2	Books to Build On	$10.95/$14.95Can

READERS:

The titles listed above are available in your local bookstore. If you are interested in mail ordering any of the Core Knowledge books listed above, please send a check or money order only to the address below (no C.O.D.s or cash) and indicate the title and ISBN book number with your order. Make check payable to Doubleday Consumer Services (include $2.50 for postage and handling). Allow 4–6 weeks for delivery. Prices and availability subject to change without notice.

Please mail your order and check to:
Doubleday Consumer Services, Dept. CK
2451 South Wolf Road
Des Plaines, IL 60018

SCHOOL DISCOUNTS FOR BULK ORDERS:

For bulk orders of quantities of 100 or more books in the Core Knowledge series (*What Your Kinder-gartner–Sixth Grader Needs to Know*), schools receive a discount on orders placed through the Core Knowledge Foundation. Call 1-800-238-3233 for information or to place an order.

FOR MORE INFORMATION ABOUT CORE KNOWLEDGE:

Call the Core Knowledge Foundation at 1-800-238-3233.